ADVANCED BIDDING

ADVANCED

A TutorText PUBLISHED BY

DOUBLEDAY & COMPANY, INC., GARDEN CITY, N.Y.

1963

BIDDING

By Charles H. Goren

PREPARED UNDER THE DIRECTION OF

EDUCATIONAL SCIENCE DIVISION

A Division of U. S. Industries, Inc.

CONTENTS

FOREWORD

In 1960, as an experiment in the field of programed instruction, I was asked to write a book on the fundamentals of the game.

This TutorText, *The Elements of Bridge,* was so successful that I agreed to undertake this second book, *Advanced Bidding,* which deals specifically with more advanced problems in bidding.

This book is intended primarily for the player who already has mastered the elementary principles of contract bridge and is now ready to acquire additional skills to carry him ahead in amateur bridge circles with relative comfort.

As you read through this book, you will find that it is impossible to reach the last page without concentrating on the material and paying attention all the way through. This is because of the unique way the material is organized.

Advanced Bidding is an "automatic tutoring" book. You will be questioned continuously on each point as you read, and only by answering each question correctly can you go on to the next point.

This method was devised by Norman A. Crowder, Vice President and Technical Director of the Educational Science Division of U. S. Industries, Inc., a psychologist and mathematician. The method has been used to teach map reading to Marines, arithmetic to grade school students, the problems of diabetes to doctors, electronics to technicians, and poetry to the uninitiated.

You will find that I am not only talking to you in the pages of this book, but even looking over your shoulder and talking back.

I am indebted to Dr. Robert E. Hall, prominent New York obstetrician and gynecologist and equally prominent amateur bridge player, for his valuable editorial assistance in suggesting ways to help other amateurs raise their skill to more sophisticated levels.

CHARLES H. GOREN

NOTE TO THE READER

This is not an ordinary book. A page may be divided into as many as three units such as occurs on the third page of this text, or it may be filled by only one unit such as on the first page. The units are numbered consecutively but they are not to be read in that order. At the bottom of each unit, there are directions telling you which unit to study next. For example, at the bottom of unit 1, there is a multiple-choice question. You are supposed to pick the answer you think is correct. When you pick your answer, you will be directed to unit 8, 14, or 20. Simply look for the unit you have selected, read it, and follow the directions given at the end of the unit. In this way you will proceed through this book.

Reading this book is very much like having an individual tutor. The book will continually ask you questions, and correct errors, as well as give information. Your progress through this course will depend entirely on your ability to think and choose right answers instead of wrong ones. The course is divided into chapters, and you will find that short learning sessions will produce better results than a few long ones.

Read the information carefully, and by the time you reach the final page you will have mastered the art of bidding in bridge. But remember—follow the instructions appearing at the bottom of each unit.

Now turn to unit 1 and begin.

CHAPTER I

OPENING BIDS

The point-count method of evaluating bridge hands has proved to be the simplest, the most effective, and the most popular yet devised. It appears to be here to stay. It is therefore appropriate in any book on bidding to review the Point-Count System.

There are 40 high-card points in the deck, ten in each suit. Points are allotted as follows:

Ace . . . . 4 points
King . . . . 3 points
Queen . . . . 2 points
Jack . . . . 1 point

Any honor other than the ace loses a point if it is unguarded or unprotected.

Singleton King . . . . 2 points
Singleton Queen . . . . 1 point
Q x . . . . 1 point
Singleton Jack . . . . no points
J x . . . . no points
J x x . . . . 1 point

These reduced values apply only when you are counting for an opening suit bid.

On almost every page of this TutorText you will find a question based on the information you are given. A different number is listed after each answer. When you turn to the unit indicated by your choice, you will find out whether your answer was correct or incorrect. If it is correct, you'll go on to the next unit of information. But if your answer is wrong, your error will be corrected before you proceed.

Now look over the three statements below. Only one of them is correct. Pick the correct statement and turn directly to the unit indicated.

The high-card value of a lone ace is four points. **8**
The high-card value of Q x x is one point. **14**
The high-card value of a singleton king is one point. **20**

You did not follow the instructions. In a TutorText you do not turn directly from one page to another unless specifically directed to do so. As you finish each unit of material you will find directions telling you which unit you should read next. There is no place in this book that directs you to this page. You should turn back to 1, therefore, and read the instructions again.

♠ A J x x x   ♡ K J x   ◇ x   ♣ Q J x x

YOUR ANSWER: This hand meets the point-count and quick-trick requirements for an opening bid.

Yes, it does. It contains only one and a half quick tricks, but it is worth 14 points and therefore *must* be opened.

But this is not the best answer. Please return to **28** and select the best answer.

♠ K Q x x x x   ♡ A x   ◇ Q x x   ♣ x x

YOUR ANSWER: I should not open the bidding with this hand.

Why not? You have 13 points and a rebiddable spade suit. If you open with one spade and partner forces you to bid again you will rebid two spades. Since you have a convenient rebid, there is no reason for passing.

Return to **27** for the right answer.

♠ K Q x x   ♡ A K x x x   ◇ x x x   ♣ x

YOUR ANSWER: I should plan to bid one spade and then rebid in hearts.

This is a bad idea.

You have a good five-card heart suit. You can't afford to hide it. If you bid spades first and then hearts, partner will assume your spades are at least as long as your hearts, if not longer, or that your hearts are weaker than they are.

Please return to **19** for the right answer.

♠ K J x x x   ♡ A K J x   ◇ x x   ♣ x x

YOUR ANSWER: I would open the bidding with one spade.

Right. With both five-card and four-card biddable suits you must try to show the former first. If you bid hearts and then spades with this hand, your partner will assume you have more hearts than spades. If you open with one spade and then later bid hearts, he will have the proper picture of your hand.

Much of your partner's subsequent bidding is predicated upon the assumption that you bid your longest suit first. If the bidding goes:

YOU	PARTNER
1 ♡	2 ♣
2 ♠	

and he has x x x in both spades and hearts, he should then bid three hearts in order to return to your longer suit.

So far, you have learned two principles of bidding: to open with the higher-ranking of two touching biddable suits and to open with the longer of two biddable suits. Obviously there must be times when these two rules seem to come into conflict. What should you do when your lower-ranking suit is longer?

This dilemma is solved in the light of the over-all strength of your hand. The stronger your hand is, the more naturally it should be bid. With strong hands, therefore, you can afford to mention your lower-ranking five-card suit before your higher-ranking four-card suit because you are not afraid of forcing partner to the three level in order to choose between them.

With weaker hands, the principle of bidding economy must take precedence over the importance of showing suit length. Hence, you sometimes have to lie about the length of your suits in order to keep the bidding down to a reasonable level. Remember this: if you must tell a falsehood, it is vastly preferable to lie about your distribution rather than to lie about the over-all strength of your hand.

With which hand would you open the bidding with one heart?

♠ A K J x   ♡ K J x x x   ◇ x x x   ♣ x **10**
♠ A K Q x   ♡ A J x x x   ◇ K x x   ♣ x **19**
♠ A J x x   ♡ A J x x   ◇ K x x   ♣ x x **24**

♠ A x x x x   ♡ K Q x   ◇ x   ♣ Q x x x

YOUR ANSWER: This hand meets the point-count and quick-trick requirements for an opening bid.

Yes, it does. There are only 13 points here, but there are also the necessary two quick tricks. Count one for the spade ace and another for the heart king-queen.

But this is not the best answer. Please return to **28** and select the best answer.

YOUR ANSWER: The high-card value of a lone ace is four points.

You are right. An ace loses none of its value by being a singleton. Any other honor must be protected or it loses one point. A king needs one card with it for protection; a queen or jack must have two accompanying cards to be guarded. Actually, of course, proper protection for a jack consists of at least three small cards; but for point-count purposes two will do.

If your hand contains all four aces, you may add an extra point. If you have no aces, you must deduct a point from your total.

After you have figured your high-card points, you may add your distribution points:

> Add three points for a void.
> Add two points for each singleton.
> Add one point for each doubleton.

These distribution points are added when counting for an opening bid. There is a special table of "dummy points" that we use when we support partner's suit. We will discuss them in the next chapter.

Look at these three hands. Including distribution, one hand has more points than the other two. Which one is it?

♠ K J x x	♡ K x x	◇ K J x	♣ Q J x **12**
♠ K	♡ A x x x x x	◇ K x x x	♣ Q x **25**
♠ Q J x x x	♡ K x x	◇ x x x	♣ A K **28**

(A) ♠ K Q x x x x   ♥ A x   ♦ Q x x   ♣ x x

(B) ♠ A Q x x   ♥ A Q x   ♦ J x x   ♣ x x x

(C) ♠ A x x x x   ♥ K Q x x   ♦ Q x x   ♣ x

YOUR ANSWER: I should not open the bidding with hand B.

We agree. Like hands A and C, this hand contains 13 points and two quick tricks; but unlike A and C it does not offer a convenient rebid. With hand A you can bid and rebid spades; with hand C you can bid spades and rebid hearts. But with hand B, if you say one spade and partner forces you to rebid by saying two hearts, you will find yourself in an embarrassing position. You may not rebid the spades; you aren't strong enough to raise hearts; and there is no bid you can make with safety.

With weak to moderate-strength hands which contain more than one biddable suit, you must plan the sequence of your bids in the most economical manner. For example, if you say one heart, partner says two clubs, and you rebid two spades, you have squandered a lot of bidding space. If partner prefers hearts, he must now say *three* hearts, which may already be too high. If, instead, you had opened with one spade, partner had responded two clubs, and you had then said two hearts, partner could have passed if he preferred hearts, or bid two spades if he preferred your first suit.

This is a classical example of bidding economy. It illustrates one of the basic rules with regard to suit selection in making opening bids: With two adjacent, biddable suits of equal length, regardless of their relative strength, bid the higher-ranking suit first.

What would be your opening bid with this hand?

♠ Q x x x x   ♥ A K J x x   ♦ x   ♣ x x

One Spade **13**

One Heart **23**

♠ A K J x   ♡ K J x x x   ◊ x x   ♣ x

YOUR ANSWER: I would open the bidding with one heart.

You'd better not.

You have two biddable major suits and only 14 points. If you open with one heart and partner responds two clubs you will be faced with a dilemma. If you now say two spades, partner will be forced to the three level if he wishes to show a preference for your hearts. With only 14 points in your hand you cannot afford this luxury.

And yet if you open with one heart and then rebid hearts over partner's two club response, you will have neglected to mention your perfectly good spade suit.

So you will have to open with one spade, treating your five-card heart holding as if it were a four-card suit.

Please go back to **6** and select the right hand for a heart opening.

♠ K Q x x   ♡ A K x x x   ◊ x x x   ♣ x

YOUR ANSWER: I should plan to bid one heart and then rebid in spades.

No. This would be *reversing,* for which you need 19 points. If your partner's hand looked like this:

♠ x x   ♡ x x x   ◊ Q x x   ♣ A K J x x

and you opened with one heart, listened to him bid two clubs, and then said two spades, you would be in trouble. He would then say three hearts because his hearts are better than his spades and you would be beyond your depth.

Please return to **19** for the right answer.

12

[from 8]

♠ K J x x   ♥ K x x   ♦ K J x   ♣ Q J x

YOUR ANSWER: This hand contains more points than the other two.

No. There is a hand with more points than this. There are just 13 points here. Perhaps you forgot to deduct one point for an ace-less hand. It is true that the hand contains 14 high-card points, but you can easily see how it is handicapped by not having an ace.

Now turn back to **8** and choose another hand.

13

[from 9]

♠ Q x x x x   ♥ A K J x x   ♦ x   ♣ x x

YOUR ANSWER: With this hand, I should open one spade.

Correct. The fact that your hearts are stronger than your spades is not nearly so important as the future of the bidding here.

You have only 13 points, so you cannot afford to waste bidding space. If the bidding goes:

YOU	PARTNER
1 ♥	2 ♣
2 ♠	

your partner will have to go to the three level to support your hearts. But if it goes:

YOU	PARTNER
1 ♠	2 ♣
2 ♥	

you can stop at the two level in either of your suits.

The length of your suits is often more important than their strength. One of the main objectives in bidding is to find a suit in which you and your partner possess eight or more cards for trump. You don't necessarily need all the top honors. Therefore, when you have more than one biddable suit, name the longest one first.

How would you open the bidding with this hand?

♠ K J x x x   ♥ A K J x   ♦ x x   ♣ x x

One Spade **6** One Heart **17**

8

YOUR ANSWER: The high-card value of Q x x is one point.

No. Any honor receives its normal value when it's guarded. These normal values were given in the table on **1**: Ace, 4; King, 3; Queen, 2; Jack, 1.

Protection for a king consists of one other card; for a queen or jack, two other cards will suffice.

Now turn back to **1** and try to pick out the correct answer.

(A)   ♠ A J x x x   ♡ K J x   ◇ x   ♣ Q J x x

(B)   ♠ A x x x x   ♡ K Q x   ◇ x   ♣ Q x x x

YOUR ANSWER: Both hands meet the requirement for an opening bid.

This is 100 per cent correct. Hand A contains only one and a half quick tricks, but it is worth 14 points and so you must make an opening bid. Hand B contains 13 points and two quick tricks.

In order to make an opening bid of one in a suit, you must, of course, have a biddable suit. A *biddable major suit* (spades or hearts) is defined as one which contains as many as four high-card points (exception: Q J 10 x) or any five-card suit. Greater liberties may be taken in opening the bidding with a minor suit.

A *rebiddable suit* is one which may be bid a second time without partner's having supported it. A four-card suit may not be rebid without a raise from partner. A five-card suit will qualify if it is Q J 9 x x or better; there must be some solidity to it as well as high-card points. Any six-card suit may be rebid.

How many biddable suits do you see in these hands?

♠ A K Q x x   ♡ x x   ◇ K x x x   ♣ K x

♠ A J x x   ♡ Q J 10 x   ◇ x   ♣ K J x x

Four **21**

Five **27**

16

[*from 27*]

♠ A x x x x ♡ K Q x x ◊ Q x x ♣ x

YOUR ANSWER: I should not open the bidding with this hand.

We think you should. You have 13 points, two quick tricks, and a convenient rebid. If you open with one spade and partner forces you to rebid by saying two clubs or two diamonds, you will rebid two hearts. If he says two hearts, of course, you will raise him; and if he says two spades, you will pass.

Return to **27** for the right answer.

17

[*from 13*]

♠ K J x x x ♡ A K J x ◊ x x ♣ x x

YOUR ANSWER: I would open the bidding with one heart.

No. This would be a poor choice.

Whenever you have two biddable suits you should try to bid the longer one first. Here you have five spades and four hearts. If you bid hearts first and then spades later, you will have misinformed your partner. He will think you have five hearts and four spades.

Please return to **13** and choose the other opening bid.

18

[*from 26*]

You bid diamonds once and then rebid hearts twice.

YOUR ANSWER: Partner will assume that I have five diamonds and four hearts.

How so? Partner knows that with only four hearts you are not going to bid them twice without support from him.

Return to **26** and reconsider your answer.

(A)	♠ A K J x	♡ K J x x x	◇ x x x	♣ x
(B)	♠ A K Q x	♡ A J x x x	◇ K x x	♣ x
(C)	♠ A J x x	♡ A J x x	◇ K x x	♣ x x

YOUR ANSWER: I would choose a one heart opening bid with hand B.

This is correct. Hand A is too weak to risk pushing your partner to the three level if he wants to express second-round preference for your first suit. Therefore, you must deliberately misdescribe the length of your heart suit by bidding spades first and hearts second.

Hand C is a standard example of two adjacent biddable suits of the same length. With this pattern you always bid the higher-ranking suit first.

Hand B, on the other hand, is worth 19 points. With this much power you can afford to bid your hand naturally. You don't care if partner has to go to the three level in order to support your first-bid suit. So, open with one heart and then bid spades on the second round. Partner will get the double message that you have more hearts than spades and that you have sufficient strength to tolerate a three-level response from him.

Bidding your lower-ranking suit first and then the higher-ranking one is the reverse of the normal sequence and is therefore known as *reversing*. Since it forces partner to the three level in order to show a preference for your first-named suit, reversing requires a good hand, a hand worth about 19 points.

In what sequence would you plan to bid the suits in this hand?

♠ K Q x x ♡ A K x x x ◇ x x x ♣ x

Spades and then hearts. **5**

Hearts and then spades. **11**

Hearts and then hearts again. **26**

20

[from 1]

YOUR ANSWER: The high-card value of a singleton king is one point.

No. A king is ordinarily worth three points. Its value is diminished by only one point if it is unguarded.

A king is unguarded only when it is a singleton, for then it may be quickly taken by the ace of the same suit. Since a king is normally worth three points, it would be worth just two points as a singleton.

An unguarded honor still gets the normal number of *distribution points* for being a singleton or doubleton. We will review this later.

Now turn back to **1** and try to pick out the correct statement.

21

[from 15]

(A) ♠ A K Q x x ♡ x x   ◇ K x x x ♣ K x
(B) ♠ A J x x   ♡ Q J 10 x ◇ x   ♣ K J x x

YOUR ANSWER: There are only four biddable suits in these hands.

Wrong. There are five.

Both spade suits qualify, of course. The club suit in hand B contains four cards and four high-card points, so it may be bid. The heart suit in hand B has only three high-card points, but you will remember that a Q J 10 x holding is the exception to the usual four-point requirement. And the diamond suit in hand A is biddable because weaker suits are acceptable in the minors.

Return to **15** for the proper answer.

22

[from 26]

You bid diamonds once and then rebid hearts twice.

YOUR ANSWER: Partner will assume that I have five hearts and four diamonds.

Never. Partner knows that with five hearts and four diamonds you would open the bidding with one heart.

Return to **26** and reconsider your answer.

♠ Q x x x x   ♡ A K J x x   ◊ x   ♣ x x

YOUR ANSWER: With this hand, I should open one heart.

No. You've missed the point. If you open with one heart and partner then responds with two diamonds or two clubs, what are you going to do? You can rebid your hearts, of course, but then partner won't hear about your spade suit. And if you rebid two spades, he will have to go to the three level in order to show a preference for hearts. Your hand is not strong enough to force the bidding to the three level.

Opening with one heart would be shortsighted.

Return to **9** and consider the better answer.

♠ A J x x   ♡ A J x x   ◊ K x x   ♣ x x

YOUR ANSWER: I would open the bidding with one heart.

Think again. You have already learned to open with the higher ranking of two touching biddable suits which are identical in length.

If you open with one heart on this hand and partner says two clubs, you will be without a convenient rebid, for by mentioning your spades on the second round you will force partner to the three level if he wishes to support your hearts. You must, therefore, bid one spade first and then two hearts over partner's response.

Please return to **6** and select the right hand for the one heart opening.

25

[*from 8*]

♠ K   ♡ A x x x x x   ◊ K x x   ♣ Q x

YOUR ANSWER: This hand contains more points than the other two.

No. First of all, there are 12 high-card points; but the spade king and club queen x are unguarded honors and so two points must be subtracted from the 12, leaving ten. Then you can add three distribution points, two for the singleton and one for the doubleton, bringing the total point count to 13.

Now turn back to **8** and choose another hand.

26

[*from 19*]

♠ K Q x x   ♡ A K x x x   ◊ x x x   ♣ x

YOUR ANSWER: I should plan to bid hearts and then, if necessary, to rebid them.

Yes, you have a rebiddable heart suit, and the hearts are superior to the spades in quality as well as quantity. You must not mention the spades after your heart opening, for this would be reversing, which requires 19 points.

In short, there is nothing mysterious about reversing. You never plan to reverse just to show a good hand; you simply avoid doing it with a poor hand. It might be more meaningful to say that 19 points are required for a bidding sequence which may push partner to the three level in order to express a preference for your first suit.

If, as in the above case, you bid a suit twice, your partner will know that you have at least five cards in that suit; if you bid the same suit three times he will know you have six cards in it.

What then will your partner assume if you bid diamonds first and then bid and rebid hearts?

That I have five diamonds and four hearts. **18**

That I have five hearts and four diamonds. **22**

That I have six diamonds and five hearts. **34**

(A)   ♠ A K Q x x   ♡ x x   ◊ K x x x   ♣ K x

(B)   ♠ A J x x   ♡ Q J 10 x ◊ x   ♣ K J x x

YOUR ANSWER: There are five biddable suits in these hands.

You are right. Spade holding A is not only biddable, it is also rebiddable. The spades, hearts, and clubs in hand B contain sufficient strength and length. The diamonds in hand A have less than four high-card points, but one may bid with such a holding in the minor suits. These weaker minor suit opening bids are often made for purposes of convenience in discovering a major suit fit, for minor suit contracts are usually avoided.

You should never open the bidding without first planning what you will say if partner forces you to bid again. This might be a good time to remind you of the *New-Suit Forcing Principle,* which provides that if partner has not passed originally and responds in a new suit, you must bid once more.

For this reason you cannot afford to open with a 13-point hand unless you have a convenient rebid. If partner's response is embarrassing to you, either you opened the bidding with the wrong suit or you should not have opened at all.

Examine these three hands. Which one should not be opened?

♠ K Q x x x x   ♡ A x   ◊ Q x x   ♣ x x

♠ A Q x x   ♡ A Q x   ◊ J x x   ♣ x x x

♠ A x x x x   ♡ K Q x x   ◊ Q x x   ♣ x

Hand A   **4**

Hand B   **9**

Hand C   **16**

28
[*from 8*]

(A)   ♠ K J x x   ♡ K x x   ◇ K J x   ♣ Q J x

(B)   ♠ K   ♡ A x x x x x ◇ K x x x ♣ Q x

(C)   ♠ Q J x x x ♡ K x x   ◇ x x x   ♣ A K

YOUR ANSWER: Hand C contains more points than the other two.

Correct. There are 13 high-card points and one distributional point, making a total of 14. Each of the other hands is worth 13 points.

Since there are 40 high-card points in the deck, the average hand should contain about ten points. You should have 13 or 14 points to open the auction with a bid of one in a suit. That is, your hand should be three or four points above average.

With 13 points you have an optional opening; you *may* bid if you have a convenient rebid and defensive strength. With 14 points you *must* open. It is your duty to tell your partner you have a hand well above average.

When you open the bidding with a 13-point hand, it must contain at least two quick tricks. A quick trick is a combination of cards that will win a trick in the first two rounds of play, even if the opponents play the hand.

A table of quick tricks is listed below. Each combination of cards must be in the same suit, of course.

Two Quick Tricks	1-½ Quick Tricks	One Quick Trick	½ Quick Trick
A K	A Q	A or K Q	K x

Look at these two hands. Which of them meets the requirements for an opening bid?

(A)   ♠ A J x x x ♡ K J x   ◇ x   ♣ Q J x x

(B)   ♠ A x x x x ♡ K Q x   ◇ x   ♣ Q x x x

Hand A   **3**   Hand B   **7**   Both hands   **15**

♠ A K x x   ♡ Q x x   ◇ x x   ♣ A x x

YOUR ANSWER: In third position, I would open with one spade.

Correct. You don't have to rebid, so you should mention your best suit immediately.

Are you ready for another quiz on opening bids? Here is a new one with some slightly stickier problems. For each hand you must select not only your opening bid, but also your rebid over any new-suit response by partner. This is actually the sort of future-bidding anticipation which you should put into practice before uttering a word at the bridge table.

(A)	♠ Q J x	♡ A Q x x	◇ Q x x	♣ K x x
(K)	♠ x	♡ Q x x x x x	◇ Q x x	♣ A K J
(G)	♠ K x x x x	♡ A x x	◇ A K J	♣ x x
(C)	♠ x	♡ Q x x x	◇ A J x x	♣ A J x x
(M)	♠ x x x	♡ A Q J x x	◇ none	♣ K Q x x x
(I)	♠ K J x x	♡ K x x x	◇ A K 10	♣ x x
(E)	♠ x x x x x x	♡ A x	◇ Q J x	♣ A x
(B)	♠ A K Q x	♡ A x x x x	◇ x x	♣ x x
(L)	♠ A K J x	♡ A Q J x x	◇ Q x x	♣ x
(H)	♠ A J x x x x	♡ x x	◇ A K x x	♣ x
(D)	♠ A K x	♡ J x x x	◇ K x x	♣ Q J x
(N)	♠ x x	♡ A Q J x	◇ K x x x	♣ K x
(J)	♠ A Q x x	♡ x x	◇ A Q J x x	♣ x x
(F)	♠ A Q 10 x	♡ A J x x x	◇ x x	♣ x x

Now check your answers on **50**.

30

[from 46]

♠ A K x x   ♡ x x   ◇ A K x x   ♣ J x x

YOUR ANSWER: I would open this hand with one spade.

No, this might lead to complications. If partner responds with two hearts, for example, you would have no convenient rebid. You are not permitted to rebid the four-card spade suit and this holding is not strong enough to justify showing a new suit at the three level.

Had you followed the bidding rule presented on **46,** this dilemma could have been avoided.

Please turn back to that page and select a better answer.

31

[from 39]

♠ A x x x   ♡ K J x x   ◇ K x   ♣ Q x x

YOUR ANSWER: This hand should be opened with one club because of the rebid problem.

No, there is no problem with this hand. It has 14 points and a convenient rebid.

You should open with one spade. If partner responds in no trump, clubs, or diamonds, you can rebid hearts. This will enable partner to take a preference for one of your suits at the two level.

Now please return to **39** and choose another answer.

32

[from 45]

♠ A x x x   ♡ A x x   ◇ A x x   ♣ x x x

YOUR ANSWER: In third position, I would make an opening bid with this hand.

No. You have 12 points but no decent suit and no special reason to direct an opening lead. This hand will probably take only three tricks on offense or defense.

Return to **45** and try again.

♠ A K x x   ♡ A Q x x   ◊ K Q x x   ♣ x

YOUR ANSWER: I would open the bidding with one diamond.

Very good. When you have this much strength you must allow for the possibility that partner is weak. If you open with one spade he may not have the values for a two-level response, yet he may have all you need for game.

Partner may, for instance, hold:

♠ x x   ♡ K J x x x   ◊ J x x   ♣ x x x

with which he would bid one heart over your one diamond opening, and you would be cold for game in hearts. Over one spade, however, he would pass.

The moral to this story: With 4–4–4–1 hands worth 20 points or more, where the normal opening would be one spade, open with a minor suit so that partner can respond at the one level.

Now look at the following hands and choose the best opening bid for each of them. Note the Answer Letter for each hand and check your answers with the corresponding letters on the following table:

(A)	♠ A K J x x	♡ x	◊ x x	♣ K x x x x
(D)	♠ x	♡ K x x x	◊ A x x x	♣ A Q x x
(F)	♠ K Q x x	♡ A J x x	◊ Q J x x	♣ x
(H)	♠ x	♡ K Q x x x	◊ A K J x x	♣ K x
(J)	♠ x	♡ K Q x x	◊ A K J x x	♣ A x x
(B)	♠ K J x x	♡ x x x	◊ A K Q	♣ x x x
(E)	♠ A Q x x	♡ K J x x x	◊ K x x	♣ x
(G)	♠ A K Q x	♡ x x	◊ x x x	♣ K x x x
(I)	♠ A K x x	♡ A J x x	◊ x x	♣ x x x
(K)	♠ K Q J x x	♡ x	◊ A Q J x x x	♣ x
(C)	♠ A Q J x x x	♡ A K x x	◊ x	♣ x x

Now turn to **38**.

34

[*from 26*]

You bid diamonds once and then rebid hearts twice.

YOUR ANSWER: Partner will assume that I have six diamonds and five hearts.

Very good. He knows that you must have more diamonds than hearts or you would have opened with one heart. He further knows that you wouldn't rebid hearts without at least five of them. Q.E.D., you must have six diamonds and five hearts.

The Choice between Two Four-Card Suits

When you hold two five-card suits, the higher ranking should be bid first. This rule generally holds for two four-card suits too, but here even greater care should be taken to prevent the bidding from getting out of hand. It takes considerable foresight to plan the bidding in the proper sequence.

These are the various distribution patterns you can hold with two four-card suits:

No.	Spades	Hearts	Diamonds	Clubs	Open with
1.	4	4	2–3	2–3	1 ♠
2.	2–3	4	4	2–3	1 ♡
3.	2–3	2–3	4	4	1 ◇
4.	4	2–3	2–3	4	1 ♣
5.	4	3	4	2	Usually 1 ♠
6.	4	2	4	3	1 ◇
7.	2–3	4	2–3	4	1 ♣

You don't have to memorize this table. You can see from it that, except for patterns 4, 5, and 6 you open with your higher-ranking suit. In each case, you will also see that this rule economizes the bidding space. If you have four-card heart and diamond suits, for example, you open with one heart and then, if partner bids one spade or two clubs you can show your diamonds and let him choose between your suits at the two level.

Go on to **35**.

With patterns 4 and 7 the same end is served by bidding clubs first. With four-card spade and club suits, for example, you open with one club and then say one spade over a heart or diamond response. Work out some of the combinations for yourself; you will find a few where the system may backfire, but very few.

What is your opening bid with this hand?

♠ A K x x   ♡ x x   ◇ K x x   ♣ K x x x

One Club **46**   One Spade **41**

(A) ♠ A x x x   ♡ A x x   ◇ A x x   ♣ x x x
(B) ♠ A K J x x   ♡ Q x x   ◇ x x   ♣ x x x
(C) ♠ x   ♡ x x x   ◇ K x x   ♣ K Q J x x x

YOUR ANSWER: In third position, I would make an opening bid with hand B only.

We agree. Hand B contains 11 points, a good suit, and some defensive value if spades are led.

Hand A is worth only three tricks no matter how you slice it. It has no suit worth mentioning.

Hand C contains 11 points and a good suit. It is not worth much on defense, however, and someone else is sure to bid spades.

A vital new feature enters the bidding when you open in third position: The new-suit forcing principle no longer applies. If you open with one heart and partner responds with one spade, for example, you are permitted to pass.

Let us see how this may influence your choice of an opening bid with this hand:

♠ A K x x   ♡ Q x x   ◇ x x x   ♣ A x x

In third position would you bid one spade? **29**

or one club? **48**

37

[from 46]

♠ A K x x   ♡ x x   ◇ A K x x   ♣ J x x

YOUR ANSWER: I would open this hand with one diamond.

We would too. Then, if partner says one heart, you can conveniently rebid one spade. If he responds with two clubs, you may raise that suit.

The Choice between Three Four-Card Suits

Here there is even greater reason to open with the suit below your shortest suit, for partner is more than likely to respond in the suit of your singleton.

There are only four possible combinations in this group:

Spades	Hearts	Diamonds	Clubs	Open With
4	4	4	1	1 ♠
4	4	1	4	1 ♣
4	1	4	4	1 ◇
1	4	4	4	1 ♡

You will see that these bids all make sense according to the principles laid down in previous pages. You open with the suit below your singleton. There is only one significant exception. Let's see if you can figure it out for yourself:

How would you open the bidding with this hand?

♠ A K x x   ♡ A Q x x   ◇ K Q x x   ♣ x

One Diamond **33**

One Spade **44**

Answer
Letter

(A) Bid one spade. If partner responds two hearts or two diamonds, rebid spades.

(B) Pass. You have 13 points but no convenient rebid.

(C) Bid one spade. If you rebid the spades and subsequently show the hearts, partner will learn that you have a 6–4 distribution.

(D) Bid one diamond. With three four-card suits you bid the suit under the singleton. The hearts are not biddable (you need four high-card points in a major suit), so you proceed to the next lower-ranking suit, diamonds.

(E) Bid one spade. With 15 points you can't reverse. If you open one heart, partner responds two clubs, and you rebid two spades, partner must go to the three level to show preference for hearts.

(F) Bid one spade. You have three four-card suits. Bid the one below your singleton.

(G) Bid one club. With two four-card suits, open with the one below your doubleton.

(H) Bid one heart. With two five-card suits, open with the higher ranking.

(I) Bid one spade. You have 13 points and a convenient rebid only if you bid spades first.

(J) Bid one diamond. With 19 points you can afford to bid a lower-ranking five-card suit first. (Contrast with E.)

(K) Bid one diamond. With this 6–5 distribution you can bid diamonds once and spades twice.

Now go on to **39.**

The Short-Club Bid

Many hands are too good to pass, but you hesitate to open them for lack of a good rebid. Some of these difficult hands can be opened with a bid of one club, even though the club suit isn't biddable. This is called the *Short-Club Bid.*

This isn't a system or convention, and you needn't ask your partner, "Do you play the short club?" It's just a convenience for the opening bidder. The responder isn't affected at all, except that he must be careful not to raise to two clubs unless he has four trumps. Look at this hand.

♠ A K J x   ♡ J 10 x   ◇ x x x   ♣ A J x

You have 14 points and must not pass. Yet a normal opening of one spade would allow you no convenient rebid if partner responded in diamonds. You should open with one club; if partner responds with one diamond or one heart, you may rebid one spade. If he responds with one spade, you will raise to two. If he responds with one no trump or two clubs, you will pass.

You may use the one club opening for problem hands like this if you have a three-card club suit headed by at least the queen.

Look at the three hands below. One of them should be opened with one club because of the rebid problem. See if you can pick it out.

♠ A x x x	♡ K J x x	◇ K x	♣ Q x x	**31**
♠ K J x x	♡ K x x	◇ Q J x	♣ Q J x	**43**
♠ K J x x	♡ x x	◇ J x x x	♣ A K J	**49**

40

[from 49]

♠ K x x x   ♡ K x x x   ◇ x x   ♣ A K x

YOUR ANSWER: I would open with one spade.

No. You may not open the bidding with a major suit which contains less than four high-card points. Neither spades nor hearts qualify.

Return to **49** and pursue the other alternatives.

♠ A K x x ♡ x x ◇ K x x ♣ K x x x

YOUR ANSWER: I would open this hand with one spade.

You'd better not. Spades are the higher-ranking suit, of course, but with four cards in spades and clubs you should open clubs.

Here's why: If you say one spade and partner responds with two hearts or two diamonds, you must go to the three level to show your clubs.

It's always preferable, especially with minimum hands such as this, to give partner as much information as possible in as little bidding space as possible.

Please go back to **35** for the better answer.

♠ x ♡ x x x ◇ K x x ♣ K Q J x x x

YOUR ANSWER: In third position, I would make an opening bid with this hand.

We wouldn't advise it. You have 11 points and a good suit, but your defensive values are poor and your suit is a minor. If you say one club, it is not unlikely that the opposition will end up in a spade contract, since they can outbid you. Or perhaps your partner will respond in spades, which is equally bad.

Your best score will result if this hand is passed out.

Return to **45** and try again.

43

[from 39]

♠ K J x x   ♡ K x x   ◊ Q J x   ♣ Q J x

YOUR ANSWER: This hand should be opened with one club because of the rebid problem.

No, this hand shouldn't be opened at all. It ostensibly has 13 points but one point must be deducted because the hand is aceless. Furthermore, it lacks the required two quick tricks. You should pass.

Now please return to **39** and choose another answer.

44

[from 37]

♠ A K x x   ♡ A Q x x   ◊ K Q x x   ♣ x

YOUR ANSWER: I would open the bidding with one spade.

This would be in accordance with the rule, but would it be the best choice? You have a big hand, worth 20 points. It is quite possible that partner has a poor hand. If you open with one spade and he wants to bid a suit of his own, he will have to do so at the two level.

As you will soon learn, a two-level response requires a better-than-minimum hand, so partner may have to pass you out at one spade with a holding that will produce a game—e.g., he might have this hand:

♠ x   ♡ K 10 x x x x   ◊ J x x   ♣ x x x

Please go back to **37** and select the correct answer.

♠ K x x x   ♡ K x x x   ◇ x x   ♣ A K x
YOUR ANSWER: I should open with one club.

Yes. With 14 points you have to open, but neither the spade nor heart suit is biddable. Here is another use of the short club.

In a nutshell, you may open with one club (1) to name a genuine club suit; (2) to avoid rebidding difficulties; or (3) to show a hand with opening-bid qualifications which lacks a truly biddable suit. You will find it a useful bid, if you adhere to these requirements.

Third-Hand Bidding

When your turn to bid is preceded by a pass by partner and a pass by your right-hand opponent, you may open the bidding with one or two points less than the usual requirements. As few as 11 points are acceptable here, or occasionally as few as ten if you have a very good suit. Without a good suit, normal requirements tend to prevail.

The rationale for these shaded third-hand bids is twofold: (1) It is fairly obvious if you have only 10–12 points after two passes that the 40 high-card points in the deck are apt to be evenly divided and probably neither partnership can make game; and (2) if the opponents buy the final contract and your partner has the opening lead, your bid will have indicated to him the best line of defense.

It should be equally obvious that there are many third-position hands worth 10–12 points which do not merit an opening bid.

With which of these hands would you consider an opening bid appropriate in the third position?

(A)   ♠ A x x x   ♡ A x x   ◇ A x x   ♣ x x x

(B)   ♠ A K J x x   ♡ Q x x   ◇ x x   ♣ x x x

(C)   ♠ x   ♡ x x x   ◇ K x x   ♣ K Q J x x x

Hand A   **32**

Hand B   **36**

Hand C   **42**

All 3 hands   **47**

46

[*from 35*]

♠ A K x x   ♡ x x   ◊ K x x   ♣ K x x x

YOUR ANSWER: I would open this hand with one club.

Right. You do so in order to be able to show your spades at the one level over a one diamond or one heart response.

Another way of stating this principle of bidding economy with two four-card suits is this: Open with the first biddable suit which ranks below the shortest suit in your hand. By referring back to the table on **34** you will see that this concept has been largely borne out by the suggested opening bids given in the right-hand column. Spades are regarded as ranking below clubs for the purposes of this rule.

The reason why this works is that partner's longest suit is mathematically most likely to be your shortest suit. If, for example, you hold:

♠ x x x   ♡ x x   ◊ A Q J x   ♣ A K Q x,

your partner's longest suit is probably hearts or spades. So if you bid one diamond and he says one heart or one spade, you can then conveniently show your clubs.

Perhaps the most difficult of the seven hand patterns given on **34** is that in which you hold four spades and four diamonds. Your common sense will come into play. Let's put it to a test:

How would you choose to open this hand?

♠ A K x x   ♡ x x   ◊ A K x x   ♣ J x x

One Spade **30**

One Diamond **37**

(A)	♠ A x x x	♡ A x x	◇ A x x	♣ x x x
(B)	♠ A K J x x	♡ Q x x	◇ x x	♣ x x x
(C)	♠ x	♡ x x x	◇ K x x	♣ K Q J x x x

YOUR ANSWER: In third position, I would make an opening bid with all three hands.

Let's hope not.

Hand A has no decent suit and it will take three tricks regardless of the opening lead.

Hand C has a good suit but poor defensive values, and either the opposition or partner is sure to bid spades.

Return to **45** and try again.

♠ A K x x   ♡ Q x x   ◇ x x x   ♣ A x x

YOUR ANSWER: In third position, I would open with one club.

In first or second position, yes. In third position, no. In the former instances you would have to say one club, in order to have a convenient rebid.

In third position, however, you are not obligated to bid again if partner mentions a new suit. You are therefore justified in bidding your best suit directly.

Please return to **36** and choose the right answer.

49

[from 39]

(A) ♠ A x x x   ♥ K J x x   ♦ K x   ♣ Q x x

(B) ♠ K J x x   ♥ K x x   ♦ Q J x   ♣ Q J x

(C) ♠ K J x x   ♥ x x   ♦ J x x x   ♣ A K J

YOUR ANSWER: Hand C should be opened with one club because of the rebid problem.

Correct. If you open with one spade you will be acutely embarrassed by a two heart response. Your spades are not rebiddable. But if you open with one club you can handle any response. After two clubs you pass; after one diamond or one heart you say one spade; and after one spade you say two spades.

Hand B should not be opened at all; it has 13 points but lacks an ace which reduces the total to 12. There is no rebid problem with hand A; you open with one spade and can rebid hearts.

As you can see, the bid of one club is made not *because* your club holding is short, but *in spite of it*. The short-club bid merely serves as a convenience to the opening bidder who would otherwise find it awkward to describe his hand.

Needless to say, a one club opening sometimes also signifies a biddable club suit. With

♠ Q x x   ♥ K x   ♦ x x   ♣ A K Q x x x,

for example, you bid and rebid clubs in order to show that your suit is genuine.

According to what you have learned so far, what would be your opening bid with this hand?

♠ K x x x   ♥ K x x x   ♦ x x   ♣ A K x

One Spade   **40**

One Club   **45**

Answer
Letter

(A)	1♣ 1♠ 1NT,	1♣ 1♡ 2♡,	1♣ 1♢ 1♡
(B)	1♠ 2♡ 3♡,	1♠ 2♣ 2♡,	1♠ 2♢ 2♡
(C)	1♢ 1♡ 2♡,	1♢ 2♣ 3♣,	1♢ 1♠ 2♣
(D)	1♣ 1♠ 1NT,	1♣ 1♡ 2♡,	1♣ 1♢ 1NT
(E)	1♠ 2♡ 2♠,	1♠ 2♣ 2♠,	1♠ 2♢ 2♠
(F)	1♠ 2♡ 3♡,	1♠ 2♢ 2♡,	1♠ 2♣ 2♡
(G)	1♠ 2♡ 3♡,	1♠ 2♣ 2NT,	1♠ 2♢ 3♢
(H)	1♠ 2♡ 2♠,	1♠ 2♣ 2♠,	1♠ 2♢ 3♢
(I)	1♠ 2♡ 3♡,	1♠ 2♣ 2♡,	1♠ 2♢ 3♢
(J)	1♢ 1♡ 1♠,	1♢ 2♣ 2♢,	1♢ 1♠ 2♠
(K)	1♡ 1♠ 2♡,	1♡ 2♣ 2♡,	1♡ 2♢ 2♡
(L)	1♡ 1♠ 4♡,	1♡ 2♣ 2♠,	1♡ 2♢ 2♠
(M)	1♡ 1♠ 2♣,	1♡ 2♣ 3♣,	1♡ 2♢ 2♡
(N)	1♡ 1♠ 1NT or 2♢,	1♡ 2♣ 2♢,	1♡ 2♢ 3♢

If you feel you have mastered the rudiments of opening bids of one in a suit, you are ready to go on to the more glamorous bids described in Chapter II, which begins on the next page.

CHAPTER II

MORE OPENING BIDS

The Two Demand Bid

Occasionally you will be dealt a hand of such strength that you will be convinced you can make a game without assistance. This does not necessarily mean you should open the bidding with some game contract. In most cases, it will be to your advantage to find out more about your partner's hand. On the other hand, it would be tempting fate to open the bidding with one of a suit for you run the risk that partner will pass your bid of one.

For these special hands we use the strongest opening bid in bridge —the opening of two in a suit. Known as the *Two Demand Bid,* it demands that both you and your partner keep the bidding open until a game contract is reached.

What are the minimum requirements for a two demand bid?

To begin with, you should have within one trick of game in your own hand. If you anticipate a major suit contract, therefore, you must have nine sure winners. You may take the calculated risk that partner will produce some holding or combination of cards that will develop the other trick. A prime requirement for the opening demand bid is the possession of four quick tricks.

During the maneuvers you must constantly be focussed on the point-count content of your hand and the length of your trump suit. Let us examine this hand:

♠ A K Q J x x x   ♡ A x x   ◇ A x   ♣ x

Can you see nine sure winners and four quick tricks?

No **55**

Yes **59**

Answer
Letter

(A) Open with one club. You have 23 points, but too many losers.

(B) Open with one spade. You have only 17 points, and lack the required four quick tricks.

(C) Open with two spades. You have 22 points, a seven-card suit, and ten winners.

(D) Open with two hearts. You have 22 points, a six-card major and game in hand.

(E) Open with two clubs. You have 29 points and ten winners.

(F) Open with one spade. You have 23 points, but too many losers.

(G) Open with two diamonds. You have 24 points, a seven-card suit, and ten sure winners (within one trick of game).

(H) Open with one diamond. You have 24 points and a six-card suit, but not enough winners to open with a demand bid in a minor suit.

(I) Open with one spade. You have just 21 points with a five-card suit.

(J) Open with two hearts. You have 22 points, a seven-card suit, and game in hand.

Now go on to **57**.

♠ x x   ♡ x x x   ◇ K J x x x   ♣ K x x

YOUR ANSWER: This hand calls for a negative response of two no trump if partner opens with two spades.

No, this hand has seven points and one quick trick, which represents the minimum requirement for a positive response.

Now, please return to **57** and select the hand that demands a negative response.

54

[from 65]

♠ x x　　♡ x x x　　◇ K J x x x　　♣ K x x

YOUR ANSWER: With this hand, I would pass in response to an opening bid of two spades.

No, no, no!

You may not pass when your partner opens with a bid of two in a suit. This is a forcing bid; he is assuming full responsibility for a game contract. And you are obliged to let him know what you have to offer.

If you have nothing in your hand—less than seven points and one quick trick, or less than eight points and one-half quick trick—make the negative response of two no trump. Otherwise, choose a positive bid: a raise of your partner's suit, a bid in a new suit, or a jump to three no trump.

You may not pass, so what would you respond? Return to **65** and decide.

55

[from 51]

♠ A K Q J x x x　　♡ A x x　　◇ A x　　♣ x

YOUR ANSWER: No. I cannot see nine sure winners and four quick tricks in this hand.

Look at the hand again—carefully.

The spades, as trump, should not lose a single trick. That makes seven tricks. In addition, you have two aces—two more sure winners. So you do have nine sure winners in the hand, one less than required for game in spades.

Quick tricks, of course, are defensive tricks. They are combinations of cards that should win tricks on the first two rounds of play. Remember, each ace and each king-queen combination equals one quick trick, each ace-king combination is two tricks, each ace-queen, one and a half, and each guarded king, one-half.

In the above hand, you have four quick tricks in the ace-king of spades, the ace of hearts, and the ace of diamonds.

Please return to **51** to choose the right answer.

Opening Pre-emptive Bids

A pre-emptive bid is an opening of three, four, or five in a suit. You may employ such a bid with a hand like this:

♠ K Q J x x x x x   ♡ x   ◇ x x   ♣ x x

With this hand, bid four spades if you are not vulnerable, or three spades if you are vulnerable.

The idea behind this strategy is to "pre-empt" or consume valuable bidding space before the opponents can get together in a suit of their own. This bid is resorted to with weak hands containing a suit of seven or more cards and not much strength on the side. It should not be employed with hands containing ten points in high cards. With a stronger holding, open with one in a suit or pass.

A pre-emptive bid is made only with a hand that has little defensive merit, but contains a long suit that will be an effective trump. If you have seven or more cards in one suit, and very little outside strength, it is quite likely that the opponents are short in your suit and have long and strong suits of their own. If you open the bidding at the three or four level, it will be difficult for the opponents to enter the auction, and if they choose to do so anyway, they may fail to find their best contract.

You should expect to be doubled whenever you make a pre-emptive bid. If you can reasonably expect to confine your losses to 500 points or less (down two, doubled and vulnerable, or down three, doubled and not vulnerable), then such action is justified.

With which of these hands would you open three hearts?

♠ x   ♡ A K x x x x x   ◇ x   ♡ A K x x **61**

♠ x x   ♡ Q J 10 x x x x x   ◇ K x   ♣ x **72**

Responses to a Two Demand Bid

When your partner opens with two in a suit, you are duty-bound to respond, no matter how poor your hand may be. Furthermore, you must keep on bidding until a game contract has been reached unless you have chosen in the meantime to double the opponents in some competitive bid.

If you have a complete bust, take consolation in the fact that the opener assumes responsibility for making the game contract.

A *positive* response to partner's opening two bid is indicated by raising his suit, bidding a new suit, or jumping to three no trump. You should have seven points and one quick trick or eight points with one-half quick trick to make a response like this. If you have less than this, you make the standard *negative* response of two no trump. When you bid two no trump, partner will not expect much help from your hand, and he probably will give up any ideas he might have had about going on to a slam. You are both still obliged to proceed to a game contract, however.

Which of these hands would call for a negative response of two no trump if partner opens with two spades?

♠ x x   ♡ x x x   ◊ K J x x x   ♣ K x x   **53**

♠ J x x   ♡ Q x   ◊ K x x   ♣ Q x x x x   **60**

♠ x x   ♡ Q x x   ◊ x x   ♣ Q J x x x x   **65**

♠ J x x   ♡ Q x   ◊ K x x   ♣ Q x x x x

YOUR ANSWER: With this hand, I would respond three no trump to an opening bid of two spades.

You have the requirements for this response, but with adequate trump support for a demand bid, this is not the best choice. It is usually more important to confirm a fit for partner's suit.

Please return to **69** and pick the correct response.

♠ A K Q J x x x   ♡ A x x   ◇ A x   ♣ x

YOUR ANSWER: With this hand, I count on nine sure winners and four quick tricks.

Correct. You can expect all seven spades to win tricks when they are trumps; add the two aces and you have your nine sure winners. The A-K of spades and your other two aces add up to four quick tricks. It would be proper to open with two spades. It is reasonable to expect some arrangement of cards in partner's hand that will enable you to pick up the extra trick needed for your four spade contract.

In terms of the point count, the requirements for an opening two bid may be given as follows:

With a good five-card major suit . . . . 25 points
With a good six-card major suit . . . . 23 points
With a good seven-card major suit . . . . 21 points
With a second good five-card suit, you may have one point less;
    with a good major two-suiter, you may have two points less.
With a minor suit holding, all requirements should be increased
    by two points.

We base these requirements on the fact that it takes about 26 points in the partners' combined hands to score a game at no trump or in a major suit, and it takes about 28–29 points to score game in a minor suit. Of course, the opening bidder should have almost the entire count in his own hand; he should rely on little or no help from partner.

Which of these hands would not be good enough for a two spade opening bid?

♠ A K J 9 x x   ♡ A Q 10   ◇ x x   ♣ A K **63**

♠ A K x x   ♡ A K x x   ◇ x   ♣ A K x x **67**

60

[*from 57*]

♠ J x x   ♡ Q x   ◇ K x x   ♣ Q x x x x

YOUR ANSWER: This hand calls for a negative response of two no trump if partner opens with two spades.

No, this hand has eight points and one-half quick trick, which warrants a positive response. Remember that the minimum requirements for a positive response are eight points with one-half quick trick or seven points with one quick trick.

Now, please return to **57** and select the hand that demands a *negative* response.

61

[*from 56*]

♠ x   ♡ A K x x x x x   ◇ x   ♣ A K x x

YOUR ANSWER: I should open three hearts on this hand.

A thousand times, no. Your hand is much too strong for a pre-emptive bid. With four quick tricks in your hand it is hardly likely that your opponents are going anywhere. And the principle behind pre-emptive bidding is to advertise a weak hand in such a way as to deprive your opponents of bidding room.

So open one heart. You need very little help to make game.

Now return to **56** and pick the right hand.

62

[*from 74*]

♠ A x   ♡ K x x   ◇ K J x   ♣ A K J x x

YOUR ANSWER: This hand qualifies for a one no trump opening.

No, it contains 19 high-card points, so it is too strong. It has the proper distribution for a no trump bid, and all four suits are well protected. However, the no trump opening is a very precise bid; it may be used with hands containing 16 to 18 high-card points, no more and no less. With a stronger hand you must open with one in a suit and show your true strength on later bidding rounds.

Now please return to **74** and choose the correct hand.

♠ A K J 9 x x   ♡ A Q 10   ◇ x x   ♣ A K

YOUR ANSWER: This hand is not good enough for a two spade opening bid.

No. This hand meets the requirement for a two spade opening bid.

It contains 23 points, a good six-card suit, and nine sure winners. The queen of spades is missing, and you may lose to it. Otherwise the spades are good; you can count on taking between five and six tricks with spades as trumps. The ace and queen of hearts are worth one and a half tricks (depending on the location of the king of hearts); the ace and king of clubs, another two.

The ace-king of spades (two), the ace-queen of hearts (one and a half), and the ace-king of clubs (two) add up to five and a half quick tricks.

Thus, the sure winner, and quick-trick point count requirements for an opening two bid are adequately fulfilled.

Please return to **59** and choose the hand which is not good enough for an opening two bid.

♠ J x x   ♡ Q x   ◇ K x x   ♣ Q x x x x

YOUR ANSWER: In response to a two spade opening bid, I would pass with this hand.

No! You must remember that an opening bid of two in a suit is absolutely forcing. You are required to make some response.

If you have seven points and one quick trick, or eight points and one-half quick trick, you must respond positively. You either raise your partner's bid, name a suit of your own, or jump to three no trump.

If you do not have a good enough hand for a positive bid, you must respond negatively. The only negative response you can make to an opening bid of two in a suit is two no trump.

How would you respond with the above hand?

Please return to **69** and choose the right answer.

(A) ♠ x x   ♡ x x x   ◊ K J x x x   ♣ K x x

(B) ♠ J x x   ♡ Q x   ◊ K x x   ♣ Q x x x x

(C) ♠ x x   ♡ Q x x   ◊ x x   ♣ Q J x x x x

YOUR ANSWER: Hand C would call for a negative response of two no trump if partner opens with two spades.

Yes, it contains only seven points and one-half quick trick. Hand A has seven points and one quick trick, and hand B has eight points and one-half quick trick, both of which warrant positive action. The proper responses with hands A and B will be discussed below.

The negative, two no trump response to an opening two bid does not in any way imply no trump distribution or the desire to reach a no trump contract. It is simply the means by which you convey the picture of a poor hand to your partner.

With anything more than a minimum holding, you should make a positive response. If you have three-card support for partner's suit, a raise is preferred, for it establishes the trump suit early in the bidding. If you have a suit of your own, you may bid it, but it should be at least as good as Q J x x x. If you have enough strength for a positive response, but no biddable suit or adequate trump support, you should respond three no trump.

What would you respond to a two spade opening bid if you held this hand?

♠ x x   ♡ x x x   ◊ K J x x x   ♣ K x x

Pass **54**

Three Diamonds **69**

Two No Trump **73**

Three No Trump **82**

♠ J x x   ♡ Q x   ◊ K x x   ♣ Q x x x x

YOUR ANSWER: I would raise to three spades if partner opens the auction with two spades.

Yes. You have eight high-card points and good trump support for a demand bid. Since it is usually important to confirm the trump fit, there is little to be gained by taking any other action.

Now for some practice. Let's say partner has opened with two hearts. What would your response be with each of these hands?

(A)	♠ x	♡ 10 x x x x x	◊ x x x	♣ x x x
(D)	♠ x x	♡ Q x x x	◊ K Q x	♣ x x x x
(F)	♠ K J x x x	♡ x x	◊ K x x	♣ x x x
(H)	♠ x x	♡ Q x x	◊ K Q x	♣ J x x x
(J)	♠ K 10 x	♡ x x	◊ A J x	♣ x x x x x
(B)	♠ A Q x x	♡ x x x	◊ K J x x	♣ x x
(E)	♠ K J x x x	♡ x x x	◊ J x x	♣ x x
(G)	♠ x x	♡ x x x x	◊ A J x	♣ Q x x x
(I)	♠ K x x	♡ x x	◊ K J x	♣ J x x x x
(C)	♠ void	♡ A x	◊ x x x x x	♣ x x x x x x

Check your answers on **70.**

67

[from 59]

(A) ♠ A K J 9 x x   ♡ A Q 10   ◇ x x   ♣ A K

(B) ♠ A K x x   ♡ A K x x   ◇ x   ♣ A K x x

YOUR ANSWER: Hand B is not good enough for an opening bid of two spades.

You are correct. Although it contains 23 points, hand B is nowhere near an opening two bid. There are only six sure winners and nine are required.

Hand A has 23 points, but it also figures to produce nine tricks. Furthermore it meets the defensive requirements for the call.

Examine these hands and see how many qualify for a two demand bid. What is the correct opening bid with each hand?

(A) ♠ x   ♡ A Q x   ◇ A Q x x   ♣ A K Q x x

(D) ♠ A K J 10 x   ♡ A K Q J x x   ◇ x   ♣ x

(G) ♠ x x x   ♡ A K   ◇ A K Q J x x x ♣ A

(I) ♠ A Q x x x   ♡ A K x   ◇ A K x   ♣ x x

(B) ♠ K Q x x x x   ♡ A Q J x x x   ◇ x   ♣ void

(E) ♠ K x   ♡ A Q J   ◇ A K Q   ♣ A K Q 10 x

(H) ♠ K x   ♡ K J x x   ◇ A K Q J 10 x ♣ A

(J) ♠ void   ♡ A K Q J 10 x x ◇ A K x x x   ♣ x

(F) ♠ A Q J 10 x   ♡ A K   ◇ K Q x x   ♣ Q x

(C) ♠ A K Q x x x x ♡ A K Q x   ◇ x x   ♣ void

Now check your answers on **52.**

Answer
Letter

(A) Bid one spade. Your hand is too strong for a three bid.

(B) Bid three spades. The bid of a new suit over a pre-emptive opening bid is forcing for one round. You may choose to show the hearts next.

(C) Bid three no trump. You have the other suits well stopped and can probably run the diamond suit.

(D) Bid three clubs. You can probably take six or seven tricks in offense, one in defense.

(E) Pass. Your partner needs all the strength you have in order to make his bid.

(F) Pass. Your diamond holding is much too weak for a pre-emptive bid.

Now go on to **74.**

♠ x x   ♡ x x x   ◇ K J x x x   ♣ K x x

YOUR ANSWER: With this hand, you should respond three diamonds after partner opens with two spades.

Correct. Your suit is good enough to show. You may bid any suit which is as good as Q J x x x.

Over an opening two spade bid, what action would you take with the following hand?

♠ J x x   ♡ Q x   ◇ K x x   ♣ Q x x x x

Three No Trump **58**

Pass **64**

Three Spades **66**

Three Clubs **71**

70

[from 66]

Answer
Letter

(A) Bid two no trump. The six hearts may look like wonderful support, but as long as you have no high-card points, you must first make a negative response. You may support hearts vigorously on the next round.

(B) Bid two spades. You have a fine hand in response to a two bid and can afford to make a temporizing response. You will support hearts subsequently.

(C) Bid two no trump. You have only four high-card points and your minor suits are too weak to mention.

(D) Bid three hearts. You have fine trump support and nine points in support of hearts. You must tell partner about this immediately.

(E) Bid two no trump. You have a good spade suit, but only six points, not enough for a positive response.

(F) Bid two spades. You have eight points and a biddable suit.

(G) Bid three hearts. You have eight points and excellent trump support.

(H) Bid three hearts. You have sound trump support and nine points.

(I) Bid three no trump. You have eight high-card points, a balanced hand and no biddable suit.

(J) Bid three no trump. With eight in high-card points and no suit worth mentioning, you have no other choice.

Now turn to **56.**

♠ J x x   ♡ Q x   ◊ K x x   ♣ Q x x x x

YOUR ANSWER: In response to a two spade opening, I would bid three clubs with this hand.

No, your hand is good enough for a positive bid, but your clubs are not good enough to mention. The suit should be at least as good as Q J x x x.

Please return to **69** and the right response.

♠ x x   ♡ Q J 10 x x x x x   ◊ K x   ♣ x

YOUR ANSWER: I should open three hearts with this hand.

Right. This is an ideal holding for a pre-emptive bid. Defensively this hand might not take a trick; played with hearts as trump it may take seven tricks. If your dummy can take two more tricks you will make the contract. But, even more important, the opponents may well have a game, or even a slam, which your bid will make it difficult for them to uncover.

In responding to pre-emptive opening bids, bear in mind that partner has promised a long trump suit and very little else, and that he is already counting on you for two or three tricks. Unless you have something in addition to this, you are bidding at your own peril.

What would be your opening bid with these hands?

(A)   ♠ Q x x x x x x   ♡ x   ◊ A Q x   ♣ K x

(F)   ♠ K x   ♡ A x   ◊ J x x x x x x ♣ x x

(D)   ♠ void   ♡ x x x ◊ K x x   ♣ K Q J x x x x

What would be your response to partner's opening bid of three diamonds?

(C)   ♠ A J 10   ♡ K Q x   ◊ x x x   ♣ A Q x x

(E)   ♠ K x x   ♡ J x x   ◊ A x   ♣ K J x x x

(B)   ♠ K Q J x x x   ♡ A K x x x   ◊ x   ♣ A

Check your answers on **68**.

73

[from 65]

♠ x x   ♡ x x x   ◊ K J x x x   ♣ K x x

YOUR ANSWER: With this hand, I would respond two no trump to a two spade opening.

No, that is a negative response and you have too good a hand for that.

You have seven high-card points and one quick trick, so you should make a positive response.

Can you raise your partner's bid? Do you have a new suit to mention? Or should you jump to three no trump?

Please decide and return to **65** to find the correct response.

74

[from 68]

No Trump Openings

The *No Trump Opening* is a specialized bid. Your hand must fit specific patterns of distribution and point-count strength, so that your partner will know just what to expect of you.

To open the auction with one no trump, your high-card content must be from 16 to 18 points, no more and no less. (In no trump bidding, only high-card points may be considered; no points are allowed for distribution.) If your hand is a little weaker than this, you must open with one in a suit. *If it is just a little stronger than this, you still must open with one in a suit.*

Furthermore, your hand must fit certain patterns of distribution. The acceptable patterns are: 4–3–3–3, 4–4–3–2, or 5–3–3–2. This means you may not bid no trump if your hand contains a singleton or more than one doubleton. And if your hand contains a doubleton, the doubleton must include a high honor—the ace, the king, or the queen.

According to this, which of these hands would qualify for a one no trump opening?

♠ A x   ♡ K x x   ◊ K J x   ♣ A K J x x **62**
♠ K J x   ♡ K x   ◊ Q J x x   ♣ A K x x **81**
♠ A x x x   ♡ A x   ◊ Q x   ♣ A K x x x **87**

♠ A J x x   ♡ A   ◊ K x x x x   ♣ A J x

YOUR ANSWER: This hand may be opened with one no trump.

No, the distribution is not proper. Possession of a singleton bars the opening bid of one no trump, even when that singleton is an ace.

Your hand must fit very special distributional patterns for a one no trump opening.

Now please return to **81** and choose the correct hand.

♠ Q x   ♡ J 10   ◊ A K x x x   ♣ x x x x

YOUR ANSWER: This hand is not suitable for a jump to three no trump.

Sorry, but this hand is quite suitable for a jump raise to three no trump. It contains ten high-card points and, though you have a good diamond suit, there is no reason to mention it. Three no trump is undoubtedly your best contract.

Go back to **90** and choose the correct answer.

♠ x x   ♡ K Q J 10 x   ◊ x x   ♣ A x x x

YOUR ANSWER: I should respond two hearts to partner's opening one no trump.

No. You have ten high-card points and should show your strength directly. Two hearts is too weak a response.

With your ten points and partner's guaranteed 16 you know that you have enough to undertake a game contract. Yet if you bid two hearts, partner is apt to pass.

Please return to **86** for the right answer.

Answer
Letter

(A) Bid one club. You have no trump distribution, but with 19 high-card points yor hand is too strong for one no trump.

(B) Bid one diamond. You have 15 points—not quite enough for one no trump.

(C) Bid one heart. You have 17 points and a balanced hand, but with a worthless doubleton, you may not open with one no trump.

(D) Bid one no trump. You have 17 points and even distribution.

(E) Bid one no trump. You have 16 points, three suits protected and a completely balanced hand.

(F) Bid one club. You have 17 high-card points, but the hand contains two doubletons.

(G) Bid one no trump. You have 17 points (one point is added for all four aces).

(H) Bid one no trump. You have 16 points and three suits protected. There is no objection to bidding one no trump with a five-card major suit.

(I) Bid one no trump. You have 17 points and three suits protected.

(J) Bid one diamond. You have 17 points, but the singleton heart ace rules out a no trump opening.

Now go on to **80.**

♠ x x   ♡ K Q J 10 x   ◇ x x   ♣ A x x x

YOUR ANSWER: I should respond three hearts to partner's opening one no trump.

Right. Two hearts would be too weak, in view of your ten high-card points. Three no trump would not tell partner of your good heart suit and unbalanced distribution.

A three heart response would give partner a clear picture of your hand. With no special fit for hearts and strength in the other suits, he may prefer to sign off at three no trump. But if he elects to raise hearts, the suit contract should be preferable. Your three heart bid has the advantage of forcing partner to game while at the same time giving him a choice between hearts and no trump.

If you have more than 14 points in your hand, you are in the slam range.

Raise to four no trump with 15 or 16 points. If partner has more than the minimum 16, he should rebid six no trump.

Raise to six no trump with 17 or 18 points. Partner is obliged to pass, for you have a maximum of 36 points, not enough to try for a grand slam.

If you hold 19 or 20 points, make a jump shift to three in a suit and then bid six no trump at your next turn. This is a stronger bid than jumping immediately to six no trump. If partner has a maximum, he should try for seven no trump.

Raise to seven no trump with 21 or more. The partnership has a minimum of 37 points. At the most, one king or a queen and a jack is out against you.

Now go on to **91**.

Responses to a One No Trump Opening

In this chapter we will include the responses to opening no trump bids, for they are also quite specific and specialized. When partner opens one no trump, you know he has 16–18 high-card points. All you have to do is count the number of points in your own hand and you can determine just what is your combined strength. It takes about 26 high-card points to score a game in no trump, 33 to make a small slam, and 37 to bring in a grand slam.

As you consider your response, bear in mind that partner may have either the maximum 18 or the minimum 16 points. Since 26 are required for game, there is no use encouraging him at all unless you have at least eight high-card points. With seven points or less, therefore, you should pass. There is one exception: you may raise partner with only seven points if you have a good five-card suit.

If your hand is fairly well balanced, and you have eight or nine high-card points (or seven points with a good five-card suit), your best response will be a single raise to two no trump. This is also true if your hand is unbalanced and its principal strength is in the minor suits, for an attempt at a nine-trick game in no trump is vastly preferable to an eleven-trick contract in the minors.

After your raise to two no trump, partner will bid three with a maximum holding and will pass with a minimum.

Look at these hands. With one of them you should raise partner's one no trump opening to two no trump. Which one is it?

♠ x x x   ♡ Q x x   ◇ A J 9 x x   ♣ x x **90**

♠ A x x x   ♡ x x x   ◇ K x x   ♣ x x x **93**

(A)   ♠ A x   ♡ K x x   ◊ K J x   ♣ A K J x x

(B)   ♠ K J x   ♡ K x   ◊ Q J x x   ♣ A K x x

(C)   ♠ A x x x   ♡ A x   ◊ Q x   ♣ A K x x x

YOUR ANSWER: Hand B qualifies for a one no trump opening.

Correct. It contains 17 high-card points, has 4–4–3–2 distribution, and the doubleton contains a high honor.

Hand A has 19 high-card points. For a one no trump opening the point count must be between 16 and 18. Hand A is too strong for one no trump and must be opened with one club with the intention of making a jump in no trump later.

Hand C contains two doubletons, which disqualifies it.

In no trump play, of course, you cannot rely on a trump suit to control the hand. You must have high cards or "stoppers" in each suit to prevent the opponents from running a series of tricks in their long suit. To bid one no trump, therefore, you must have protection or stoppers in at least three of your suits (and if you have a doubleton, it *must* contain one of the three high honors). In case you have to play the hand at no trump, you hope that your partner has a stopper in your unprotected suit or at least that he has some length in it so that the opponents cannot win too many tricks in that suit.

Which of these hands may be opened with one no trump?

♠ A J x x   ♡ A   ◊ K x x x x   ♣ A J x   **75**

♠ x x x x   ♡ A x x   ◊ K Q x   ♣ A Q J   **85**

♠ A x x   ♡ K x   ◊ A J x x x   ♣ K x x   **94**

82

[from 65]

♠ x x   ♡ x x x   ◇ K J x x x   ♣ K x x

YOUR ANSWER: With this hand, I would respond three no trump to an opening bid of two spades.

You do have enough strength to respond positively, and a jump to three no trump would, of course, be a positive response. However, such a bid would not best describe your hand to your partner.

Please return to **65** and choose a better answer.

83

[from 103]

♠ A x x   ♡ K x x   ◇ A K x   ♣ Q J x x

YOUR ANSWER: With this hand the response to a two club convention bid would be two hearts.

According to the provisions of the two club convention, a biddable suit should usually have at least four cards to the queen. In this hand both major suits have only three cards, so two hearts is not the correct rebid.

To let your partner know that you have no biddable major suit, you should make the artificial bid of two diamonds.

Please return to **103** for the two heart response hand.

84

[from 106]

♠ Q x x   ♡ J x   ◇ A x x x x   ♣ Q x x

YOUR ANSWER: With this hand, I would bid two diamonds in response to a one no trump opening.

No. This would be an underbid.

With nine high-card points a raise to two no trump is called for. You have a balanced holding and there is no reason to look for a suit contract.

Please return to **106** for the hand that calls for a diamond response.

(A)	♠ A J x x	♡ A	◇ K x x x x	♣ A J x
(B)	♠ x x x x	♡ A x x	◇ K Q x	♣ A Q J
(C)	♠ A x x	♡ K x	◇ A J x x x	♣ K x x

YOUR ANSWER: Hand B could be opened with one no trump.

Yes, this is correct. Hand B contains 16 high-card points, even distribution, and protection in three suits.

Hand A doesn't qualify because it contains a singleton; one diamond is the proper opening. Hand C has acceptable distribution and protection in all suits, but it has only 15 points and therefore should also be opened with one diamond.

Here again are the requirements for an opening bid of one no trump:

1. 16–18 points in high cards.
2. Balanced distribution (4–3–3–3, 4–4–3–2, 5–3–3–2).
3. Protection in at least three suits; any doubleton must contain the ace, king, or queen. (Protection in a suit is defined as A x, K x, Q x x, J x x x.)

Now look at the following hands and choose the proper opening bid.

(A)	♠ A x	♡ K x x	◇ K J x	♣ A K J x x
(D)	♠ K J x	♡ K x	◇ Q J x x	♣ A K x x
(F)	♠ A x x x	♣ A x	◇ Q x	♣ A K x x x
(H)	♠ A K Q x x	♣ x x x	◇ K x	♣ K J x
(J)	♠ A J x x	♡ A	◇ K x x x x	♣ A J x
(E)	♠ x x x	♡ A x x	◇ K Q J x	♣ A Q x
(B)	♠ A x x	♡ K x	◇ A J x x x	♣ K x x
(G)	♠ A x x x	♡ A x x	◇ A x x	♣ A x x
(I)	♠ A Q x x	♡ A K x x	◇ x x x	♣ K J
(C)	♠ J x x x	♡ A Q J x	◇ A K Q	♣ x x

Check your answers on **78**.

53

86

[from 90]

(A) ♠ Q x   ♡ J 10   ◇ A K x x x   ♣ x x x x

(B) ♠ A K x x x   ♡ x x x x   ◇ Q   ♣ J 10 x

(C) ♠ Q x x   ♡ A x x   ◇ J x x x x   ♣ K x

YOUR ANSWER: Hand C is not suitable for a jump to three no trump.

Right. All three hands contain ten high-card points, which is the minimum for the jump to three no trump (after an opening one no trump), and with A and C there is no point in showing the diamonds, because we usually prefer no trump to trying for a minor suit game.

With an unbalanced hand whose principal strength is in the *majors,* however, such as B, you don't raise in no trump without first investigating the possibility of a game contract in hearts or spades. See **99** for the technique of conducting this investigation.

With ten points or more, an unbalanced hand, and a good suit, it is advisable to make a jump shift in that suit. This bid is forcing to game but it gives partner a chance to decide whether he prefers to play at three no trump or to raise your suit.

How would you respond to one no trump opening with this hand?

♠ x x   ♡ K Q J 10 x   ◇ x x   ♣ A x x x

Two Hearts **77**   Three Hearts **79**

Three No Trump **95**

87

[from 74]

♠ A x x x   ♡ A x   ◇ Q x   ♣ A K x x x

YOUR ANSWER: This hand may be opened with one no trump.

No. It has two doubletons. In order to qualify for a one no trump opening, the distribution of a hand must be either 4–3–3–3, 4–4–3–2, or 5–3–3–2, besides the prerequisite of 16–18 high-card points. In other words, a sound no trump bid must not contain either a singleton or two doubletons.

Now return to **74** and choose the correct hand.

Answer
Letter

(A) Jump to three no trump. You have 13 high-card points and no suit worth showing.

(B) Raise partner to four no trump. You have 16 high-card points. You know that partner has at least 16. If he has 17 or 18 points, he is expected to bid six no trump. If he has only 16, he should pass.

(C) Jump to three no trump. You have ten high-card points, which is the minimum for the jump raise.

(D) Raise to two no trump. You have eight high-card points. If partner has a maximum he will carry on to game.

(E) Make a jump takeout to three diamonds. You have 20 high-card points, and should look for a grand slam. After partner's rebid, you will bid six no trump. This invites him to go on to seven if he has a near maximum.

(F) Pass. You have just seven high-card points and no very attractive suit. Remember partner has at most 18 points.

(G) Jump to six no trump. You have 18 high-card points and balanced distribution. Partner should pass, for even if he has a maximum of 18, it is not likely that you will have a good play for a grand slam.

Go on to **99.**

89

[*from 111*]

♠ A x x   ♥ J x x   ♦ K x x x   ♣ Q x x

YOUR ANSWER: With this hand, a response of three diamonds to a two no trump opening would be incorrect.

No, this response is right.

With this strong balanced hand you would certainly want to play the game in no trump. But to let partner know that you have exactly ten high-card points, you should first bid a suit. Your longest suit is diamonds, so you would respond first with three diamonds. Partner will know what kind of a hand you have when you say four no trump on your next bid.

Please return to **111** and select the *incorrect* response.

90

[*from 80*]

(A)   ♠ x x x   ♥ Q x x   ♦ A J 9 x x   ♣ x x

(B)   ♠ A x x x   ♥ x x x   ♦ K x x   ♣ x x x

YOUR ANSWER: With hand A, you should raise partner's one no trump opening to two no trump.

Yes, you have seven high-card points, a good five-card suit, and no trump distribution.

Hand B has only seven points and no five-card suit so with it you should pass. Game is very improbable even if partner has the maximum 18 points.

If your hand contains 10–14 points and balanced distribution, you are assured of a combined total of at least 26 points, even if partner has only the minimum 16. Therefore, you should jump directly to three no trump. You are not encouraging partner to go any higher, because you have, at most, 32 points (even if partner has the maximum 18), and so a small slam isn't likely.

Which hand is *not* suitable for a jump to three no trump?

♠ Q x   ♥ J 10   ♦ A K x x x   ♣ x x x x   **76**
♠ A K x x x   ♥ x x x x   ♦ Q   ♣ J 10 x   **86**
♠ Q x x   ♥ A x x   ♦ J x x x x   ♣ K x   **98**

Let's practice a little. After partner's one no trump opening, what is your response with each of these hands?

(A)	♠ A x	♡ x x x x x	◊ K x x	♣ K Q J
(D)	♠ x x x	♡ Q x x x	◊ A Q 10	♣ Q x x
(F)	♠ x x x	♡ K J x x	◊ Q x x	♣ J x x
(B)	♠ K x	♡ A x x	◊ K J x x	♣ K Q x x
(E)	♠ K Q x	♡ A J x	◊ K J x x	♣ A Q x
(G)	♠ K Q x	♡ K x	◊ A x x x	♣ A Q x x
(C)	♠ K x x	♡ x x x x	◊ Q J x x	♣ A x

Check your answers on **88**.

♠ A K x x   ♡ x x   ◊ A Q J x x   ♣ J x

YOUR ANSWER: With this hand, I would bid two diamonds in response to a one no trump opening.

No, you certainly shouldn't do that.

This is a *strong* unbalanced hand, and you should not make the weak takeout to two in a suit. Such a bid would completely mislead your partner. He would think it was a desperation measure to escape from no trump. He might pass, and your two excellent hands would be wasted.

With this strong holding, game is assured and you will wish to investigate slam possibilities. The correct procedure is to make a jump shift to three diamonds.

Please return to **106** and select a different answer.

93

[from 80]

♠ A x x x   ♡ x x x   ◇ K x x   ♣ x x x

YOUR ANSWER: With this hand, I should raise partner's one no trump opening to the two level.

No. With only seven high-card points and no five-card suit, you should pass. Remember that without a good five-card suit you need a high-card point count of at least eight to raise partner. With less than eight, game is very improbable even if partner has the maximum 18 points.

Please return to **80** and pick the hand that is appropriate for a two no trump raise.

94

[from 81]

♠ A x x   ♡ K x   ◇ A J x x x   ♣ K x x

YOUR ANSWER: This hand may be opened with one no trump.

No. The distribution is all right for no trump, and each suit is fairly well stopped, but the hand contains only 15 high-card points.

For an opening of one no trump the hand must have exactly 16, 17, or 18 high-card points. This makes the no trump opening a very precise and descriptive bid. Partner will know just what to expect, and he can gear his bidding accordingly.

Now return to **81** and choose the correct hand.

95

[from 86]

♠ x x   ♡ K Q J 10 x   ◇ x x   ♣ A x x x

YOUR ANSWER: I should respond three no trump to partner's opening one no trump.

You have the proper high-card count to make this response, but it would not be the best choice. You must choose a bid which best describes not only your point count but your distribution as well.

Please return to **86** for the right answer.

♠ K Q x x   ♡ A J x x   ◇ A J   ♣ Q J x

YOUR ANSWER: With this hand, the response to a two club convention bid would be two hearts.

No. Both major suits are biddable in accordance with the provisions of the two club convention—Q x x x or better. Therefore, the *higher*-ranking suit should be mentioned first:

The correct rebid here is two spades, not two hearts.

Return to **103** for the hand that demands the two heart response.

♠ A J x x   ♡ A Q x   ◇ A J x   ♣ K J x

YOUR ANSWER: This hand calls for a two no trump opening.

Although this hand has the proper distribution, it should not be opened in no trump. To qualify for a no trump opening a hand must meet very specific point-count requirements. For one no trump, the high-card point requirement is 16–18; for two no trump, 22–24; and for three no trump, 25–27.

The above hand has a high-card point count of 20, too strong for one no trump and not strong enough for two no trump. It must, therefore, be opened in a suit—in this case clubs. You will have an opportunity to rebid in no trump on the next round.

Please return to **107** to find the two no trump bid.

♠ Q x x   ♡ A x x   ◇ J x x x x   ♣ K x

YOUR ANSWER: This hand is not suitable for a jump to three no trump.

As a matter of fact, it is quite suitable for a jump raise. It contains ten high-card points and no suit worth mentioning. Ten points plus opener's minimum of 16 makes 26, enough for game.

Please go back to **90** for the hand that is not suitable for a jump raise to three no trump.

The Two Club Convention

Sometimes when partner opens with one no trump, you may feel that your hand would be better fitted for suit play rather than for no trump. This is especially true when you have one or both major suits well represented in your hand, since a major suit game is available at the four level.

In order to find out whether partner's hand contains a biddable major suit, you may employ what is known as the *Two Club Convention*. You do this, by responding two clubs after the one no trump opening.

This is an artificial bid; and has nothing to do with the clubs in your hand. It shows, rather, that you have around eight high-card points and at least four cards in one of the major suits. In short, it tells your partner that you would prefer to play the hand in a suit rather than no trump and that you are searching for one of the major suits in which your combined holding amounts to eight or more cards.

This two club response is forcing. Partner must answer in a major suit if he has one that is Q x x x or better.

With which of these hands should you bid two clubs in response to a one no trump opening?

♠ K Q x x x	♡ A x x x	◊ x	♣ J x x	**103**
♠ Q x x x	♡ Q x x	◊ Q x x	♣ K x x	**109**
♠ J x x x	♡ Q x x x	◊ J x	♣ x x x	**114**

     ♠ A K J 10   ♡ Q x x x x   ◊ x x   ♣ x x
YOUR ANSWER: I should now bid three hearts.

No. If you do this your partner will assume you have only eight or nine points and may well pass. You have ten high-card points and 13 points in support of hearts.

You must make a stronger bid.

Return to **110** and choose the right answer.

♠ Q x x   ♡ x   ◊ J x x x x x   ♣ x x x

YOUR ANSWER: With this hand, I would bid two diamonds in response to a one no trump opening.

Yes, this hand might not take a single trick as dummy in a no trump contract. It has only three high-card points. But with diamonds as trump you are assured of taking several trump tricks in your own hand.

If you have a strong unbalanced hand with ten or more high-card points and a good suit of five or more cards, you may take out to three of your suit. This is forcing to game and offers partner a choice of contracts.

If your hand has a good major suit of at least six cards but less than ten points in high cards, you may jump to four in the suit. Partner is obliged to pass.

To summarize, a takeout to two diamonds, two hearts, or two spades in response to a one no trump opening is a show of weakness. A jump takeout to three of a suit shows strength, a good five-card suit and ten or more high-card points, and is forcing to game. A jump takeout to four of a suit shows less than ten high-card points and a suit of at least six card length.

Now turn to **104**.

102

[*from 107*]

♠ A K J x   ♡ A x x   ◇ K x x   ♣ Q J x

YOUR ANSWER: This hand calls for a two no trump opening.

This is a good no trump hand, but it has only 18 high-card points and therefore cannot be opened at the two level. Since it falls within the required 16–18 range of a one no trump opening bid, that is the correct call.

Please return to **107** to find the two no trump bid.

103

[*from 99*]

♠ K Q x x x   ♡ A x x x   ◇ x   ♣ J x x

YOUR ANSWER: I should bid two clubs with this hand in response to a one no trump opening.

Right.

It has a high-card point count of ten, which is adequate for a raise to three no trump, but with an unbalanced hand and good holdings in both of the majors, you should make every effort to ferret out a suit contract first. To start communication with your partner and find out what he has in the major suits, you use the two club convention. After your two club bid, if he has no biddable major suit (and a biddable suit according to the provisions of this convention should be at least Q x x x), your partner will bid two diamonds, another artificial bid which has nothing to do with the diamonds in his hand but merely denies having a major suit.

If he has four of each major he will first mention the higher-ranking suit and bid two spades. With this you will know that he has spades; you will not yet know if he also has biddable hearts. If partner bids two hearts in response to your two club convention bid, you will know that he has hearts but not spades.

With which of these hands would you rebid two hearts to a two club convention bid?

♠ A x x   ♡ K x x   ◇ A K x   ♣ Q J x x   **83**
♠ K Q x x   ♡ A J x x   ◇ A J   ♣ Q J x   **96**
♠ A Q x   ♡ A J x x   ◇ K x   ♣ K x x x   **110**

How would you respond with these hands when partner opens with one no trump?

(A) ♠ x	♡ A K 10 x x	◊ K x x	♣ J x x x
(D) ♠ K Q J x x x x	♡ x x	◊ x x x	♣ x
(F) ♠ A K x x	♡ x x x	◊ x x x	♣ x x x
(H) ♠ x x	♡ K x	◊ A Q J 10 x	♣ Q x x x
(J) ♠ x	♡ J 10 x x x	◊ Q x x x	♣ Q x x
(B) ♠ x x x	♡ K Q	◊ x x x	♣ Q J 10 x x
(E) ♠ K x	♡ x x x	◊ J x x	♣ A Q x x x
(G) ♠ A K x x	♡ A	◊ x x x x	♣ x x x x
(I) ♠ A x x x x x	♡ x	◊ x x x	♣ x x x
(C) ♠ x	♡ x x x x	◊ Q x x	♣ K x x x x

Go on to **112** to check your answers.

♠ Q J x x   ♡ K x x   ◊ Q x x   ♣ A x x

YOUR ANSWER: With this hand, a response of six no trump to a two no trump opening would be incorrect.

No, that would be the correct bid.

This hand is balanced and has 12 high-card points. With 11 or 12 points, the correct response is six no trump.

The combined strength in your hand and partner's amounts to at least 34 points, at most 36. Partner must therefore pass your six no trump bid regardless of his point count.

Please return to **111** for the *incorrect* response.

♠ A K J 10   ♡ Q x x x x   ◊ x x   ♣ x x

YOUR ANSWER: I should now bid four hearts.

Correct. You have found the major suit fit you were looking for. There are at least nine hearts in your combined hands.

To mention your spades now would mean you had five of them and that your spades were better than your hearts. To bid only three hearts would show eight or nine points. You have 13 points in support of hearts, so game is virtually assured.

If you have a weak, unbalanced hand, and partner opens with one no trump, you may be afraid your hand will make a very poor dummy at no trump. At such times the partnership may do better at the two level in a suit contract. As you know, you may raise to two no trump with only seven points and a good five-card suit. But if your hand is weaker than this—say you have less than seven points with an unbalanced hand, containing a five-card suit—you may make a simple takeout to two diamonds, two hearts, or two spades. This is definitely a weak response; partner is urged to pass and let you play the hand right there.

Your contract should be relatively safe, even if you have a very weak hand. You know that partner must have at least two cards in your suit, and if he has but two, he should have a high honor. So you will have at least seven trumps between you, possibly more.

With which of these hands would you bid two diamonds in response to a one no trump opening?

♠ Q x x   ♡ J x   ◊ A x x x x   ♣ Q x x   **84**

♠ A K x x   ♡ x x   ◊ A Q J x x   ♣ J x   **92**

♠ Q x x   ♡ x   ◊ J x x x x x   ♣ x x x   **101**

Openings of Two and Three No Trump

Like the one no trump opening, opening bids of two and three no trump show a precise range of high-card strength. For two no trump, your hand must be balanced, all four suits must be protected, and the high-card point count must be 22, 23, or 24.

The opening bid of two no trump, unlike an opening bid of two in a suit, is not forcing. If partner has nothing, he may pass.

If your hand contains 25, 26, or 27 points, is well balanced, and offers protection in all four suits, you may open with three no trump. Partner, of course, may pass if he has little or nothing. He should, however, remember that only 33 or 34 points are required for a small slam, and 37 or 38 points for a grand slam. After your opening bid of two or three no trump, he should know almost exactly the number of points in the two combined hands and be guided accordingly.

Which of these hands calls for a two no trump opening?

♠ A J x x   ♡ A Q x   ◇ A J x   ♣ K J x **97**

♠ A K J x   ♡ A x x   ◇ K x x   ♣ Q J x **102**

♠ K Q x   ♡ K Q x x   ◇ A K J   ♣ K Q x **111**

♠ A K Q   ♡ A K J   ◇ K Q J x   ♣ x x x **115**

♠ Q x x   ♡ J x x   ◇ A x x   ♣ Q x x x

YOUR ANSWER: With this hand, a response of four no trump to a two no trump opening would be incorrect.

No, that would be the correct bid.

The hand is balanced and has nine high-card points. By your direct raise beyond game, partner will know your exact strength and can decide the fate of the hand himself. If he has the maximum of 24 points, making a combined total of 33, he will go on to slam.

Please return to **111** for the *incorrect* response.

109

[from 99]

♠ Q x x x   ♡ Q x x   ◇ Q x x   ♣ K x x

YOUR ANSWER: I should bid two clubs with this hand in response to a one no trump opening.

No. This is an evenly balanced hand with a high-card point count of nine. With 4–3–3–3 distribution you should prefer a no trump contract.

This hand calls for a raise to two no trump.

Please go back to **99** for the hand that is appropriate for the two club convention.

110

[from 103]

♠ A Q x   ♡ A J x x   ◇ K x   ♣ K x x x

YOUR ANSWER: With this hand, the response to a two club convention bid would be two hearts.

Right. This hand has a biddable heart suit, but not a biddable spade suit. To be biddable according to the convention, a suit should contain at least four cards headed by the queen.

After the no trump bidder responds to the two club inquiry, the responder must take control. If you are responder and partner has denied a major suit by giving you a two diamond response, you may show a major of your own only if you have at least five cards in the suit; you should not show a four-card major.

With ten points or more (which means that you and your partner have a combined point count of at least 26), you should make a jump bid to assure reaching a game contract. With eight or nine points you may invite a game raising partner's major to three if you have uncovered a fit, or by returning to two no trump if you haven't.

Partner opens with one no trump. You respond two clubs, and partner rebids two hearts. What do you do?

♠ A K J 10   ♡ Q x x x x   ◇ x x   ♣ x x

Bid Three Hearts **100**   Bid Four Hearts **106**

Bid Two Spades **113**

♠ K Q x   ♡ K Q x x   ◇ A K J   ♣ K Q x

YOUR ANSWER: This hand calls for a two no trump opening.

Right. This hand meets all the requirements for a two no trump opening. It is well balanced, has a point count of 23, and affords protection in all four suits.

Responses to Two No Trump Opening Bids

If partner opens with two no trump and you have a *balanced* hand, you can either pass or raise no trump. Count your own high-card points, and remember that partner has 22–24 points himself.

With less than four high-card points, you should pass.

With four–eight points, which would give you a combined total of 26–32, raise to three no trump.

With nine points, raise to four no trump. If partner has the maximum of 24 points, the total will be 33 and he should bid a small slam.

With ten points, unless partner has the minimum 22 points, you will certainly have a slam. You should first bid a suit, and then raise to four no trump. This shows greater strength than a direct raise to four no trump.

With 11 or 12 points, bid six no trump. The combined number of points will be 33–36.

With 13–14 points, first bid a suit and then six no trump. Again, this is a stronger bid than an immediate raise to six no trump. It asks partner to bid seven if he has a maximum.

With 15 points in your hand, the opponents have three points at most, so you may bid seven no trump yourself.

Which of the following responses to a two no trump opening is incorrect?

SPADES	HEARTS	DIAMONDS	CLUBS	RESPONSE	
A x x	J x x	K x x x	Q x x	3 ◇	**89**
Q J x x	K x x	Q x x	A x x	6 NT	**105**
Q x x	J x x	A x x	Q x x x	4 NT	**108**
Q x x	J x x x	Q x x	K x x	4 NT	**116**

Answer
Letter

(A) Bid three hearts. You have eleven high-card points and a good five-card suit, so you should make a game-forcing response.

(B) Bid two no trump. You have eight points and a good five-card suit.

(C) Pass. A two club bid would be interpreted as an employment of the two club convention.

(D) Jump to four spades. You have only six high-card points, but your spade suit will take six tricks.

(E) Jump to three no trump. You have ten high-card points.

(F) Pass. You have just seven points.

(G) Bid two clubs. If your partner has a four-card spade suit, it will be preferable to contract for a game in spades. Otherwise, you will carry on to three no trump.

(H) Jump to three no trump. You have 12 high-card points. Although your hand is slightly unbalanced, with minor suit holdings we usually prefer to try the shorter road to game.

(I) Bid two spades. Your singleton heart will be useful in spade contract but it might prove disastrous in no trump.

(J) Bid two hearts. You have only five high-card points, but with an unbalanced holding, a heart contract would appear to be safer with your hand.

Turn to **107.**

♠ A K J 10   ♡ Q x x x x   ◇ x x   ♣ x x

YOUR ANSWER: I should now bid two spades.

No, this is not permitted. Partner has denied the spade suit by bidding hearts. You should not bid a suit of your own here unless it contains five good cards.

You have ten high-card points and you know that partner has at least four hearts headed by a high honor.

Since partner has at least 16 points, you must insist on a game contract, for you have a minimum of 26 points in your combined hands.

Now return to **110** and choose another answer.

♠ J x x x   ♡ Q x x x   ◇ J x   ♣ x x x

YOUR ANSWER: I should bid two clubs with this hand in response to a one no trump opening.

You have a point count of only four, so you should not bid at all.

With a balanced hand and less than eight points it is better to pass in response to a one no trump opening.

Please return to **99** for the hand that is appropriate for the two club convention.

♠ A K Q   ♡ A K J   ◇ K Q J x   ♣ x x x

YOUR ANSWER: This hand calls for a two no trump opening.

Although this is a balanced hand with a high-card point count of 23, it should not be opened with two no trump. For a two no trump opening bid, all four suits must be protected. The clubs in this hand are unstopped.

The proper opening bid for this hand is one diamond.

Please return to **107** to find the two no trump bid.

♠ Q x x   ♡ J x x x   ♢ Q x x   ♣ K x x

YOUR ANSWER: With this hand, a response of four no trump to a two no trump opening would be incorrect.

You are right. This would be an incorrect bid.

You have only eight high-card points, which would give the partnership at most a total of 32 points, not enough for a slam. With 4–8 points, the rule is to bid three no trump in response to a two no trump opening.

If partner opens with two no trump and you have an *unbalanced* hand, bid any six-card major suit regardless of your high-card count, or any five-card major if you have at least four high-card points (or, with a highly unbalanced hand, with three points). If you have a good six-card major and about eight high-card points, make a jump suit bid to four.

If you have four-card holdings in either or both major suits, you may respond with three clubs to probe for a major suit fit. This is similar in nature to the two club convention after a one no trump opening. (Over three clubs, partner will show a biddable four-card major suit, or without a major he will rebid three diamonds.)

If partner opens with three no trump, you know that he has 25–27 high-card points in his hand, and that he does not require a great deal of support from you. Remember that 33 points are enough for a small slam and 37 for a grand slam. With seven points and no five-card suit, bid four no trump; with eight or nine points, bid six no trump; with ten or 11 points, first bid four diamonds* and then six no trump on the next round; with 12 points bid seven no trump.

Now please go on to Chapter III, which contains more about responses to opening bids.

---

* The four diamond bid is artificial. If you bid four of a major partner may pass, and the four club bid is part of another convention (see **367**).

CHAPTER III

RESPONSES TO OPENING BIDS

When your partner has made an opening bid of one in a suit you know that he has some length in that suit (unless he has opened with one club) and that he has somewhere between 13 and about 23 points. At this stage, that's all you know about his hand. But by combining this knowledge with an appraisal of the cards which were dealt to you, you are in a position to make the first rough estimate of what your combined holdings are worth and to guide your own bidding accordingly.

With the equivalent of an opening bid in your own hand, for example, you can expect, as a rule of thumb, to reach and make a game contract. With an average hand (ten points) you will not know whether a game is available until you learn more about your partner's holding. With a minimum hand (six–ten points), game is not too likely unless partner has a strong hand, but even so you want to end up in the best possible contract and, to do so, you want to exchange as much information as possible with partner at a low level. With a bust (zero–five points), of course, you pass.

Minimum Responses

Let us first deal with the very important group of responses which are used to describe hands of minimum strength. These are the six–ten point hands. If ever you are tempted to pass with such seemingly insignificant cards, just put yourself in your partner's place. Imagine how you would feel if you were left in a one bid with 20 points in your hand, staring at a six-point dummy, which might be all you require to make game. For this reason, if no other, *you must never pass with six or more points.*

Please go on to **118**.

There are three different bids you can make with a mediocre holding:

1. One no trump, with six–ten high-card points.
2. A single raise, with seven–ten "dummy points."
3. The bid of a new suit, with six or more points counting high cards as well as distribution.

One No Trump

In order to make a response of one no trump you must have six–ten points in *high cards*. (You will remember that distribution points are not counted in making opening no trump bids; the same rule applies to the responder and on all subsequent rounds of bidding.) A one no trump response also carries certain negative inferences. It usually signifies the absence of a suit that can be shown at the level of one and it also implies an indifferent fit for the opening bidder's suit.

It is important to realize that this one no trump response does not necessarily indicate a desire on your part to play the hand in a no trump contract. It does not promise stoppers in every suit. It is merely a means of (1) keeping the bidding open with six–ten points, (2) denying trump support, and (3) denying possession of another suit which you can bid at the one level.

When partner opens the bidding with one spade, with which of these hands should you respond one no trump?

(A) ♠ x x x   ♥ Q x x x   ♦ J x x   ♣ K x x

(B) ♠ x x   ♥ x x   ♦ Q x x x   ♣ A J x x x

(C) ♠ x x x   ♥ K x x   ♦ A x x   ♣ K x x x

Hand A   **122**

Hand B   **130**

Hand C   **136**

All three hands   **141**

♠ x   ♡ Q x x x   ◇ K x x   ♣ Q x x x x

YOUR ANSWER: This hand contains exactly ten points in support of partner's one heart bid.

No. Count again. Three points for the diamond king, plus two for the club queen, plus three for the promoted heart queen, plus three for the singleton equals 11.

Please return to **133** for the correct answer.

(A)   ♠ A Q x x x   ♡ x   ◇ Q x x x   ♣ x x x

(B)   ♠ A 10 x x x   ♡ x x   ◇ Q x x   ♣ x x x

Partner opens with one club and your right-hand opponent overcalls one heart.

YOUR ANSWER: I should respond one spade with hand A.

Right you are. You have ten points; nine or more are needed for this free response at the one level. Hand B contains only seven points and therefore does not qualify for a free bid.

Needless to say, if your free bid must be made at the two level, even greater strength is required.

Go on to **152**.

♠ A Q x x   ♡ x x x   ◇ x x x   ♣ x x x

YOUR ANSWER: I should respond one spade to partner's opening one diamond bid.

Your answer is right, as far as it goes. With six points and a biddable suit you have a minimum one-over-one response here.

But your answer is incomplete. Please return to **143**.

122

[from 118]

♠ x x x   ♥ Q x x x   ♦ J x x   ♣ K x x

Partner opens with one spade.

YOUR ANSWER: I should respond one no trump.

That's right. You have six high-card points, which meets the minimum requirement for this response.

But this is not the entire answer. Please return to **118**.

123

[from 126]

(A)   ♠ J x x x   ♥ x   ♦ K J x x   ♣ x x x x

(B)   ♠ K x x x   ♥ x x   ♦ J x x x   ♣ Q x x

Partner opens with one spade and your right-hand opponent bids two hearts.

YOUR ANSWER: I should bid two spades with hand **A**.

Yes. You have adequate trump support and nine points in support of spades, which meets the minimum requirements for a free raise. Hand B contains only eight points, which is one point shy, therefore you should pass.

One-Over-One Suit Bids

When your partner opens with one of a suit, you may bid a new suit *at the one level* with as few as six points and a suit which is composed of Q x x x or better. However if you are obliged to bid at the two level in order to show your suit, your hand must contain greater strength.

Remember, whenever you bid no trump, only high-card points are counted. When there is a choice between bidding one of a suit and responding with one no trump, the suit bid is normally preferred.

How would you respond to partner's opening bid of one diamond with this hand?

♠ Q x x   ♥ K J x x   ♦ Q x x   ♣ J x x

One No Trump **128**   Two Diamonds **140**   One Heart **143**

(A)	♠ A x x	♡ K x x	◇ Q J x	♣ x x x x
(B)	♠ K Q x	♡ Q J 10 x	◇ J x x	♣ x x x
(C)	♠ Q x x	♡ K x x	◇ J x x	♣ Q x x x

YOUR ANSWER: Hand A calls for a one no trump response to partner's one club opening.

Right. You have ten high-card points and a balanced hand. The one no trump response will describe your hand with a single stroke and put partner in a position to assess accurately the combined potential of your holdings.

With hand B you should bid one heart, for a possible suit contract should be explored first. With hand C you have only eight points so that the hand does not qualify for a one no trump response.

Free Bids of One No Trump

When your right hand opponent has opened the bidding and you chose to compete with a suit of your own, this is referred to as an overcall. In other words you are calling over a bid made by your right-hand adversary.

If your partner's opening bid is overcalled by the opponent on your right the need for you to keep the bidding open has been removed, for partner will have a chance to bid again even if you pass. Any response you make now is known as a "free bid," the requirements for which are a bit stronger than they are for an ordinary response.

In order to bid one no trump under these conditions you should have from 10–12 points in high cards and a stopper in the adverse suit.

Partner opens with one diamond and the opponent on your right bids one heart. With which of these hands would it be proper for you to respond one no trump?

♠ Q J x	♡ K x x	◇ x x x	♣ Q x x x	129
♠ K x x x	♡ K J x	◇ x x x	♣ Q J x	142
♠ K x x	♡ J x x	◇ Q x x x	♣ K J x	147

125

[from 143]

♠ A K Q x x   ♡ K Q J x x   ◊ x   ♣ x x

YOUR ANSWER: I should respond one spade to partner's opening one diamond bid.

Yes, you should. You have a strong hand. You want to know more about your partner's hand. Even with your 18 points you can afford to bid only one spade and then show the extent of your power later. Partner may not pass your spade bid, for whenever the responder mentions a new suit, the opening bidder is obliged to bid again.

But your answer is only 50 per cent right. Please return to **143**.

126

[from 133]

(A) ♠ x   ♡ Q x x x   ◊ K x x   ♣ Q x x x x

(B) ♠ void   ♡ Q J x x   ◊ J x x x   ♣ x x x x x

(C) ♠ x x x   ♡ K x x   ◊ A x x x   ♣ Q x x

YOUR ANSWER: Hand B contains exactly ten points in support of partner's heart bid.

Quite right. One point for the diamond jack, plus four for the promoted heart queen-jack, plus five for the void in spades. There are 11 dummy points in hand A and nine in hand C.

The Free Raise to the Two Level

If his opening bid is overcalled by the opponent on your right, your partner will automatically have the opportunity to bid again even if you pass. For this reason you need a better hand to support partner's suit after an overcall. For a free raise, you should have 9–12 dummy points instead of seven–ten.

With which of these hands is a free raise of partner's one spade opening permissible after an overcall of two hearts?

♠ J x x x   ♡ x   ◊ K J x x   ♣ x x x x   **123**

♠ K x x x   ♡ x x   ◊ J x x x   ♣ Q x x   **148**

♠ K Q x   ♡ Q J 10 x   ◊ J x x   ♣ x x x

YOUR ANSWER: This hand would call for a one no trump response to partner's one club opening bid.

No, that would be the wrong response.

After a one club opening you should not suppress a biddable major suit. Therefore, you should bid one heart. There may be an opportunity to try no trump later if partner does not like hearts.

Please return to **141** and select the correct answer.

♠ Q x x   ♡ K J x x   ◊ Q x x   ♣ J x x

YOUR ANSWER: In response to partner's opening bid of one diamond, I would say one no trump.

No. You have nine high-card points, and even distribution, but if you say one no trump partner will probably never hear about your heart suit and a superior contract may be missed. It is usually preferable to explore suit possibilities first before trying no trump.

Please return to **123** and select the correct response.

♠ Q J x   ♡ K x x   ◊ x x x   ♣ Q x x x

Partner opens with one diamond and the opponent on your right bids one heart.

YOUR ANSWER: I should respond one no trump.

Not quite. You have a heart stopper but only eight points. In the absence of the one heart overcall, you would have responded with one no trump. But since the opposition has relieved you of the responsibility to keep the bidding open, greater strength is required to make a "free bid." With this hand, you should pass and bid only if partner requests you to do so by some form of action.

Now please return to **124** and select another answer.

130

[from 118]

    ♠ x x   ♡ x x   ◇ Q x x x   ♣ A J x x x

Partner opens with one spade.

YOUR ANSWER: I should respond one no trump.

Yes, you should. Your hand has only seven high-card points. Even when valued for a suit bid it has just nine points, which isn't enough to mention clubs at the two level.

But this is not the entire answer. Please return to **118**.

131

[from 143]

(A)   ♠ A Q x x   ♡ x x x   ◇ x x x ♣ x x x

(B)   ♠ A K Q x x ♡ K Q J x x ◇ x   ♣ x x

    YOUR ANSWER: In response to partner's opening one diamond bid, I should say one spade with either of these hands.

No doubt about it. Hand A has six points; you will say one spade and then take no further positive action. Hand B has 18 points; a one spade response will suffice for the time being until you hear further from your partner. He may not pass your bid of a new suit, so you can show the extent of your power later.

Free One-Over-One Bids

When your right-hand opponent overcalls partner's opening bid you are no longer under pressure to keep the bidding alive and should not speak, even at the one level, unless you have a fairly good hand. Nine or more points are now necessary for a one-over-one response.

Partner opens with one club and your right-hand opponent overcalls with one heart. With which of these hands would you bid one spade?

   ♠ A Q x x x ♡ x ◇ Q x x x ♣ x x x **120**

   ♠ A 10 x x x ♡ x x ◇ Q x x ♣ x x x **144**

♠ Q x x ♡ K x x ◇ J x x ♣ Q x x x

YOUR ANSWER: This hand would call for a one no trump response to partner's one club opening.

No, that would be the wrong response.

This hand contains only eight high-card points. You must have nine to eleven points to make a one no trump response to an opening one club bid.

Please return to **141** and select the correct answer.

♠ x x x ♡ Q J x x ◇ x ♣ x x x x

YOUR ANSWER: With this hand, I could give a single raise to partner's one heart opening.

Yes, you may. In dummy points the Q J in partner's suit are worth four and the singleton is worth three more, making a total of seven points, which meets the minimum requirement for this response.

There is one additional distinction to be made in calculating dummy points, i.e., when you are contemplating a raise of partner's suit, you must deduct a point for each of the following "flaws":

1. Possession of only three trumps.
2. 4–3–3–3 distribution.
3. An unguarded honor.

(Note that not having an ace in dummy is not considered a flaw, as it is in the evaluation of opening hands.)

After partner's one heart opening, which of these hands contains exactly ten dummy points?

♠ x ♡ Q x x x ◇ K x x ♣ Q x x x x **119**

♠ void ♡ Q J x x ◇ J x x x ♣ x x x x x **126**

♠ x x x ♡ K x x ◇ A x x x ♣ Q x x **149**

134

[from 161]

YOUR ANSWER: Yes, if the opening bidder has 16 points and his partner responds with two in a suit, he can expect to reach a game contract.

Quite right.

When partner responds with two in a suit, the opening bidder can count on him for at least ten points; together they have at least 26 points. This is enough to try for game in a major suit or at no trump.

Since the new-suit forcing principle applies here, there is practically no upper limit to the number of points you may have to mention a new suit at the two level. But where part of your values are distributional and there is a choice between responding with two of a suit and one no trump you should favor the latter bid, for it does not force partner to bid again.

Look at this hand, for example:

♠ 10 x x   ♡ x x   ◊ A x x   A J x x x

Partner has opened with one heart. Your hand is valued at nine points for a no trump bid, but valued at clubs, your hand is worth ten points.

If partner opens with one spade what is your response with these hands?

(A)	♠ x x	♡ A J x x x	◊ Q x x x	♣ K x
(D)	♠ x x	♡ A J x x x	◊ K x x	♣ Q x x
(F)	♠ x x	♡ A J x x x	◊ A x x	♣ x x x
(B)	♠ K x x x	♡ A x x x	◊ K x x	♣ x x
(E)	♠ x x x	♡ A K x x x	◊ K x	♣ x x x
(G)	♠ x x x	♡ A Q J x	◊ x x x	♣ Q x x
(C)	♠ x x	♡ A x x x x	◊ K x x	♣ Q x x

Check your answers on the facing page.

Answer
Letter

(A) Bid two hearts. This hand is worth 12 points valued at hearts.
(B) Bid two hearts. In support of spades the hand has 12 points. This makes it slightly too strong for a simple raise in spades and so you temporize with a bid in your best suit.
(C) Bid one no trump. You have just nine high-card points.
(D) Bid two hearts. You have ten high-card points and one for distribution, plus a reasonable five-card suit, making your hand a little strong for one no trump.
(E) Bid two hearts. You have no trump distribution, but with ten high-card points and a fine major suit, the heart bid is preferable.
(F) Bid one no trump. The heart suit is attractive, but with only nine high-card points and a balanced hand, you are not quite strong enough to increase the level of bidding.
(G) Bid one no trump. You have just nine high-card points and even distribution.

Go on to **151**.

♠ x x x   ♡ K x x   ◇ A x x   ♣ K x x x

Partner opens with one spade.

YOUR ANSWER: I should respond one no trump.

Correct. You have ten points and no biddable suit. This is the maximum holding with which you can respond one no trump.
But this is not the entire answer. Please return to **118**.

137

[from 152]

Answer
Letter

(A) Bid one heart. Always show a major suit if you can.

(B) Bid one spade. You can support hearts later. You may safely respond at the one level with a strong hand, for partner cannot pass when you bid a new suit.

(C) Bid two diamonds. You have 11 points in support of diamonds.

(D) Bid one diamond. With 11 points you are too strong for two clubs, and not strong enough for three clubs. You must therefore make a temporizing response in diamonds first.

(E) Bid two hearts. You have ten points, enough for one constructive bid. The raise of partner's major is preferred to bidding a suit of your own.

(F) Bid one spade. You have 16 points but need more information from partner. The bid of a new suit forces him to bid again.

(G) Bid one no trump. You have ten points and a balanced hand. There's little to be gained by mentioning your diamonds.

(H) Bid one no trump. There's no alternative. You can't pass with six high-card points.

(I) Pass. You should not make a free bid with only eight points.

(J) Pass. You have only five points.

(K) Pass. You have only five high-card points and no eligible response.

(L) Pass. In support of diamonds, this hand is worth only seven points (one point is subtracted for 4–3–3–3 distribution when contemplating a raise), not nearly enough for a free bid.

Go on to **138.**

Answer
Letter

(M) Bid two clubs. You have seven points in support of clubs, counting one for the doubleton and one for the promoted queen of clubs.

(N) Bid one spade. Your diamonds are better, but this hand is not strong enough to bid at the two level, and the one spade response is preferred to a bid of one no trump.

(O) Bid one no trump. You have ten high-card points and good heart protection.

(P) Bid one spade. You have 17 points and game is assured, but there is no need to rush matters until you find out where you are going. A simple forcing response fills the bill at this point.

(Q) Bid two hearts. You have nine dummy points and heart support.

(R) Bid one no trump. You have ten high-card points and two heart stoppers.

Go on to **161**.

♠ x x x x   ♡ Q J x x   ◇ x   ♣ x x x x

YOUR ANSWER: With this hand, I could not give a single raise in response to partner's opening bid of one heart.

Wrong. You have seven dummy points, which justifies a single raise. Promote the Q J of hearts to four points and count three for the singleton diamond. Seven dummy points are not much, but they might be enough to produce a game if partner has a very strong hand.

Please return to **142** for the right answer.

140

[from 123]

    ♠ Q x x   ♡ K J x x   ◊ Q x x   ♣ J x x

YOUR ANSWER: In response to partner's opening bid of one diamond, I would say two diamonds.

No. It is more important to explore for a major suit contract first. Although you have support for your partner's diamonds, you also have a major suit worth mentioning.

Please return to **123** and select the correct response.

141

[from 118]

(A)   ♠ x x x   ♡ Q x x x   ◊ J x x   ♣ K x x
(B)   ♠ x x   ♡ x x   ◊ Q x x x   ♣ A J x x x
(C)   ♠ x x x   ♡ K x x   ◊ A x x   ♣ K x x x

Partner opens with one spade.

YOUR ANSWER: I should respond one no trump with each of these hands.

This is 100 per cent correct. Hand A meets the minimum requirement (six points) and hand C the maximum (ten points). Hand B is intermediate in strength and contains a fair club suit, but clubs cannot be mentioned without going to the two level, which requires an above-average hand.

There is a slight but important difference in making a one no trump response to an opening bid of one club, as opposed to saying one no trump after an opening of one in some other suit. Since it is so easy to respond in diamonds, hearts, or spades following a one club bid, and since these responses are preferable with a reasonable suit, the requirements for a one no trump response to a one club opening are 9–11 high-card points (instead of the normal six–ten points).

Which of these hands would call for a one no trump response to partner's one club opening bid?

  ♠ A x x   ♡ K x x   ◊ Q J x   ♣ x x x **124**

  ♠ K Q x   ♡ Q J 10 x   ◊ J x x   ♣ x x x **127**

  ♠ Q x x   ♡ K x x   ◊ J x x   ♣ Q x x x **132**

(A)	♠ Q J x	♡ K x x	◇ x x x	♣ Q x x x
(B)	♠ K x x x	♡ K J x	◇ x x x	♣ Q J x
(C)	♠ K x x	♡ J x x	◇ Q x x x	♣ K J x

Partner opens with one diamond and the opponent on your right bids one heart.

YOUR ANSWER: I should respond one no trump with hand B.

Correct. You have ten points and a sure heart stopper. Hand A is two points short; hand C lacks a heart stopper.

Raising Partner's Suit to the Two Level

This is another response available with hands of mediocre strength. It takes a better hand to go to the two level in a new suit, but if you can support your partner's suit a single raise may be offered with seven–ten points. Adequate trump support consists of Q x x, J 10 x, x x x x, or better.

In anticipation of supporting partner's suit, you evaluate your hand in terms of *dummy points,* which are slightly different from the usual high-card and distribution points. For example, when raising partner, a doubleton, singleton, and void are valued at one, three and five points respectively, instead of one, two, and three. And the honors in partner's suit are promoted in the following manner: a king counts four instead of three, a queen counts three instead of two, and a jack counts two instead of one.

There is a limit to this promotion business. If your trump holding is already worth four points no promotion takes place. K Q J x, for example, cannot be promoted at all, for there are already more than four points here, so count this normally. A x x and K J x already equal four points, so there is no more room for promotion. But Q J x or K x x are normally worth only three points and should be promoted to four in support of an opening bid by partner in the same suit.

In response to an opening bid of one heart, could you give a single raise with this hand?

♠ x x x x ♡ Q J x x ◇ x ♣ x x x x

Yes **133** No **139**

♠ Q x x   ♡ K J x x   ◊ Q x x   ♣ J x x

YOUR ANSWER: In response to partner's opening bid of one diamond, I would say one heart.

Right. A response of one no trump would ignore your heart holding and might result in the loss of a superior suit contract. A diamond raise would be the least informative bid of all; minor suit contracts are usually avoided where another possibility exists.

The one heart response serves another purpose, which should be constantly borne in mind. It uses up a minimum of bidding space. It is quite possible that partner might wish to make his rebid in the spade suit; if so, he will appreciate your one heart bid, which enables him to say one spade instead of two.

Here is an important point: *The one no trump and single raise responses should not be made on hands with more than ten points.* These bids denote a moderate holding and hence they do not force partner to bid again. But there is no such limit to the strength of your hand when you respond in a new suit, even at the one level. A new-suit response therefore may denote strength or weakness and partner is obligated to bid again under the new-suit forcing principle. Furthermore, he must continue to bid once more after each and every new-suit bid you make.

Which of these hands calls for a response of one spade to partner's opening bid of one diamond?

(A)   ♠ A Q x x   ♡ x x x   ◊ x x x   ♣ x x x

(B)   ♠ A K Q x x   ♡ K Q J x x   ◊ x   ♣ x x

Hand A   **121**

Hand B   **125**

Hands A and B   **131**

♠ A 10 x x x ♡ x x ◇ Q x x ♣ x x x

Partner opens with one club and your right-hand opponent over-calls with one heart.

YOUR ANSWER: I should respond one spade.

No. You have only seven points. This hand would suffice for a one-over-one response without an intervening bid, but you need at least nine points to bid after an overcall.

Please return to **131** for the right answer.

YOUR ANSWER: No, even though the opening bidder has 16 points when his partner responds with two in a suit, he cannot ex-pect to reach game contract.

Don't be so pessimistic.

When partner responds with two in a suit, the opening bidder knows he has at least ten points. Between them they have at least 26 points—probably enough for game in a major suit or no trump.

Please return to **161** for the other answer.

♠ x x x ♡ A 10 x x x x ◇ Q x x ♣ x

YOUR ANSWER: After partner opens one club, and opponent over-calls one spade, this hand warrants a free bid.

No, there is no safe way of showing this heart suit. A bid of two hearts would force partner to the three level if he desired to re-turn to clubs, and your hand isn't strong enough to permit such drastic action.

There is, however, a hand on which you may make a free bid. Return to **168** and pick it out.

147

[from 124]

♠ K x x   ♡ J x x   ◇ Q x x x   ♣ K J x

Partner opens with one diamond and the opponent on your right bids one heart.

YOUR ANSWER: I should respond one no trump.

Not so fast. You have the proper point count for this response, but you have no stopper in the opponent's suit. A free bid of one no trump absolutely promises a stopper in the opponent's suit. You have enough to enter the auction freely, but with this hand the best choice is a raise to two diamonds.

Now please return to **124** and select another answer.

148

[from 126]

♠ K x x x   ♡ x x   ◇ J x x x   ♣ Q x x

Partner opens with one spade and your right-hand opponent bids two hearts.

YOUR ANSWER: With this hand, I should bid two spades.

No. Your spade support is good, but you have only eight points. You should pass. You need at least nine points for a free raise.

Please return to **126** for the right answer.

149

[from 133]

♠ x x x   ♡ K x x   ◇ A x x x   ♠ Q x x

YOUR ANSWER: This hand contains exactly ten points in support of partner's heart bid.

No. Count again. Four points for the diamond ace, plus two for the club queen, plus four for the promoted heart king, minus one for having only three trumps and minus one more for 4–3–3–3 distribution equals eight.

Please return to **133** for the right answer.

♠ K J x x x   ♡ x   ◊ Q J 10 x x   ♣ x x

YOUR ANSWER: This hand calls for a jump raise from one to four spades.

Yes, it certainly does. It has less than nine high-card points, five of partner's suit, and a singleton. (The total dummy point count is 11.)

Nevertheless, you must have been a bit careless, because this is not the answer we wanted you to give.

So please go back to **155**, look at the question again, and pick the best answer.

A Free Response of Two in a Suit

When an opponent overcalls your partner's opening, you may want to bid a suit of your own at the two level. You may do so with as few as ten or 11 points, provided your suit is of lower rank than your partner's suit. That is, if your response allows partner to return to his own suit at the *two* level, you are not promising any more than the ten-point minimum required for a normal takeout at the two level.

Partner has opened with one heart and the overcall has been one spade. With this 11-point hand,

♠ x x x   ♡ x x   ◊ A Q 10 x x   ♣ K J x

you may bid two diamonds because you are permitting partner to return to his suit without increasing the level of the contract.

If partner opens with one diamond and the overcall is one spade, may you bid two hearts with this hand?

♠ x x x   ♡ A K x x x   ◊ x x   ♣ K x x

Yes   **160**

No   **168**

152

[from 120]

Quiz on Responses

Partner opens with one club. You hold:

(A) ♠ x x x   ♡ Q x x x   ◊ x x x   ♣ A K x

(G) ♠ Q J x   ♡ A x x   ◊ K x x x   ♣ x x x

(M) ♠ x x   ♡ x x x   ◊ K x x x   ♣ Q x x x

(D) ♠ x x   ♡ x x   ◊ K x x x   ♣ A Q x x x

(P) ♠ K Q J x x   ♡ A Q x x   ◊ x x   ♣ K x

(J) ♠ Q x x   ♡ Q x x   ◊ J x x x   ♣ x x x

Partner opens with one heart. You hold:

(B) ♠ A K J x x   ♡ A J x x   ◊ Q x x   ♣ x

(H) ♠ Q x x   ♡ x x   ◊ K x x x x   ♣ J x x

(N) ♠ K x x x   ♡ x x   ◊ A x x x x   ♣ x x

(E) ♠ K x x x   ♡ A x x x   ◊ Q x x   ♣ x x

(Q) ♠ x   ♡ K x x x   ◊ Q x x x x   ♣ x x x

(K) ♠ K x x   ♡ Q x x   ◊ x x x x   ♣ x x x

Partner opens with one diamond. Right-hand opponent bids one heart. You hold:

(C) ♠ A Q x   ♡ x   ◊ J x x x   ♣ x x x x x

(I) ♠ A x x x x   ♡ x x   ◊ K x x   ♣ x x x

(O) ♠ K J x   ♡ K J x   ◊ x x x   ♣ Q x x x

(F) ♠ K J x x   ♡ x x   ◊ Q x x x   ♣ A K Q

(R) ♠ K x x   ♡ A K   ◊ x x x   ♣ x x x x x

(L) ♠ x x x   ♡ x x x   ◊ A K x x   ♣ J 10 x

Check your answers on **137**.

♠ x x x   ♡ K Q 10 x x   ◇ Q J x x   ♣ x

YOUR ANSWER: After partner opens one club, and opponent over-calls one spade, this hand warrants a free bid.

No, you have no safe way of taking immediate action on this ten-point holding. A response of two hearts is out of the question, even though you have a very good suit. This response would force partner to the three level in case he wanted to return to clubs, and your hand isn't strong enough to permit such drastic action. A bid of one no trump is not advisable either, for you lack protection in the adverse suit (spades).

There is, however, a hand on which you may make a free bid. Return to **168** and pick it out.

Choice of Responses

Often your hand will meet the textbook requirements for more than one response. In these cases a little common sense will come in handy, but here are a few additional suggestions to guide you.

Choice between a Single Raise and One No Trump

Since the point-count requirements are so similar for a one no trump response (six–ten) and a single raise (seven–ten), you may find that there are many hands which qualify well for either bid. Distributional factors will frequently determine your choice. With truly indeterminate hands—hands which qualify equally well for either bid—it is well to forecast the over-all future of the bidding.

With which of these hands would you favor a one no trump response to an opening one spade bid?

♠ Q x x x   ♡ x   ◇ K x x x   ♣ x x x x   **158**
♠ J 10 x   ♡ J x x   ◇ K x x x   ♣ A x x   **167**
♠ J x x x   ♡ x x x   ◇ K x x   ♣ K x x   **173**

155

[from 164]

(A)	♠ K Q x x ♡ x	◇ A J x x x	♣ x x x
(B)	♠ A J x x ♡ K x x	◇ Q J x x	♣ x x
(C)	♠ A Q x x ♡ x x x x	◇ K Q x x	♣ A

YOUR ANSWER: With hand A, I should make a jump raise to three spades.

Right. You have four good cards in spades and 13 dummy points (count three for the heart singleton). With partner's minimum of 13 points, you can probably fulfill a game contract. Your jump raise will alert partner, and he will rebid until a game or slam contract is reached.

Hand B is too weak (12 points) for a jump raise, and calls for a temporizing bid in diamonds. Hand C is too strong (18 points) for a jump raise, calling again for a temporizing bid in diamonds with the intention of supporting spades vigorously on the next round.

The Triple Raise

A triple raise from one to four in a major suit is made with a hand that is fairly weak in high cards but long in partner's trump suit. It is a pre-emptive type of bid; there is always the possibility the opponents have a good suit of their own and you are trying to pre-empt the bidding space. In these cases, naturally you have a reasonable expectation of fulfilling your contract.

This type of bid has been called a "shut out," in that you are supposed to be shutting out any further bidding from either side. However, we do not like this term. There is nothing in this bid that should discourage partner from going on and trying for a slam if all he needs is long trump support and good distribution. The bid is quite descriptive. It tells partner that you have plenty trumps and not too much high-card strength.

To qualify for this double jump of one to four in a major suit, your hand must contain at least five cards in partner's suit, though occasionally it might be done with four very good trumps, a singleton or a void, and no more than nine high-card points.

If partner opens with one spade, which of the hands below would qualify for a jump to four spades?

♠ K J x x x   ♡ x   ◇ Q J 10 x x   ♣ x x   **150**
♠ A x x x x x   ♡ x   ◇ x x   ♣ Q J x x   **159**
Both hands qualify.   **163**

(A)	♠ K J x x	♡ K x x x x	◊ void	♣ Q x x x
(B)	♠ K J x x	♡ A x x x	◊ x	♣ Q x x x

YOUR ANSWER: Hand A is worth a raise to four hearts after an original pass and partner's third-hand opening of one heart.

Right you are. Although these hands are similar, there is a small but significant difference in point count.

Hand A has a total of 12 high-card and distributional points, not enough to open, but it has 15 dummy points when the trump king is promoted to four points and the diamond void is assigned five distributional points.

Hand B also has 12 high-card and distribution points, but only 13 dummy points.

The Jump Takeout in No Trump

Some hands are best described by the jump response of two no trump. For this bid your hand must contain exactly 13–15 high-card points, no trump distribution, at least two cards in your partner's suit, and protection in each of the other three suits. Like any other single jump bid by responder, this commits you and partner to a game contract.

If partner opens with one spade, with which of these three hands may you jump to two no trump?

♠ Q x x	♡ x x x x	◊ K J x	♣ A K x **174**
♠ 10 x	♡ K J x	◊ K J 10 x	♣ A J x x **178**
♠ x x	♡ A x x x	◊ A x x	♣ K J x x **184**

93

157

[from 167]

♠ Q x x   ♥ J x x   ♦ Q x x x   ♣ Q x x

YOUR ANSWER: With this hand, I would raise partner's opening one diamond bid.

This would be doubtful technique. Whenever possible, the minor suits are avoided in probing for a possible game. A two diamond bid on this seven-point hand is not apt to lead anywhere for partner would have to have 22 points to produce game in diamonds.

Please go back to **167** and reconsider your answer.

158

[from 154]

♠ Q x x x   ♥ x   ♦ K x x x   ♣ x x x x

YOUR ANSWER: In response to a one spade opening, I would bid one no trump with this hand.

Never. Your hand is worth nine points in support of spades and only five points in no trump. Furthermore, a one no trump response might provoke partner to try another suit and you are more than satisfied with the one he has already bid. Tell him so. Bid two spades.

Please return to **154** for the best one no trump hand.

159

[from 155]

♠ A x x x x x   ♥ x   ♦ x x   ♣ Q J x x

YOUR ANSWER: This hand calls for a jump raise from one to four spades.

Yes, it certainly does. It has less than nine high-card points, six cards in partner's suit, and a singleton. (The total dummy point count is 11.)

Nevertheless, you must have been a bit careless, because this is not the answer we wanted you to give.

So please go back to **155,** look at the question again, and pick the best answer.

♠ x x x   ♡ A K x x x   ◇ x x   ♣ K x x

YOUR ANSWER: Yes, I can respond two hearts with this hand if partner opens with one diamond and opponent overcalls with one spade.

Sorry, but you shouldn't.

With only 11 points in your hand, you must be careful about your bids at the two level. A bid of two hearts would force partner to go to the *three* level to return to his diamond suit. Such a bid would lead him to believe you had greater strength than you do. He would think you could well afford the quick rise in bidding levels.

Obviously you can't. So you should refrain from mentioning your hearts. You should pass and await further developments.

Please go back to **151** for the correct choice.

Responses of Two in a Suit

As you remember, with a hand of moderate strength you may bid at the two level in your partner's suit.

In order to mention a *new* suit at the two level, however, you must have ten or more points. For instance, if partner opens with one heart, you may bid two clubs with this hand, for it is worth 11 points.

♠ x x x   ♡ x x   ◇ A x x   ♣ A Q x x x

If the opening bidder has a hand worth 16 points and his partner responds with two in a new suit, may he expect to reach a game contract?

Yes **134**

No **145**

162

[from 165]

YOUR ANSWER: After partner's jump to three no trump, I would need 13 points in my hand for a slam bid.

You'd better be more cautious.

Partner has 16, 17, or 18 points—but you can be sure of only 16. Thirteen added to 16 is only 29, and that is four points short of what you need in order to bid a small slam.

Please return to **165** for the right answer.

163

[from 155]

♠ K J x x	♡ x	◇ Q J 10 x x	♣ x x
♠ A x x x x x	♡ x	◇ x x	♣ Q J x x

YOUR ANSWER: Both of these hands call for a raise from one to four spades.

Right. Both hands have fewer than nine high-card points, five or more cards in partner's suit, and a singleton. Thus both hands would qualify for the jump from one to four spades.

If you pass at your first bidding opportunity and then your partner opens the bidding, you may find that your hand is quite well suited for play at his trump suit. Although not strong enough for an opening bid, you may now discover you have enough dummy points to be virtually certain of a game contract.

In order to be sure you reach this contract, you must do more than jump to three in partner's suit. After you have passed originally, a jump response is not forcing on partner, and if he opened with only 12 points he is permitted to pass. Therefore, when a hand is worth 14 dummy points, a triple raise from one to four is in order. In other words, a triple raise after an original pass is a stronger bid than a double raise.

After your initial pass and partner's opening bid of one heart, which of these hands would be worth a triple raise to four hearts?

♠ K J x x	♡ K x x x x	◇ void	♣ Q x x x	**156**
♠ K J x x	♡ A x x x	◇ x	♣ Q x x x	**166**

Both of these hands **176**

(A)   ♠ x x x   ♡ A 10 x x x x   ◇ Q x x   ♣ x

(B)   ♠ x x x   ♡ K Q 10 x x   ◇ Q J x x   ♣ x

(C)   ♠ K J x   ♡ A Q x x x   ◇ x x x   ♣ x x

YOUR ANSWER: After partner's one club opening and opponent's one spade overcall, hand C warrants a free bid.

Yes, you may bid one no trump for you have a balanced hand with ten high-card points and the adverse suit is safely stopped. A two heart response is not recommended with either A, B, or C, for this would force partner to the three level to rebid his own suit. None of these hands is strong enough for such drastic action. And furthermore, if you bid two hearts and partner then said three clubs, what now?

We have spent so much time on responses with poor hands that you may have forgotten all about good hands. Cheer up. We're now going to discuss those happy occasions when partner opens the bidding while you're still adding up the points in your own hand.

If your hand is worth 13 points or more, you should make it your objective to reach a game contract. In some cases you will wish to convey this information to partner at once. You may do so by making some sort of a jump bid.

Any jump bid by the responder (unless he has previously passed) is forcing to game. That is, the opening bidder and responder both are obliged to keep bidding until a game contract is reached.

In order to make a jump raise from one to three in partner's suit, responder's hand must be valued at precisely 13–16 dummy points and must contain at least four reasonably good trumps. Neither partner may thereafter stop the bidding short of game.

Look at these hands. Partner opens with one spade.

With which hand should you jump to three spades?

♠ K Q x x   ♡ x   ◇ A J x x x   ♣ x x x   **155**

♠ A J x x   ♡ K x x   ◇ Q J x x   ♣ x x   **169**

♠ A Q x x   ♡ x x x x   ◇ K Q x x   ♣ A   **183**

♠ A Q x x   ♡ K J x   ◊ A x   ♣ x x x x

YOUR ANSWER: This hand calls for a one spade response in preference to a call of two no trump after partner opens with one club, because it is desirable to show the spade suit first.

Yes. Although the hand is strong enough for the jump to two no trump and it qualifies in every other way, you must waste no time in showing your good major suit if you can do so conveniently. Your new-suit bid is a one-round force, and you will get to a game contract eventually, but meanwhile you can try to determine whether the contract should be in spades or no trump.

With more than 15 points you may not bid two no trump. With 16–18 points and no trump distribution, you respond with three no trump. In other words, to qualify for the jump to three no trump, your hand must be the equivalent of an opening one no trump hand.

This is also a very descriptive bid. Your hand must have a 4–3–3–3 distribution, and you should be very careful to have protection in all unbid suits.

If partner has opened with one spade, and you have this hand, you may bid three no trump:

♠ Q x x   ♡ A Q x   ◊ K x x x   ♣ A Q x

The hand has 4–3–3–3 distribution, 17 high-card points, and good protection in the unbid suits.

If you were the opening bidder and partner made a jump take-out to three no trump, what would be the least number of points you could hold in your hand to feel reasonably confident of fulfilling a small slam contract?

Thirteen **162**

Fifteen **175**

Seventeen **186**

♠ K J x x   ♡ A x x x   ◊ x   ♣ Q x x x

YOUR ANSWER: After an original pass, and partner's third-hand opening bid of one heart, this hand would be worth a raise to four hearts.

No, you need more points to make a triple raise after you have originally passed. Your hand is worth 13 points in support of hearts, not quite enough to insist on game if partner has made a shaded opening bid in the third seat. With this hand you may jump to three hearts, of course. Then partner can go on if he so desires.

Please return to **163** for the correct answer.

(A)   ♠ Q x x x   ♡ x   ◊ K x x x   ♣ x x x x
(B)   ♠ J 10 x   ♡ J x x   ◊ K x x x   ♣ A x x
(C)   ♠ J x x x   ♡ x x x   ◊ K x x   ♣ K x x

YOUR ANSWER: In response to a one spade opening, I should bid one no trump with hand B.

Right. Hand B contains eight points in support of spades and nine points in no trump. With hands of this type where the range is from six–eight points we prefer the one no trump response. With nine or ten points it is better to raise partner since that is more apt to encourage him.

Hand A is worth nine points in spades and is unsuitable for no trump so a spade raise is in order. Hand C is valued at seven points in both spades and no trump but the raise of a major suit is usually preferable with four trumps.

If partner has opened with a minor suit bid, you should mention a major or bid no trump if you can.

Would you raise partner's opening one diamond bid with this hand?

♠ Q x x   ♡ J x x   ◊ Q x x x   ♣ Q x x

Yes **157**
No **188**

♠ x x x   ♡ A K x x x   ◇ x x   ♣ K x x

YOUR ANSWER: No, I can't respond two hearts with this hand if partner opens with one diamond and opponent overcalls with one spade.

Right. You should not bid two hearts because you have only 11 points and can't afford to push partner's next bid to the *three* level. In case he wants to return to diamonds, that's where he would have to go.

Without support for partner's suit, and without protection in opponent's suit for a no trump bid, you have no choice but to pass.

Sometimes you have to resort to other measures when the opponent's overcall robs you of your normal response. Look at this hand:

♠ K Q x x x   ♡ 10 x x   ◇ A x x   ♣ x x

If partner opens with one heart, you would naturally respond with one spade. But if there is a two club overcall, you may not bid spades for this would force partner to the three level on the next round. You may not bid no trump, and you are a little too strong to pass. Therefore, a raise to two hearts (even though you don't quite have normal trump support) would be the most expedient course of action.

As you examine the following hands, assume that partner opens one club, and the next hand overcalls with one spade. Pick out the hand that warrants a free bid.

♠ x x x   ♡ A 10 x x x x   ◇ Q x x   ♣ x   **146**

♠ x x x   ♡ K Q 10 x x   ◇ Q J x x   ♣ x   **153**

♠ K J x   ♡ A Q x x x   ◇ x x x   ♣ x x   **164**

♠ A J x x   ♡ K x x   ◇ Q J x x   ♣ x x

YOUR ANSWER: I should make a jump raise to three spades.

No. Unfortunately, this hand falls one point short of the prescribed 13 dummy points required for a jump raise, so it is not good enough.

Count five points for ace-jack of spades, three for the king of hearts, three more for the queen-jack of diamonds, and one for the doubleton. Thus, the count comes to only 12.

The 12 dummy points make the hand too strong for a single raise to two spades. You may not make a single raise with more than ten dummy points. You should temporize with a bid in diamonds intending to raise spades subsequently.

Please return to **164** for the correct answer.

♠ K x x x x   ♡ x x   ◇ K x x   ♣ A 10 x

YOUR ANSWER: After partner's one spade opening, this hand calls for a single raise.

No. You have 12 dummy points, counting one for the promoted king of trump. This hand is too strong for a single raise. You have adequate trump support but not enough over-all strength to jump to three spades.

Yet you are strong enough for two forward-going bids and should name a suit of your own first. Even though you don't have a biddable suit according to the book definition you must make the temporizing bid of two clubs and then support spades at your next opportunity. This will give partner an accurate picture of your over-all strength; there is no danger that you will play the hand in clubs, and telling a "little white lie" about the length of a suit is infinitely preferable to lying about the strength of your hand.

Return to **188** and see if you can find a hand that allows for only a single raise.

♠ A K x x x   ♡ A Q x   ◊ Q J   ♣ K x x

YOUR ANSWER: Yes, I should make a jump shift with this hand, if partner opens with one diamond.

Certainly.

You have 20 points, 19 in high cards. You know that partner has at least 13 points, and that makes an assured total of 33. You have good spades, well-distributed values and some fitting cards in diamonds.

Partner may have a long diamond suit or he may have spade support. Or his values may be evenly distributed, in which case you may have a slam in no trump.

If partner opens with one spade, what is your response with each of these hands?

(A)	♠ A Q 10 x	♡ x	◊ A K J x	♣ Q 10 x x
(D)	♠ A Q 10 x	♡ x x x	◊ A Q x	♣ Q 10 x
(F)	♠ A x x x x	♡ x	◊ K x x	♣ J x x x
(H)	♠ A x x	♡ K Q x x	◊ K x x	♣ Q J x
(B)	♠ x	♡ A Q 10 x	◊ A K J x x	♣ x x x
(E)	♠ Q 10 9 x	♡ A K 10 x	◊ A Q x x	♣ x
(G)	♠ A x x	♡ K J x	◊ A Q J x	♣ K x x
(C)	♠ x x x	♡ A Q x	◊ K x	♣ K J 10 x x

Check your answers on the facing page.

Answer
Letter

(A) Bid three diamonds. With 19 dummy points and such magnificent spade support, it is almost certain that you will reach a slam contract in spades. The jump shift will best describe your strength to partner.

(B) Bid two diamonds. This hand is worth just 16 points and does not qualify for any jump bid. You may force the opener to bid again by naming a new suit. A game contract, of course, is assured.

(C) Bid two no trump. You have 13 high-card points and the other three suits are protected. Possession of a five-card minor suit is no deterrent to the two no trump response.

(D) Bid three spades. The hand contains 13 dummy points. Deduct one point for 4–3–3–3 distribution. Game is assured, but a slam is not likely unless partner has considerable excess values.

(E) Bid three hearts. Your hand is worth 19 dummy points and a slam in spades is almost certain. Your jump shift will convey this message to partner.

(F) Bid four spades. You have just eight high-card points, five of partner's trumps, and a singleton.

(G) Bid three no trump. You have 18 high-card points and even distribution.

(H) Bid two no trump. You have 15 high-card points and all suits well protected.

Go to **154.**

173

[*from 154*]

♠ J x x x   ♥ x x x   ♦ K x x   ♣ K x x

YOUR ANSWER: In response to a one spade opening, I would bid one no trump with this hand.

Here the choice is a fine one. You have seven points in support of spades, seven points for no trump. But with very good support for your partner's *major* suit we would recommend a raise to two spades. If your spade and diamond holdings were reversed, a one no trump response would be preferable.

Please return to **154** for the best one no trump hand.

174

[*from 156*]

♠ Q x x   ♥ x x x x   ♦ K J x   ♣ A K x

YOUR ANSWER: After partner's one spade opening, I would jump to two no trump with this hand.

Sorry, but no.

It has enough high-card points (13) for the jump, but it lacks protection in hearts.

You need to have at least two cards in partner's suit, but not necessarily any protection there. You must have protection in the other three suits, however, and you don't in hearts.

Please go back to **156** for the hand that does qualify for this response.

175

[*from 165*]

YOUR ANSWER: After partner's jump to three no trump, I would need only 15 points in my hand for a small slam bid.

No, that would be a bit risky.

You can depend on only 16 points in partner's hand, and 15 added to 16 makes only 31 points. You should be sure of at least 33 high-card points to make a small slam with any confidence.

So please return to **165** for the right answer.

♠ K J x x   ♡ K x x x x   ◊ void   ♣ Q x x x

♠ K J x x   ♡ A x x x   ◊ x   ♣ Q x x x

YOUR ANSWER: Both of these hands are worth a raise to four spades after an original pass and partner's third-hand opening of one heart.

Your answer is not correct. Only one of these hands is worth the triple raise.

Although the hands are similar in general strength and distribution, look them over again and count the points carefully. You will see that there is enough difference to make one of the hands qualify for a triple raise in this situation. Remember, you need more strength for a triple raise after an opening pass than you would for a triple raise after a simple opening bid.

Now return to **163** and choose the correct answer.

♠ Q J x   ♡ x x   ◊ K 10 x x x   ♣ A x x

YOUR ANSWER: After partner's one spade opening, this hand calls for a single raise.

No. This hand is worth 11 points in support of spades. There are ten points in high cards and one for the doubleton. The one-point promotion for your holding in spades is canceled by the fact that you are raising with only three trumps.

With 11 dummy points, this hand is too strong for a single raise. Yet you are strong enough to make two bids and should name a suit of your own first. So bid two diamonds and then support spades on the next round. This will give partner an accurate picture of your over-all strength.

Return to **188** and see if you can find a hand that allows for only a single raise.

178

[from 156]

(A) ♠ Q x x   ♥ x x x x   ♦ K J x   ♣ A K x

(B) ♠ 10 x   ♥ K J x   ♦ K J 10 x   ♣ A J x x

(C) ♠ x x   ♥ A x x x   ♦ A x x   ♣ K J x x

YOUR ANSWER: After partner's one spade opening, I would jump to two no trump with hand B.

Yes. Hand B fulfills all the requirements for this type of jump bid. It has 13 high-card points, no trump distribution, two cards in partner's suit, and good protection in the other three suits.

Hand C qualifies in every way except that it is short in high-card strength; it has only 12 points. Hand A also qualifies in every respect but one; the hearts are unprotected.

If you have a choice between making a jump to two no trump and responding at the one level in a good four-card major suit, you should give preference to the major suit. Even though you have not told partner immediately that your hand warrants a game contract, your new-suit bid is forcing for one round and you can continue to make forcing bids until you reach the desired contract.

Assume partner has opened the bidding with one club.

(A) ♠ K x x   ♥ A Q x   ♦ K J 10 x   ♣ x x x

(B) ♠ A Q x x   ♥ K J x   ♦ A x   ♣ x x x x

Holding hand A you respond two no trump, but with hand B the preferred bid is one spade.

Why was the bid two no trump bypassed with hand B?

Because it is preferable to show your major suit first. **165**

Because hand B is weaker and is not worth a jump. **191**

Because two no trump requires greater strength after a one club opening bid. **196**

♠ A x x x   ♡ x   ◇ A 10 x x x   ♣ x x x

YOUR ANSWER: After partner's one spade opening, this hand calls for a single raise rather than a bid in my own suit.

No, it's a little better than that. The hand has 11 dummy points, so it is strong enough for two bids. And it is only sensible to take full advantage of this.

To communicate this information about your strength to partner, and to let him know about the shape of your hand, first bid your diamonds at the *two* level.

Partner is forced to bid again, and regardless of what his bid is, you can then support his spades.

Return to **188** and see if you can find a hand that allows for only a single raise.

♠ A J x x   ♡ K 10 x x   ◇ x x x   ♣ x x

YOUR ANSWER: After partner's one club opening, this hand calls for a one spade response.

No, the hand contains only nine points and is worth only one constructive effort. Ordinarily you name your higher-ranking suit, but you must also try to envision further bidding developments. If you say one spade here and partner has four hearts he would like to mention, he may not be able to do so at the two level and so the heart suit will be lost. But if you say one heart he can raise if he has hearts too, or he can bid one spade himself, if he has four of that suit.

Now return to **198** and choose the proper answer.

181

[from 187]

♠ K x x x   ♡ x x   ◊ K 10 x x   ♣ A x x

YOUR ANSWER: After partner's third-hand opening of one spade, the best bid with this hand would be two diamonds.

This would be your proper response had you not passed originally. The bid of a new suit would force partner to bid again and you could support spades later. But having passed originally, your two diamond bid is no longer forcing on partner and you may be left there when you prefer to be in spades.

Go back to **187** and try to find the best bid for this hand.

182

[from 186]

♠ A K x x x   ♡ A Q x   ◊ Q J   ♣ K x x

YOUR ANSWER: No, I should not make a jump shift with this hand if partner opens with one diamond.

Why not?

You have 20 points. You know that partner has at least 13 points, and that makes a total of 33. You have impressive spades and well-distributed values with a couple of fitting cards in partner's suit.

Slam prospects are very attractive, and a jump shift will inform partner of your interest.

So please go back to **186** for the correct answer.

183

[from 164]

♠ A Q x x   ♡ x x x x   ◊ K Q x x   ♣ A

YOUR ANSWER: I should make a jump raise to three spades.

Definitely not. This hand is worth 18 dummy points. You should not make a jump raise with less than 13 or more than 16. With this hand you must temporize first by bidding diamonds.

If you make the double raise with more than 16 points, partner will underestimate your strength and you may miss a slam.

Please return to **164** for the correct answer.

♠ x x   ♡ A x x x   ◇ A x x   ♣ K J x x

YOUR ANSWER: After partner's one spade opening, I would jump to two no trump with this hand.

No.

Remember you need 13–15 high-card points for a jump to two no trump, and this hand contains only 12. Otherwise, with the two cards in partner's spades, and with no trump distribution and good protection, the hand would qualify.

Please go back to **156** for the hand that does qualify for a jump to two no trump.

(A)   ♠ K x x x x   ♡ x x   ◇ K x x   ♣ A 10 x

(B)   ♠ Q J x   ♡ x x   ◇ K 10 x x x   ♣ A x x

(C)   ♠ A x x x   ♡ x   ◇ A 10 x x x   ♣ x x x

YOUR ANSWER: After partner's one spade opening, all three of these hands call for a single raise rather than any other bid.

No, not at all.

If the choice is between raising partner's suit and bidding a new suit, and your hand is worth 11 or 13 points, then you should plan on making two bids. Mention your own suit first, and the next time around raise partner's suit.

If you will look these hands over carefully, you will see that each one is worth at least 11 points when valued as a dummy; every one of them is too strong for a single raise.

In the case of hands B and C, bid two diamonds first. With hand A you will have to improvise a temporizing response of two clubs.

Go back to **188** for the correct answer.

YOUR ANSWER: After partner's jump to three no trump, I would need 17 points in my hand to make a slam bid.

Right. And it's just a matter of simple arithmetic.

You need a total of about 33 points for a small slam. You know from partner's jump to three no trump that he has 16 to 18 points, but you can depend on only 16. Subtract 16 from 33 and that leaves 17; you would need at least 17 points in your hand to be sure of a slam at this point in the bidding.

The Jump Shift

With more than 18 points you must not respond with three no trump. Instead you make a jump shift in a new suit—the strongest response in bridge. This bid carries slam connotations, for responder knows, with 19 points in his hand and a minimum of 13 in partner's, that the total can be no less than one point removed from small slam requirements. Aside from the 19-point minimum there is one other prerequisite to making this bid: You have to know where the hand can conveniently be played. This means that either you can support partner's suit, or you have a self-sustaining suit of your own, or else you have enough general high-card strength to warrant a slam in no trump. Without this assurance of a satisfactory fit, you should be content to make a simple forcing response; then if your probing produces promise of a fit you can jump at a later opportunity.

If you have this hand, which has a value of 20 points:

♠ A K Q 10 x   ♡ x   ◊ A K J x x   ♣ x x

and partner opens with one heart, a jump shift to two spades is in order. You have no support for partner's suit, of course, but you have two suits which are virtually self-sufficient.

If partner opens with one diamond, should you make a jump shift with this hand?

♠ A K x x x   ♡ A Q x   ◊ Q J   ♣ K x x

Yes **171**

No **182**

110

(A)   ♠ A J x x   ♡ K 10 x x   ◇ x x x   ♣ x x
(B)   ♠ A Q 10 x   ♡ K Q J x   ◇ x x   ♣ x x x

YOUR ANSWER: After partner's one club opening, hand B calls for a one spade response but not hand A.

Very good.

Hand B has 13 points and is strong enough for two forward-going bids, thus enabling you to show both the hearts and the spades. And, since the two suits are of equal length, spades should be bid first and the hearts on the next round.

Hand A has only nine points and merits only one constructive effort. If you say one spade here and partner has four hearts he would like to mention, he may be too weak to do so at the two level. So it is more practical to say one heart with this hand. Partner can raise hearts if he fits that suit or he can bid spades himself if he has a four-card suit.

Partner might have a moderate hand like this:

♠ x x   ♡ Q J x x   ◇ K x x   ♣ A K x x

If you chose to bid spades with hand A, he will feel obliged to rebid one no trump, and the heart suit will be lost.

Responding When You Have Previously Passed

Under these circumstances you must bear these two facts in mind: (1) partner may have opened with as few as 10–11 points, and (2) the only forcing response you can make after originally passing is to jump in a new suit.

Let's say that partner opens with one spade in third position and you have this hand:

♠ K x x x   ♡ x x   ◇ K 10 x x   ♣ A x x

What would your response be? Try to think this through on your own, and then see if you arrive at the right answer.

The best bid would be:

Two Diamonds   **181**
Two Spades   **189**
Three Spades   **199**

188

[from 167]

♠ Q x x   ♡ J x x   ◇ Q x x x   ♠ Q x x

YOUR ANSWER: With this hand, I would not raise partner's opening bid of one diamond.

You are so right. A two diamond bid is not apt to be productive since a game in diamonds would require a combined partnership total of about 29 points. Bid one no trump and leave the rest to partner.

Choice between Raising Partner and Bidding Your Own Suit

If partner opens in a minor suit you will naturally mention any biddable major if you have six or more points.

If partner opens in hearts and you have both heart support and a biddable spade suit you will mention the spades only if you can afford to make a second bid. Generally speaking, you can afford the luxury of a second bid only when blessed with more than ten points, so with a hand of moderate strength, it is better to ignore your spades and say two hearts.

If your own suit is of lower rank than partner's, you must, of course, have a minimum of ten points to mention it, for to do so you will have to bid at the two level.

Let us assume that partner has opened with one spade. With which of these hands should you give a single raise instead of naming your own suit?

♠ K x x x x   ♡ x x   ◇ K x x   ♣ A 10 x **170**

♠ Q J x   ♡ x x   ◇ K 10 x x x   ♣ A x x **177**

♠ A x x x   ♡ x   ◇ A 10 x x x   ♣ x x x **179**

All of them **185**

None of them **195**

♠ K x x x   ♡ x x   ◊ K 10 x x   ♣ A x x

YOUR ANSWER: After partner's third-hand opening of one spade, the best response with this hand would be two spades.

You're on the right track, but this is not the best response.

With only 11 points, you correctly passed originally instead of opening the bidding. But now your hand becomes worth 12 points when valued as a dummy and if partner has anything more than the barest minimum you can make game in spades. So you must tell him this by making a more vigorous bid than two spades.

Go back to **187** and see if you can now figure out which of the other two bids it should be.

♠ J x x x x   ♡ x   ◊ A K J 10 x x   ♣ x

YOUR ANSWER: Having passed on the first round, I should respond to partner's one spade opening with a bid of three diamonds.

Yes, with 16 dummy points and a fine distributional fit, you can afford to probe the possibilities of slam and the only response which will enable you to do this is a jump in a new suit. When you raise spades on the next round, partner will have a good picture of your distribution, and he will be in a better position to appraise the potentialities of the hand.

Now go on to Chapter IV, on **200,** to learn about rebids by the opening bidder.

191

[from 178]

♠ A Q x x   ♡ K J x   ◊ A x   ♣ x x x x

YOUR ANSWER: This hand calls for a one spade response in preference to a two no trump response after partner opens with one club because it is too weak for the jump.

No. This hand is quite strong enough for the jump to two no trump; it has protection in each of the other suits, no trump distribution, and 14 high-card points. There is a valid reason however why this jump is not preferred.

Turn back to **178** and see if you can pick out the real reason why you make the bid of one spade.

192

[from 195]

♠ A x x   ♡ void   ◊ K x x x x x   ♣ A x x x

YOUR ANSWER: Yes, this hand calls for a raise of partner's one spade opening to three spades.

Not quite. Even though this hand has the required count (15 dummy points, counting five for the heart void and one deduction for only three trumps) for a jump raise, it does not have the necessary four good trumps. While game is probable in spades, you must bid two diamonds first and save the spade raise for later.

Please return to **195** for the other answer.

(A)   ♠ A J x x   ♡ K 10 x x   ◇ x x x   ♣ x x

(B)   ♠ A Q 10 x   ♡ K Q J x   ◇ x x   ♣ x x x

YOUR ANSWER: After partner's one club opening, both hands would call for a one spade response.

No, hand A contains only nine points and is worth only one constructive effort. Ordinarily you name your higher-ranking suit first, but you must also try to envision further bidding developments. If you say one spade here and partner has four hearts he may not be able to mention them at the two level and so the heart suit will be lost. But if you say one heart he can raise if he has hearts too, or he can bid one spade himself if he has four of that suit.

Now return to **198** and choose the proper answer.

♠ J x x x x   ♡ x   ◇ A K J 10 x x   ♣ x

YOUR ANSWER: Having passed on the first round, I should respond to partner's one spade opening with a bid of three spades.

No, the hand is much too good for this. Your hand has become worth 16 points in support of spades which assures you of a game contract and warrants slam investigation. A three spade bid might be passed by partner and you cannot afford to take this risk.

Now return to **199** and pick out the right response.

195

[from 188]

(A) ♠ K x x x x   ♡ x x   ◊ K x x   ♣ A 10 x
(B) ♠ Q J x   ♡ x x   ◊ K 10 x x x   ♣ A x x
(C) ♠ A x x x   ♡ x   ◊ A 10 x x x   ♣ x x x

YOUR ANSWER: None of these hands calls for an immediate raise to partner's one spade opening.

Congratulations. That is correct.

If the choice is between raising partner's suit and bidding a new suit, and your hand is worth 11 or 12 points, you must plan on making two bids. Mention your own suit first, and then raise partner's.

Each of these hands is worth at least 11 points when valued as a dummy, which makes every one of them too strong for a simple raise. With hands B and C, bid two diamonds first. With hand A you will have to invent a temporizing response of two clubs. It doesn't matter that the suit is not biddable. The two club bid is part of a campaign to give partner an accurate idea of your over-all strength, and there is no likelihood of your having to play a club contract.

Choice between a Double Raise and a New-Suit Bid

Sometimes, with 13 or more points, the choice may be between giving a double raise and naming a new suit. Either bid may be correct, but you should try to give the one that best describes your hand. For instance, with this hand:

♠ J x x x x   ♡ x   ◊ A Q x x   ♣ K x x

you might consider a two diamond response after partner has opened with one spade. However, this is not recommended because the jump to three spades is more descriptive of your values. When there is a direct bid that precisely describes your hand, it is preferable to indirect action.

Partner opens with one spade, and you hold:

♠ A x x   ♡ void   ◊ K x x x x x   ♣ A x x x

Does this hand call for a jump to three spades?

Yes **192**

No **198**

116

♠ A Q x x   ♡ K J x   ◇ A x   ♣ x x x x

YOUR ANSWER: This hand calls for a one spade response instead of a two no trump response after partner opens with one club because two no trump requires greater strength after a one club bid.

This answer is wrong.

Perhaps you were influenced by the fact that the one no trump response requires greater strength when the opening is one club. However, the same rule does not apply to a two no trump response.

Turn back to **178** and see if you can pick out the real reason why you make the bid of one spade.

♠ J x x x x   ♡ x   ◇ A K J 10 x x   ♣ x

YOUR ANSWER: Having passed on the first round, I should respond to partner's one spade opening with a bid of four spades.

No, the hand is too good for this. With 16 dummy points you will settle for no less than a game contract, but first you should probe the possibilities of slam. If you bid four spades partner may be obliged to pass even though he knows you are making a strong bid.

Now return to **199** and pick out the right response.

♠ A x x ♡ void ♢ K x x x x x ♣ A x x x

YOUR ANSWER: No, this hand does not call for a raise of part-ner's one spade opening to three spades.

Right you are.

Even though this hand has the required count for a jump raise (you have 15 dummy points counting five for the heart void and one deduction for only three trumps), it does not have the necessary four trumps. While game is probable in spades, you must bid two dia-monds first and save the spade raise for later.

Responding with Two-Suiters

When you have two suits of your own and feel that your hand is good enough to show both of them, you should mention them in the orthodox sequence. That is, with suits of equal length, bid the high-ranking first; with suits of unequal length, bid the longer first. But remember, this is only if you intend to show both of them.

If partner has opened with one heart and you hold this hand:

♠ A K J x ♡ x x ♢ x x ♣ K 10 x x x

you are strong enough to show both black suits, so your response should be two clubs. After you bid spades at your next opportunity, partner will have an accurate picture of your distribution.

If partner opens with one club, which of these hands calls for a one spade response?

♠ A J x x ♡ K 10 x x ♢ x x x ♣ x x **180**

♠ A Q 10 x ♡ K Q J x ♢ x x ♣ x x x **187**

Both of them **193**

♠ K x x x ♡ x x ◇ K 10 x x ♣ A x x

YOUR ANSWER: After partner's third-hand opening of one spade, the best bid with this hand would be three spades.

Right.

Your hand is worth 12 points as a dummy and is too good for a single raise. A double raise will tell partner that you have a good hand despite your original pass. If he has a full opening bid he can now bid game; if he made a shaded third-hand opening however, he is at liberty to pass.

If you had not already passed, your best response would be two diamonds. This would force partner to bid again and consequently afford you the opportunity to support spades on the next round. After your original pass, however, your new-suit bid is no longer forcing. If you make a two diamond bid now, you may find yourself left in it.

When you have previously passed, a jump in a new suit is absolutely forcing and announces that you insist upon reaching an eventual game contract. Obviously, since you were unable to open the bidding, your enthusiasm must be based upon a great satisfaction in partner's suit. In fact, you might have chosen to jump to game in his suit, but because of your great distribution you desired to alert partner of the possibilities of a slam.

Let's say you hold this 13-point hand and choose to pass:

♠ J x x x x ♡ x ◇ A K J 10 x x ♣ x

If partner happens to open in third position with one spade, things look considerably brighter. What should your response be?

Three Diamonds **190**

Three Spades **194**

Four Spades **197**

CHAPTER IV

REBIDS BY THE OPENING BIDDER

It has long been our impression that a great many "readers" of bridge books never get past the first few chapters. They probably reason that they should know something about opening bids and responses but that after that the bidding process sort of takes care of itself.

Nothing could be further from the truth. Just as many bridge auctions are mishandled on the second round of bidding as on the first round—perhaps more. If you neglect even a single aspect of this bidding business your entire game will suffer.

Rebids are no more difficult to master than are opening bids. They are a logical continuation of the same thought process. And they are just as vitally important to the outcome of the final contract.

As you know, opening bids of one in a suit may be made with hands containing anywhere from 13 to about 23 points. At his second turn to bid, the opener has his first and best opportunity to pinpoint his point count more precisely. Here's how it's done:

First of all, for purposes of analysis, opening hands can be classified into these four groups:

A. *The Minimum Hand,* with 13, 14, 15, and sometimes 16 points.
B. *The Good Hand,* with 16, 17, 18, and sometimes 19 points.
C. *The Very Good Hand,* with 19, 20, or 21 points.
D. *The Rock Crusher,* with 22 or more points.

Already you can sense that each of these four types of hands calls for a different type of rebid. So let's test your instincts right now, before we give you any further information.

Having opened this hand with one spade, what is your rebid after partner's response of two spades?

♠ A Q J x x   ♡ x x x   ◇ A x x x   ♣ x

Pass **208**   Three Diamonds **211**
Three Spades   **216**

120

♠ x x   ♡ A K J x   ◇ K J x   ♣ K x x x

You opened with one heart and partner bid one spade.

YOUR ANSWER: I should now bid two clubs.

This would not be the worst bid in the world, but there is a better call with a balanced hand of minimum proportions.

After this slight hint you may return to **222** and find the right answer.

♠ A Q x x x x   ♡ x   ◇ x x   ♣ K Q x x

You opened with one spade and partner bid two spades.

YOUR ANSWER: I should now pass.

Your slide rule must be broken.

Your hand was worth 14 points originally, and now revalues to 17 points when partner raises your suit (add one for your fifth spade and two more for your sixth). Partner has promised from seven–ten points, so your combined total lies between 24 and 27. With only 26 points needed for game, you should not stop now.

Return to **208** and pick a better rebid.

♠ A K x x x x   ♡ A J x   ◇ x x x   ♣ x

You opened with one spade and partner bid one no trump.

YOUR ANSWER: I should now pass.

No. Your hand is unbalanced, and your spade suit is rebiddable. Despite your minimum strength you should warn partner that your hand will play better in spades rather than in no trump. With this hand you should rebid two spades.

Please return to **206** and look for the hand which calls for a pass.

204

[from 212]

♠ A K x x   ♡ K J x   ◇ A Q x x   ♣ x x

YOUR ANSWER: I should raise partner's one no trump response to three no trump.

You'd better recount your points.

Partner has shown six–ten high-card points. You have 17 high-card points. You need nine more for game. So instead of making any assumptions, why not ask partner if he has nine points?

If you say two no trump, partner will know that you want to go on. If his one no trump response was in the minimum range, he will decline your invitation and pass. If he has a near maximum, he will carry on to three no trump.

Go back to **212** and choose the correct answer.

205

[from 213]

♠ x   ♡ A K x x   ◇ K J x x   ♣ K J x x

The bidding between you and your partner has gone:

SOUTH	WEST	NORTH	EAST
1 ♡	Pass	2 ♡	Pass
3 ♣	Pass	3 ♡	Pass
?			

YOUR ANSWER: I should now pass.

Right. You have shown your interest in a game bid by bidding again after partner's simple raise. Even with this knowledge he has been unable to carry on to game. In other words, if he had a good raise—nine–ten points, he should have done something more enthusiastic than merely returning to three hearts. He is, therefore, marked with about seven–eight points, and the combined hands do not add up to 26. You are obliged to pass.

Go on to **206**.

Rebids after a One No Trump Response

When partner responds one no trump you know he has six–ten high-card points and probably no special support for your suit. Your appraisal of game possibilities is based upon the same sort of point-count mathematics as after a single raise. But even if you are not contemplating a game, you will wish to determine the best place to play the hand, and in order to do this there are three questions you must ask yourself:

(1) Is my hand suitable for no trump play?

(2) Is my original suit strong enough to rebid in the light of the knowledge that partner may not have any support for it?

(3) Do I have a second suit which he might like better?

In order to pass or raise the no trump response you must reassess your hand in terms of high-card points, suit protection, and distribution. Remember that a one no trump response does not show stoppers in every suit. Broadly speaking, with a balanced minimum hand you pass, and with a hand which is unsuitable for no trump play, you rebid your original suit or name a new one.

Having opened one spade, with which of these hands should you pass partner's one no trump response?

♠ A K x x x x   ♡ A J x   ◇ x x x   ♣ x   **203**

♠ A K J x x   ♡ x x   ◇ K J x   ♣ J x x   **212**

♠ A K x x x   ♡ A Q J x   ◇ x x   ♣ x x   **219**

♠ x x   ♡ A K J x   ◇ K J x   ♣ K x x x

You opened with one heart and partner bid one spade.

YOUR ANSWER: I should now bid two hearts.

With what? ♡ A K J x ? Not at all.
Your hearts are not rebiddable.
Return to **222** and try again.

208

[from 200]

♠ A Q J x x   ♡ x x x   ◊ A x x x   ♣ x

You opened with one spade and partner bid two spades.

YOUR ANSWER: I should now pass.

You are so right.

This little hand illustrates three enormously important points: (1) If you have already shown the full value of your hand, and partner has not invited you to go on, *don't bid again.* (2) We have here a graphic demonstration of the usefulness of the upper limits which are placed on responder's minimum bids. You *know* partner has no more than ten points and that you therefore *cannot* make game. (3) Once you have found a suitable place to play the hand, and you know that game is impossible, there is no point in raising the level of the contract.

Rebids after a Single Raise by Partner

After a single raise by partner, the trump suit is usually established. Now that a fit has been found and your suit solidified, you must re-evaluate your hand in terms of *rebid points*. In addition to your original high-card and distributional points, you add one point if you have a fifth trump, two more points for a sixth, two more for a seventh, et cetera. Having done this, you now add your total rebid points to the seven–ten promised by partner to determine your future action.

If you open with one spade and partner raises to two spades, what would be your rebid with the following hand?

♠ A Q x x x x   ♡ x   ◊ x x   ♣ K Q x x

Pass **202**

Three Spades **213**

Four Spades **217**

♠ A x x   ♡ x   ◊ A K J x x   ♣ x x x x

YOUR ANSWER: If I opened the bidding with one diamond and partner responded one spade, I should not raise partner's bid.

Your hand is worth 14 points valued as a dummy, which is ample for a raise to two spades. In raising your partner's suit, you let him know that you have at least a trifle more than a bare minimum in over-all strength or trump support. This information enables him to bid his hand more accurately.

Remember, with just 13 dummy points you may raise your partner's suit provided you have four of his trumps. If you have 14 or more dummy points, you may raise with only three trumps.

Now return to **229** and choose the right answer.

♠ x   ♡ A K x x   ◊ K J x x   ♣ K J x x

The bidding between you and your partner has gone:

SOUTH	WEST	NORTH	EAST
1 ♡	Pass	2 ♡	Pass
3 ♣	Pass	3 ♡	Pass
?			

YOUR ANSWER: I should now bid four diamonds.

By no means.

You have bid your hand to its limit and partner has shown no inclination to proceed. If he had more than a minimum raise he would have shown it by making a more constructive bid than a mere return to three hearts.

Please go back to **213** and choose another answer.

211

[from 200]

♠ A Q J x x   ♡ x x x   ◇ A x x x   ♣ x

You opened with one spade and partner bid two spades.

YOUR ANSWER: I should now say three diamonds.

We hope that no one turns to this page.

You have 13 points . . . a bare minimum. You know partner has seven–ten dummy points for his raise. At most the partnership has a total of 23 points. Already you're at the two level and a fit has been established. Mentioning a brand-new suit a level higher is well calculated to get you overboard.

Return to **200** and try again.

212

[from 206]

(A)	♠ A K x x x x	♡ A J x	◇ x x x	♣ x
(B)	♠ A K J x x	♡ x x	◇ K J x	♣ J x x
(C)	♠ A K x x x	♡ A Q J x	◇ x x	♣ x x

You have opened with one spade and partner bid one no trump.

YOUR ANSWER: I should pass with hand B.

Right. With hand A you should rebid two spades; with hand C you should say two hearts. With hand B there is no reason to escape from no trump. True, your spades are rebiddable, but the hand is balanced and in the minimum-strength range.

Here is a tip worth remembering: *The best place to play an indifferent hand is one no trump.*

Sometimes, of course, a raise of the no trump is indicated. Where your hand is well suited for no trump play, this decision rests on simple arithmetic.

After having opened the bidding with one spade, with which of the following hands would you raise partner's one no trump response to three no trump?

♠ A K x x   ♡ K J x   ◇ A Q x x   ♣ x x   **204**

♠ A K x x x   ♡ A Q x   ◇ A x x   ♣ K x   **222**

♠ A Q x x x x   ♡ x   ◊ x x   ♣ K Q x x

You opened with one spade and partner bid two spades.

YOUR ANSWER: I should now bid three spades.

You should do just that.

Your hand was originally worth 14 points but you have 17 rebid points (when partner raises, you add one for the fifth spade, two more for the sixth), and partner has promised from seven–ten points. If he has a minimum response (seven–eight points) he will pass your three spade bid; if he has a maximum (nine–ten points) he will raise you to four spades. Simple, isn't it?

Pursuing the same train of thought, it should be already obvious that if the rebid value of your hand amounts to 19 points you can jump directly to game after partner's raise, for you are assured of the necessary 26 points. With more than 22 points, of course, you will want to explore slam possibilities.

Don't get the impression that you must always stick to the same suit just because partner has raised it. If, for example, you had opened one spade with

♠ A K x x   ♡ A Q J x   ◊ x x   ♣ Q x x

and partner had raised to two spades with

♠ Q x x   ♡ K x x x x   ◊ x x x   ♣ K x

you might miss the boat if you rebid three spades. You have nothing to lose by making your rebid in hearts. Partner will be delighted to assist you in your second suit.

In the next example the bidding proceeds:

You	Partner
1 ♡	2 ♡
3 ♣	3 ♡

What do you bid next, if this is your hand?

♠ x   ♡ A K x x   ◊ K J x x   ♣ K J x x

I should pass **205**
I should bid four diamonds **210**
I should bid four hearts **218**

214

[from 226]

Answer
Letter

(A) Two diamonds. Diamonds are lower ranking than your first suit, and can therefore be shown conveniently.

(B) One spade. The convenient opportunity to show a four-card major suit at the one level should not be bypassed.

(C) Pass. Your spades are rebiddable but you aren't going anywhere, and your hand is suited for no trump.

(D) Two clubs. This hand is slightly unbalanced and you should offer partner a choice of suits. He may like clubs, or he may have a good red suit.

(E) One no trump. You have a minimum hand of balanced proportions.

(F) Four hearts. You have 21 points. Partner has announced at least six so that game is assured.

(G) Two diamonds. With 16 high-card points and a singleton, you should probe further.

(H) Two diamonds. This is preferable to two hearts, for it gives partner a choice of two suits for parking purposes.

(I) Two spades. This hand is worth 14 points in support of spades, sufficient for an immediate raise with three-card trump support.

(J) Pass. You're too weak for game aspirations after this response. With a balanced hand, don't rebid a five-card suit over one no trump.

(K) One spade. The rebid of a new suit at the one level promises no more than minimum values.

(L) Two diamonds. This hand is worth 18 points in support of spades, so it is a little too strong for an immediate raise. A temporizing rebid is called for.

(M) One no trump. This is preferable to two diamonds with such a balanced holding.

(N) Two no trump. The one no trump response over one club shows 9–11 high-card points. You have 15, which means there is a good chance for game, if partner has more than a minimum.

Go on to **215**.

Jump Rebids in Partner's Suit

When partner bids a new suit at the one level he has six or more points. If you have 17–19 points in support of his suit you may give him a double raise. This is not a forcing bid. With a bare response partner may pass; with anything in excess he will bid game in a major suit; if he has the equivalent of an opening bid himself, he may look for a slam.

In contrast to the rules for responder, a raise of partner's suit from one to four by opener is stronger than a raise from one to three. This is because the double raise by opener is not forcing; if he is sure of game, therefore, he must bid it himself, or make a bid which is absolutely forcing upon partner. The raise from one to four of responder's suit requires 20 or 21 dummy points.

Having opened with one diamond, with which of these hands would you not raise partner's one spade response to the four level?

♠ A J x x ♡ x x ◇ A K J x ♣ A Q x **223**

♠ K x x x ♡ A ◇ A K x x ♣ K x x x **232**

♠ A Q J x ♡ K x ◇ A Q J x ♣ J x x **236**

♠ A Q J x x ♡ x x x ◇ A x x x ♣ x

You opened with one spade and partner said two spades.

YOUR ANSWER: I should now say three spades.

If you would voluntarily go to three spades with this hand, you need to read this chapter even more than we suspected.

You have 13 points—a bare minimum opening. You know partner has a maximum of ten dummy points, and maybe only seven. With at most a combined partnership total of 23 points, you are already high enough.

Return to **200** and try again.

217

[*from 208*]

♠ A Q x x x x   ♡ x   ◊ x x   ♣ K Q x x

You opened with one spade and partner bid two spades.

YOUR ANSWER: I should now say four spades.

Not so fast.

Your hand was worth 14 points originally, and revalues to 17 points when partner raises your suit. (Add one for your fifth spade and two more for your sixth.) Partner has promised from seven–ten points, so your combined total lies between 24 and 27. If partner has nine–ten points you will have the necessary 26 for game, but if he has only seven–eight points you will be short of the requirements. Why not find out first whether he has a maximum or a minimum?

Return to **208** and pick a better rebid.

218

[*from 213*]

♠ x   ♡ A K x x   ◊ K J x x   ♣ K J x x

The bidding between you and your partner has gone:

SOUTH	WEST	NORTH	EAST
1 ♡	Pass	2 ♡	Pass
3 ♣	Pass	3 ♡	Pass
?			

YOUR ANSWER: I should now bid four hearts.

You didn't get your partner's message.

You showed an interest in getting to game when you bid again after his simple raise. He could do no better than return to your original suit, thereby announcing a minimum raise.

So you can rely on only seven–eight points in the dummy. With 17 points in your own hand and a maximum of 25 points in the combined hands, do you wish to contract for game? No.

Please go back to **213** and choose another answer.

♠ A K x x x   ♡ A Q J x   ◇ x x   ♣ x x

You opened with one spade and partner bid one no trump.

YOUR ANSWER: I should now pass.

No. Holding two doubletons your hand is slightly unbalanced, and you should look for a suit fit. Since you have already shown the spades and partner may have no particular liking for that, you should try hearts next. If partner holds something like:

♠ x x   ♡ K 10 x x x   ◇ x x   ♣ A x x x

he would have been unable to say two hearts over one spade, but by bidding two hearts now, you can uncover a game-sized fit.

Please return to **206** and look for the hand which calls for a pass.

♠ x x   ♡ A K J x   ◇ K J x   ♣ K x x x

You opened with one heart and partner bid one spade.

YOUR ANSWER: I should now pass.

You must be too tired to concentrate if you've turned to this answer.

Have you forgotten that when partner responds in a new suit after your opening bid, you MUST bid again?

Now turn back to **222** and try again.

221
[from 236]

♠ J x   ♥ A x x   ♦ A K Q x x   ♣ A Q x

You opened with one diamond and partner responded with one spade.

YOUR ANSWER: I would choose two no trump as a rebid.

So would we.
You have 20 high-card points, no trump distribution, and stoppers, in the unbid suit.

Jump Rebids in Opener's Suit

You have already learned to think in terms of rebid points after partner has raised your suit, thereby increasing your point count by one if you hold five trump cards, by three if you hold six, by five if you hold seven. These additional rebid points may also be counted without a raise from partner if your suit is self-sustaining. In order to qualify as self-sustaining, your suit must be a solid five-carder or a very strong six- or seven-carder.

If your suit is this good and your count amounts to 19–21 rebid points, you may make a jump rebid in your own suit. You will note that such a hand must be above the minimum range to begin with; i.e., 16–19 points in original valuation. Such hands will produce about seven tricks in play.

The jump rebid is not forcing when made over a one-level response, for partner may have minimum values and poor fit for your suit.

Let's see how you can put this knowledge to work. Suppose you have opened with one heart and partner responded one spade. With which of these hands would you not rebid three hearts?

♠ x x x   ♥ A K Q 10 x   ♦ K Q x   ♣ A x **230**

♠ x   ♥ A K Q x x x   ♦ Q x x   ♣ Q x x **235**

♠ x x   ♥ A Q J x x x   ♦ A Q x   ♣ K x **237**

(A)   ♠ A K x x   ♡ K J x   ◊ A Q x x   ♣ x x

(B)   ♠ A K x x x   ♡ A Q x   ◊ A x x   ♣ K x

YOUR ANSWER: I should raise partner's one no trump response to three no trump with hand B.

Correct. You have 20 high-card points. Partner has promised at least six, so you may bid game yourself. Hand A contains only 17 high-card points. With it, you should say two no trump and let partner carry on to game if his response was in the upper range (nine–ten points).

Rebids after a One Level Suit Response

When you open with one in a suit and partner responds with one in another suit you are, of course, duty-bound to bid again. Chapter II was largely dedicated to preparing you for this eventuality. Fortunately, there are various bids available to you. With minimum-strength (13–16 point) hands you may choose between rebidding:

   (1) one no trump,
   (2) two of your original suit,
   (3) two of partner's suit,
   (4) one of a new suit,
   (5) two of a new suit if it is lower-ranking than your opening suit.

You have already learned most of this. Each of these five types of rebids carries its own special meaning.

Having opened with one heart, how would you rebid this hand after partner's one spade response?

    ♠ x x   ♡ A K J x   ◊ K J x   ♣ K x x x

Two Clubs **201**

Two Hearts **207**

Pass **220**

One No Trump **228**

223

[from 215]

♠ A J x x   ♡ x x   ◇ A K J x   ♣ A Q x

YOUR ANSWER: I would not raise partner's spade response from one to four.

Why not?

You have 20 points. This is all partner needs for game even if he has only six points.

If you say only three spades, partner will pass with

♠ K x x x x   ♡ x x x x   ◇ Q x   ♣ x x

and you will miss a sure game.

Return to **215** and pick another hand.

224

[from 235]

♠ A K x x   ♡ x x   ◇ x x x x   ♣ K x x

Partner opened with one heart, you bid one spade, and he then jumped to four hearts.

YOUR ANSWER: I should now pass.

Not unless you want to risk missing a slam.

You have ten high-card points. Thus far your partner is counting on your having only six. You must tell him that you have something extra. You know that partner has at least 22 rebid points. Maybe he has 23 or 24, in which case the prospects for slam will be very good.

Don't worry about your lack of trump support. Partner's suit is self-sufficient.

Now return to **235** and select another alternative.

(A) ♠ A x x   ♡ x   ◇ A K J x x   ♣ x x x x

(B) ♠ A x x   ♡ x x   ◇ A K J x x   ♣ x x x

(C) ♠ A x x x   ♡ x x   ◇ A K J x   ♣ x x x

(D) ♠ A x x   ♡ x x   ◇ A K x x   ♣ K J x x

YOUR ANSWER: If I opened with one diamond and partner responded one spade, only hand B would not justify a raise of partner's bid.

Correct. This hand is not strong enough to raise partner's suit since it contains only three trumps and 13 points. You need four-card trump support to raise partner with a bare minimum opening bid. With hand B you should rebid two diamonds.

Hand A is worth a raise of partner's suit since it has 14 dummy points. Hand C contains four of partner's suit and so qualifies for a raise with only 13 points. Hand D has 16 points and hence is strong enough to support spades with three trump.

So far we have concentrated primarily on rebids with hands of minimum strength.

The minimum rebids are as follows:

(1) one no trump,
(2) two of your original suit,
(3) two of partner's suit,
(4) one of a new suit,
(5) two of a new suit which is lower-ranking than your original suit.

The responder should interpret opener's minimum rebids as showing no more than 16 points. The only significant exception to this occurs in cases (4) and (5), where opener rebids in a new suit. With either of these rebids opener may have as many as 18 points. But since *new-suit rebids by the opening bidder are not forcing upon the responder,* the opener should choose a stronger call if he has more than 18 points. And, contrariwise, he should never make a minimum-strength rebid (one no trump, two of his original suit, or two of responder's suit) with more than 16 points.

Now you should be ready for a fairly advanced quiz on rebids. Go on to **226.**

226

[*from 225*]

Choose the best rebid for these hands:

(A) ♠ x x x ♡ A J x x x ◇ A K x x ♣ x
Opening: one heart Response: one spade

(E) ♠ x x ♡ A K J x ◇ K J x ♣ K x x x
Opening: one heart Response: one spade

(K) ♠ A Q x x ♡ x ◇ A K x x ♣ x x x x
Opening: one diamond Response: one heart

(G) ♠ Q J 9 x x ♡ x ◇ A Q J x ♣ A Q x
Opening: one spade Response: one no trump

(C) ♠ A K J x x ♡ K x ◇ J x x ♣ J x x
Opening: one spade Response: one no trump

(I) ♠ Q x x ♡ A x x x x ◇ A J x x ♣ x
Opening: one heart Response: one spade

(M) ♠ K J x ♡ x x ◇ A K J x x ♣ J x x
Opening: one diamond Response: one heart

(B) ♠ Q J 10 x ♡ Q ◇ A Q x x x ♣ A x x
Opening: one diamond Response: one heart

(F) ♠ K x ♡ A J x x ◇ A 10 x x x ♣ A K
Opening: one diamond Response: one heart

(L) ♠ K x x ♡ A Q x x x ◇ A Q x x ♣ x
Opening: one heart Response: one spade

(H) ♠ Q x ♡ A K x x x ◇ A 10 x x ♣ x x
Opening: one heart Response: one spade

(D) ♠ K Q J x x ♡ Q x ◇ x x ♣ A J x x
Opening: one spade Response: one no trump

(J) ♠ A Q 10 x x ♡ x x x ◇ A K J ♣ x x
Opening: one spade Response: one no trump

(N) ♠ K x ♡ A x x ◇ A x x ♣ K J x x x
Opening: one club Response: one no trump

Check your answers on **214**.

♠ J x ♡ A x x ◊ A K Q x x ♣ A Q x

You opened with one diamond and partner responded with one spade.

YOUR ANSWER: I would not choose two no trump as a rebid.

Well, we would.

You have 20 high-card points, no trump distribution, and stoppers in the unbid suits.

Backtrack to **236** and try again.

♠ x x ♡ A K J x ◊ K J x ♣ K x x x

You opened with one heart and partner bid one spade.

YOUR ANSWER: I should now bid one no trump.

You are right.

With 15 high-card points your hand is in the minimum range. You may not rebid hearts, you obviously may not pass, and since you have balanced distribution, your hand may be best described by a rebid of one no trump.

You have already learned how to handle the following rebid problems. They were all discussed in Chapter I, for it was necessary to teach these rebid principles in order for you to select the proper opening bid. But lets us review them here. Select the proper rebid for each hand.

(A) ♠ x x ♡ A K J 10 x ◊ A x x x ♣ x x
You open with one heart. Partner responds with one spade.
(C) ♠ A K x x ♡ x x ◊ x x x ♣ A Q x x
You open with one club. Partner responds with one diamond.
(B) ♠ x x ♡ A Q x x x ◊ A K J x ♣ x x
You open with one heart. Partner responds with one spade.
(D) ♠ A Q x x ♡ x ◊ x x x ♣ A Q x x x
You open with one club. Partner responds with one spade.

Check your answers on **229**.

Answer
Letter

(A) Rebid two hearts. This will show partner that you have re-biddable hearts, you have no spade support, and you have a minimum hand.

(B) Rebid two diamonds. Even with minimum hands, you may show a second suit at the two level if it is lower-ranking than your original suit.

(C) Rebid one spade. The naming of a second suit at the one level requires no additional strength.

(D) Rebid two spades. There should be no explanation needed here. You have found a major suit fit.

With regard to raising your partner's suit, there are a few additional fine points to learn. First of all, you must revalue your hand in terms of *dummy points*. Second, you must, of course, have at least Q x x, J 10 x, or x x x x as trump support. And third, you should have at least 14 dummy points or else at least four trumps to offer an immediate raise.

Suppose with the following hands you have opened the bidding with one diamond and partner has responded one spade. Which one of the hands is NOT suitable for a raise to two spades?

	♠	♡	◇	♣	
(A)	A x x	x	A K J x x	x x x x	**209**
(B)	A x x	x x	A K J x x	x x x	**225**
(C)	A x x x	x x	A K J x	x x x	**233**
(D)	A x x	x x	A K x x	K J x x	**241**

♠ x x x   ♡ A K Q 10 x   ◇ K Q x   ♣ A x

You opened with one heart and partner responded one spade.

YOUR ANSWER: I would not rebid three hearts.

We would. You have a solid five-card suit, 19 points by original valuation, and 20 points when the heart suit is revalued as self-sustaining. This hand should take seven tricks all by itself. If partner holds as little as

♠ K Q J x   ♡ x x   ◇ x x x   ♣ Q x x x

you will have a good play for game.

Please return to **221** and look for the hand which does not warrant a three heart rebid.

♠ A Q x   ♡ A Q J x x   ◇ K J x   ♣ x x

YOUR ANSWER: With this hand, the two no trump rebid is recommended over the rebid of the heart suit because the heart suit is not rebiddable.

No. This is a fine rebiddable suit. Even a five-card suit headed by only the queen-jack is usually considered good enough for a rebid. But just because a suit is rebiddable does not mean that you are obliged to rebid it. Sometimes other calls are available, which reveal more information about your strength. There is a very important reason why you should avoid rebidding your own suit with the above hand.

Return to **247** and choose the correct answer.

232

[from 215]

♠ K x x x   ♥ A   ♦ A K x x   ♣ K x x x

YOUR ANSWER: I would not raise partner's spade response from one to four.

We would. You have 21 dummy points in support of spades. This is all partner needs to make game even if he has only six points.

If you say only three spades, partner will pass with

♠ Q J x x x   ♥ x x x   ♦ x x   ♣ Q x x,

although game is almost assured.

Return to **215** and pick another hand.

233

[from 229]

♠ A x x x   ♥ x x   ♦ A K J x   ♣ x x x

YOUR ANSWER: If I opened the bidding with one diamond and partner responded one spade, I should not raise partner's bid.

Look at your hand again. You hold four good trumps and 13 dummy points. This is adequate for a raise to two spades.

Remember, with just 13 dummy points you may raise your partner's suit, provided you have four of his trumps. If you have 14 or more dummy points, you may raise with only three trumps.

Now return to **229** and choose the right answer.

234

[from 258]

♠ J x   ♥ x x   ♦ A K x x x   ♣ A J x x

You opened the bidding with one diamond and your partner jumped to two no trump.

YOUR ANSWER: I should now rebid three diamonds.

Why? You don't want to direct the bidding toward a game contract in diamonds. With only 14 points you aren't interested in contracting for 11 tricks.

There is a way of assuring an easier contract. Return to **258** and see if you can find it.

(A)   ♠ x x x   ♡ A K Q 10 x   ◇ K Q x   ♣ A x
(B)   ♠ x   ♡ A K Q x x x   ◇ Q x x   ♣ Q x x
(C)   ♠ x x   ♡ A Q J x x x   ◇ A Q x   ♣ K x

You opened with one heart and partner responded one spade.

YOUR ANSWER: I would not rebid three hearts with hand B.

We agree with you. This hand qualifies for a jump rebid on only one count: it contains a self-sustaining six-card suit. But it fails to fulfill the other prerequisites for this type of bid: it was worth only 15 points originally, whereas at least 16 are required; it contains only 18 rebid points, whereas at least 19 are required; and it can hardly be expected to produce the necessary seven tricks. You must be satisfied with a simple two heart rebid with this hand.

Hand A, on the other hand, contains a solid five-card suit and 20 rebid points; hand C has a good six-card suit and 21 rebid points. Both of these hands should take seven tricks in play.

More strength is required of the opening bidder to jump from one to four than from one to three in his partner's suit. This also applies to opener's jump rebids in his own suit. To jump directly to game in his own suit, the opening bidder must have at least 22 rebid points and a hand which contains eight and a half or nine winners.

A good example:

♠ x   ♡ A K Q J 10 x   ◇ A x x   ♣ K Q x

If you open with one heart and partner responds one spade, you should be unwilling to play this hand for less than game no matter how weak a response partner makes. You should rebid four hearts.

This double jump by opener is strong rather than pre-emptive (in contrast to responder's double jump) because opener's single-jump rebid is not forcing. With a powerhouse the opener must jump directly to game because a three-level jump may be passed out.

Such a double jump by opener cannot possibly be regarded as a "shutout" bid. With appropriate values partner may go on bidding.

Partner opened with one heart; you responded one spade; partner jumped to four hearts. With which of these hands would you now pass?

♠ A K x x   ♡ x x   ◇ x x x x   ♣ K x x   **224**
♠ K Q J x   ♡ x x x x   ◇ x x   ♣ x x x   **239**
♠ A Q x x x   ♡ x x   ◇ K Q x x   ♣ K x   **251**

(A) ♠ A J x x ♡ x x ◇ A K J x ♣ A Q x

(B) ♠ K x x x ♡ A ◇ A K x x ♣ K x x x

(C) ♠ A Q J x ♡ K x ◇ A Q J x ♣ J x x

YOUR ANSWER: With hand C, I would not raise partner's one spade response to four.

You are correct.

Hand C is the only hand with less than 20 points in support of spades. With it you should say three spades and give partner a chance to pass if he responded with a bare minimum. With the other hands, however, you should want to be in game even if partner has only six points.

Jump Rebids in No Trump (by Opener)

You have already learned that when partner's response to your opening bid is one no trump you need 17–19 high-card points to raise him to two no trump, and 20 or more points to say three no trump.

If partner's response is one of a suit, however, you need 19–20 high-card points to rebid two no trump, 21 or 22 points to say three no trump. The reason for the higher requirement in this case is very simple: in calculating his suit response, partner may well have included distributional points, whereas for a no trump response his points are all in high cards. Needless to say, for a jump rebid in no trump you also should have a balanced hand with protection in all the unbid suits.

When partner has responded with one spade to your opening bid of one diamond, would you now bid two no trump with this hand?

♠ J x ♡ A x x ◇ A K Q x x ♣ A Q x

Yes **221**

No **227**

♠ x x   ♡ A Q J x x x   ◇ A Q x   ♣ K x

You opened with one heart and partner responded one spade.

YOUR ANSWER: I would not rebid three hearts.

Well, we would. You are staring at a classic example of a jump rebid. It contains a very good six-card suit, 21 rebid points, and the power to take seven tricks all by itself.

If partner made his one spade response on

♠ A x x x x   ♡ x x   ◇ K x x   ♣ x x x,

he will carry on to four hearts.

Please return to **221** and look for the hand which does not warrant a three heart rebid.

♠ K x   ♡ x   ◇ A Q x x x   ♣ A Q x x x

You opened with one diamond, your left-hand opponent bid one spade, and partner bid two hearts.

YOUR ANSWER: I should now say two no trump.

No. In the first place your hand is highly unbalanced and is therefore not well suited for no trump. You have 15 points for no trump, 18 for suit play.

Secondly, you have a biddable suit which you haven't shown. Partner hasn't supported your diamonds and you don't like his hearts. Perhaps you can find a fit in clubs. There is no danger in searching for a fit since you both have shown good hands and a possible game contract in clubs is not out of reach.

Now return to **262** and study the other hands.

239

[*from* 235]

(A)   ♠ A K x x   ♡ x x   ♢ x x x x   ♣ K x x

(B)   ♠ K Q J x   ♡ x x x x   ♢ x x   ♣ x x x

(C)   ♠ A Q x x x   ♡ x x   ♢ K Q x x   ♣ K x

Partner opened with one heart, you bid one spade, and he then jumped to four hearts.

YOUR ANSWER: I should now pass with hand B.

You would be right in so doing. This hand is worth only seven points in support of hearts. Partner would therefore need 26 points to consider slam, and if he had 26 points he would have opened with a demand bid originally. Your heart support is of no special value to him, for his hearts are solid.

With hand C you have 16 points and you must keep bidding to slam. With hand A you have ten high-card points and should bid again to show your excess values. If partner holds more than 22 points he will surely be interested in slam. Don't worry about your lack of trump support; partner has all the hearts he needs.

The Jump Shift by Opening Bidder

Here at last is the one rebid which absolutely forces responder to speak again. Jump rebids in your own or partner's suit reveal strength, but, as you have already learned, they may be passed by partner if he has a bare minimum. A jump shift *in a new suit*, however, is just as forcing as an opening bid of two in a suit. Partner may not pass until a game contract is reached. For example:

♠ K x x x   ♡ A K J x x   ♢ A K J   ♣ x

Although this hand contains 21 points including high cards and distribution, it does not qualify for an opening bid of two hearts because it contains too many losers. If you open with one heart and partner responds one spade, however, the picture suddenly changes. Now your spade holding has been greatly enhanced, and you know that a game contract must be reached.

Go on to **240**.

So what call do you select as your rebid? Three spades or three hearts? Neither, for these bids are not forcing. How about four spades? Well, this automatically gets you to game but it does not do full justice to your holding. Valued as a dummy your hand is worth 23 points in support of spades. In order to convey your full strength to partner you should make a jump shift to three diamonds. On the next round you will raise spades. If partner has a few key values above a bare minimum response, your sequence of bids may serve to uncover a slam.

Which of these three hands best qualifies for the following bidding sequence:

Opening: one heart. Response: one spade. Rebid: three clubs.

♠ A x   ♥ A K Q x   ♦ K x x   ♣ A K J x   **246**

♠ A x   ♥ A K Q x x x   ♦ x   ♣ A K Q x   **255**

♠ J x   ♥ A K J x x   ♦ x   ♣ A K Q x x   **259**

♠ A x x   ♥ x x   ♦ A K x x   ♣ K J x x

YOUR ANSWER: If I opened the bidding with one diamond and partner responded one spade, I should not raise partner's bid.

You didn't check your point count. Your hand had an original valuation of 16 points and is worth 15 points in support of spades.

Remember, with just 13 dummy points you may raise your partner's suit, provided you have four of his trumps. If you have 14 or more dummy points, you may raise with only three of his trumps.

Now return to **229** and choose the right answer.

242

[*from* 249]

♠ K x   ♡ A Q x x x   ◇ Q x x   ♣ K x x

You opened with one heart and partner responded two clubs.

YOUR ANSWER: I would now say three clubs.

This would be wrong. This hand is worth only 15 points in support of clubs which classifies it as a minimum opening bid, and you shouldn't go to the three level with a hand in this range.

Return to **249,** reread the lesson, and try to choose a better answer.

243

[*from* 245]

♠ A K J x x   ♡ A x x   ◇ x x x   ♣ x x

You have opened with one spade and partner has responded two hearts.

YOUR ANSWER: I would now say three hearts.

No, your hand is too weak. You have rebiddable spades and heart support, but only 13 points. In order to underline the bare minimum nature of your opening bid, you must make the meekest of rebids —two spades. It is better to conceal your heart support than to encourage partner to believe you have more than a minimum hand. There is a better hand for a raise to three hearts on **245.** Please go back and look for it.

♠ J x   ♡ x x   ◇ A K x x x   ♣ A J x x

You opened the bidding with one diamond and your partner responded two no trump.

YOUR ANSWER: I should now rebid three no trump.

We agree. You have a minimum opening bid and your best suits are the minors. You don't want to seek an 11-trick game contract. Partner has promised 13–15 high-card points. With your 13 high-card points he should be able to make game in no trump. Once again we see an illustration of the principle of looking for no trump contracts when your strength is in the minor suits.

Choose your rebid for the hands below:

♠ A x x x   ♡ K Q J x   ◇ K x x x   ♣ x   (A)
  You opened: one spade   Response: two spades

♠ x x   ♡ A K Q x x   ◇ A J x x x   ♣ x   (D)
  You opened: one heart   Response: one no trump

♠ K Q x   ♡ A x   ◇ Q J 9 x x   ♣ A J x   (G)
  You opened: one diamond   Response: two clubs

♠ A J 10   ♡ Q x   ◇ A K J x   ♣ Q J x x   (I)
  You opened: one diamond   Response: two clubs

♠ x x   ♡ A K 10 9 x x   ◇ K x   ♣ A Q x   (B)
  You opened: one heart   Response: one spade

♠ A K Q x x   ♡ K x x   ◇ K x x   ♣ x x   (E)
  You opened: one spade   Response: two hearts

♠ A Q x   ♡ A Q J x x   ◇ K J x   ♣ x x   (H)
  You opened: one heart   Response: two clubs

♠ A K J x x   ♡ K x x   ◇ x x   ♣ Q x x   (J)
  You opened: one spade   Response: two hearts

♠ x   ♡ A 10 x x x   ◇ K x   ♣ A K 10 x x   (F)
  You opened: one heart   Response: two diamonds

♠ A K J x x x   ♡ x   ◇ K x x   ♣ Q x x   (C)
  You opened: one spade   Response: two spades

Go on to **265** to check your answers.

245

[from 261]

The Choice between Rebidding Your Suit and Raising Partner's

You will often face this dilemma. The solution is not so difficult as it may seem. It depends on the over-all strength of your hand. If you have a rebiddable suit of your own as well as support for partner's suit, you should rebid your own suit with a bare minimum. Support of partner's suit usually implies slight additional values.

If, on the other hand, you have a second biddable suit in your own hand as well as support for partner's suit, you must settle for a raise with a minimum holding. Naming a third suit frequently implies dissatisfaction with partner's suit or a desire to promote another round of bidding. With minimum hands you cannot afford to suggest a strong willingness to go on.

With the following hands you have opened with one spade and partner has responded two hearts. With which of them would you raise to three hearts?

♠ A K J x x   ♡ A x x   ◇ x x x   ♣ x x **243**

♠ A Q J x x   ♡ Q x x   ◇ x   ♣ A K x x **257**

♠ A K Q x x   ♡ K x x   ◇ K x x   ♣ x x **263**

246

[from 240]

♠ A x   ♡ A K Q x   ◇ K x x   ♣ A K J x

Opening: one heart. Response: one spade. Rebid: three clubs.

YOUR ANSWER: This hand is well suited to this bidding sequence.

You'd better go back to Chapter I and review a bit. This hand contains 24 high-card points, balanced distribution, and stoppers in all four suits. It should be opened with two no trump.

There is a hand better suited for the sequence on **240**. Please go back and find it.

♠ K x   ♡ A Q x x x   ◇ Q x x   ♣ K x x

You opened with one heart and partner responded two clubs.

YOUR ANSWER: I would now say two hearts.

Quite right. This is a minimum opening bid, so you must not make an aggressive-sounding rebid. Either two no trump or three clubs would imply a stronger holding. Your hearts are rebiddable and since partner has to have at least ten points for his two-level response, your two heart contract should be reasonably secure.

Following a two-level response by partner, the requirements for a two no trump rebid are 15–18 high-card points. This is not a jump bid, and is not forcing. But since partner has already promised ten points (in high cards and distribution), game should be reached if a satisfactory contract can be found.

♠ A Q x   ♡ A Q J x x   ◇ K J x   ♣ x x

You open one heart with the hand above. Partner responds with two clubs, which is your only unprotected suit. You have 17 high-card points and should rebid two no trump. Why did we not suggest that you rebid your hearts instead?

The heart suit is not rebiddable. **231**

We think this hand should be played in no trump. **252**

We want to describe the hand's over-all strength. **262**

♠ J x   ♡ x x ◇ A K x x x ♣ A J x x

You opened the bidding with one diamond and your partner jumped to two no trump.

YOUR ANSWER: I should now rebid three clubs.

This would be ill-advised. You have only 13 high-card points and all your strength is in the minor suits. You are too weak to think in terms of an 11-trick game contract in either clubs or diamonds.

Return to **258** and find a better rebid for this hand.

Rebids by Opener after a Takeout to Two of a Suit

If you choose your opening bid properly, you will have already planned your rebid. Even if partner bids a new suit at the two level. The principal things to remember are these:

A rebid of your original suit or the bid of another suit which permits partner to return to your first suit at the two level, does not promise additional strength.

A bid of two no trump, a rebid at the three level, or any rebid which forces partner to the three level to return to your first suit, denotes a stronger hand.

How would you put this lesson to use with this hand? You have opened the bidding with one heart and partner has responded two clubs.

♠ K x   ♡ A Q x x x   ♢ Q x x   ♣ K x x

Your rebid is:

Three Clubs **242**
Two Hearts **247**
Two No Trump **253**

♠ A K x x   ♡ A J x x   ♢ J x x x   ♣ x

You opened with one spade; partner responded with two diamonds.

YOUR ANSWER: I would now bid three diamonds.

Well, this would not be a bad bid, but we should not prefer it. It would be better, we think, to continue the search for a major suit fit by rebidding two hearts. If partner can now support either of your suits you will have a good chance for game, for he has already shown at least ten points by his two-level response. A game in diamonds is less likely.

Now please return to **263** and try another answer.

♠ A Q x x x   ♡ x x   ◇ K Q x x   ♣ K x

Partner opened with one heart, you bid one spade, and he then jumped to four hearts.

YOUR ANSWER: I should now pass.

Not on your life.

You have 16 points. For his four heart bid partner is counting on you for only six points. You know that he has 22 rebid points and maybe more. Your combined values are definitely in the slam zone. If you pass, partner will be very unhappy when he sees the dummy.

Please go back to **235** and choose another alternative.

♠ A Q x   ♡ A Q J x x   ◇ K J x   ♣ x x

YOUR ANSWER: With this hand I opened one heart and partner responded two clubs. A rebid of two no trump is recommended because the hand should be played at no trump.

Not necessarily. Partner has responded in your only unprotected suit, so no trump is certainly a possibility, but you should not be ready to give up on a suit contract. You don't know too much about partner's hand as yet. It may be worth ten or 18 points. It may contain four hearts or more. It may be balanced or unbalanced. Therefore you should make an effort to further describe your holding to partner, and then wait to hear more about his.

There is a valid reason why the two no trump rebid was chosen at this point. Return to **247** and see if you can determine what it is.

253

[from 249]

♠ K x   ♡ A Q x x x   ◊ Q x x   ♣ K x x
You opened with one heart and partner responded two clubs.

YOUR ANSWER: I would now say two no trump.

No. This hand contains only 14 high-card points which classifies it as a minimum opening bid, and you should not rebid two no trump with a minimum hand.

Please return to **249** and look for a better rebid.

254

[from 263]

♠ A Q x x   ♡ K x   ◊ K x x x   ♣ K x x
You opened with one spade; partner responded with two diamonds.

YOUR ANSWER: I should now bid three diamonds.

No. It would be better tactics to conceal your diamond support, at least for the time being. A preferable rebid would be two no trump. Holding 15 high-card points and protection in the other suits, this call will give more information to partner while at the same time steering him toward a nine-trick game contract.

Now please return to **263** and look for a better answer.

255

[from 240]

♠ A x   ♡ A K Q x x x   ◊ x   ♣ A K Q x
Opening: one heart.   Response: one spade.   Rebid: three clubs.

YOUR ANSWER: This hand is well suited to this bidding sequence.

Perhaps you should go back to Chapter II for a little review. This is an ideal hand with which to open two hearts. It contains 25 points, a good six-card suit, and it should win ten tricks without any assistance from partner.

There is a hand better suited for the sequence on **240**. Please go back and look for it.

♠ A x x   ♡ J x x x   ◇ A K J x x   ♣ x

You opened with one diamond, your left-hand opponent bid one spade, and partner bid two hearts.

YOUR ANSWER: I should now say two no trump.

Certainly not. This would be the weakest bid you could make. Partner has shown a strong hand by bidding two hearts, thereby forcing you to bid again and at the same time preventing you from rebidding diamonds at the two level. You, too, have a good hand and, what's more, an excellent fit with partner's hearts. Valued as a dummy your hand is worth 17 points. You must show him this by saying four hearts.

Now return to **262** and study the other hands.

♠ A Q J x x   ♡ Q x x   ◇ x   ♣ A K x x

You opened with one spade and partner responded two hearts.

YOUR ANSWER: I should now say three hearts.

No. This hand is too strong for a mere single raise. Your hand is worth 19 points in support of hearts. You may either raise partner directly to four hearts, or preferably bid three clubs first with the intention of showing the heart support near.

There is a better hand for a raise to three hearts on **245**. Please go back and look for it.

258

[from 263]

(A) ♠ A K x x   ♡ A J x x   ◇ J x x x   ♣ x
(B) ♠ A Q x x   ♡ K x   ◇ K x x x   ♣ K x x
(C) ♠ A Q J x x   ♡ x x   ◇ A Q J x   ♣ K x

You opened with one spade; partner has responded with two diamonds.

YOUR ANSWER: I should now bid three diamonds with hand C.

Quite right. Holding 19 points in support of partner, you might be tempted to jump to four diamonds, but a four diamond call would deprive partner of the opportunity to try three no trump himself. Avoid getting beyond the three level in minor suits without first having ruled out the possibility of playing the hand in no trump.

With hand A it is best to continue the search for a major suit fit by saying two hearts. With hand B you should conceal your diamond support, at least temporarily, in favor of a two no trump rebid.

Rebids after Forcing Responses

When you open the bidding and partner makes a jump response (a double raise, two no trump, or a jump shift), you know that you will reach a game contract at least. Your rebids now must show where you feel the hand should be played. For example:

♠ A J x x   ♡ A K x x   ◇ J x x x   ♣ x

You open with one spade and partner raises to three spades. You should rebid four spades despite the four-card suit. Since you have found a satisfactory major suit fit (remember that you can count on partner for at least four trumps if he gives you a double raise) there is no occasion to bid your hearts. Since the trump suit has already been established, partner would interpret a heart rebid as a slam try, and you are too weak to suggest a slam. If partner's response had been two no trump you would have then bid three hearts, because you would still be looking for the best contract and with a singleton club no trump would not be to your taste.

How would you handle the rebid with this hand? Partner said two no trump after your one diamond opening.

♠ J x   ♡ x x   ◇ A K x x x   ♣ A J x x

Rebid Three Diamonds? **234**   Three No Trump? **244**
Three Clubs? **248**

154

(A) ♠ A x   ♡ A K Q x   ◊ K x x   ♣ A K J x
(B) ♠ A x   ♡ A K Q x x x   ◊ x   ♣ A K Q x
(C) ♠ J x   ♡ A K J x x   ◊ x   ♣ A K Q x x

Opening: one heart. Response: one spade. Rebid: three clubs.

YOUR ANSWER: Hand C is well suited to this bidding sequence.

Yes, it is. Although it contains 21 points, it is not quite good enough for an opening two demand bid. But after partner's response you are unwilling to settle for less than game, so you jump in a new suit to prevent partner from passing while you try to determine whether your best contract is hearts, clubs, spades, or no trump. A jump shift rebid by the opening bidder is forcing to game.

Hand A should be opened with two no trump, hand B with two hearts.

What is your rebid with each of these hands? In each case you have opened with one heart and partner has responded one spade.

(A) ♠ x x   ♡ A Q J x x   ◊ A K x   ♣ K Q J
(C) ♠ A Q x x   ♡ A Q x x x   ◊ x x   ♣ A Q
(E) ♠ K x x x   ♡ A K Q x x   ◊ x   ♣ A K x
(B) ♠ K x   ♡ A Q J 10 x x ◊ A Q x   ♣ x x
(D) ♠ K J x x   ♡ A Q J x x   ◊ x   ♣ K J x
(F) ♠ K x   ♡ A K J x x   ◊ K Q x   ♣ A J x

(A) Two no trump. You have 20 high-card points.
(B) Three hearts. You have 21 rebid points, a strong six-card suit, and a reasonable expectation of winning seven tricks.
(C) Four spades. You have 20 dummy points and a good major suit fit.
(D) Three spades. You have 18 dummy points and the necessary four-card trump support.
(E) Three clubs. With 23 dummy points your hand is too strong to merely give a direct raise to four spades. You should therefore first jump in a new suit, even if it involves manufacturing a bid, and then raise partner on the next round.
(F) Three no trump. You have 21 high-card points and stoppers in every suit.

Go to **249**.

260

What are the *minimum* requirements for the opening bidder to make these rebids?

	Opening	Overcall	Response	Rebid
(A)	1 ♦	. . . .	1 ♡	1 ♠
(I)	1 ♡	. . . .	2 ♣	2 ♦
(E)	1 ♡	. . . .	2 ♡	3 ♡
(M)	1 ♠	. . . .	2 ♡	3 ♡
(Q)	1 ♡	2 ♣	2 ♦	2 NT
(C)	1 ♡	2 ♦	2 ♠	2 NT
(K)	1 ♠	2 ♣	2 ♡	2 ♠
(G)	1 ♡	2 ♣	2 ♦	2 ♠
(O)	1 ♡	. . . .	2 ♣	3 ♣
(B)	1 ♠	. . . .	2 ♦	3 ♣
(J)	1 ♡	. . . .	2 ♣	2 ♠
(R)	1 ♡	. . . .	2 ♣	2 NT
(F)	1 ♡	, . . .	1 ♠	2 ♡
(N)	1 ♡	. . . .	1 ♠	3 NT
(D)	1 ♠	. . . .	1 NT	2 NT
(L)	1 ♡	. . . .	1 ♠	2 NT
(H)	1 ♣	. . . .	1 ♦	2 ♡
(P)	1 ♡	. . . .	1 ♠	3 ♡

Check your answers on **261**.

Answer
Letter

(A) 13 points are all that's needed to mention a new suit at the one level.

(B) 17 points are required to show a new suit at the three level.

(C) 13 points; this is the cheapest call available. Remember, partner has a good hand to force you past two hearts.

(D) 17 high-card points and a balanced hand.

(E) 17 rebid points; if partner has raised with nine or ten points he can bid game.

(F) 13 points and a rebiddable suit.

(G) 19 points; this is a reverse. Remember, you are forcing partner into the three level merely to show a preference for hearts. With a minimum hand you must rebid your hearts.

(H) About 21 points; this is a jump shift which is forcing to game.

(I) 13 points; you are rebidding in a lower-ranking suit.

(J) 19 points; this is a reverse.

(K) 13 points; a simple rebid of your suit may be made with a bare minimum.

(L) 19 high-card points, no trump distribution, stoppers in the unbid suits.

(M) 14 dummy points are required to raise partner's major suit from two to three.

(N) 21 high-card points, no trump distribution, stoppers in the unbid suits.

(O) 16 dummy points are required to raise partner's minor suit from two to three.

(P) 16 points by your original valuation, 19 rebid points, a solid five-carder or a very good six-carder; seven playing tricks in your own hand.

(Q) 15 high-card points and a club stopper; with less you may rebid hearts.

(R) 15 high-card points and some protection in the unbid suits.

Go on to **245.**

262

[from 247]

♠ A Q x   ♡ A Q J x x   ◊ K J x   ♣ x x

YOUR ANSWER: With this hand a rebid of two no trump is recommended because this better describes the over-all strength of the
hand.

Yes. Your hearts are rebiddable, of course, but a rebid of your
own suit indicates a minimum hand. This hand is definitely in a
stronger category, and you *must* avoid a minimum-sounding rebid. You may or may not be interested in a no trump contract.
Partner's next bid will serve as a guide. Here, as always, it is more
important to show your over-all strength in preference to some distributional feature.

Sometimes the two no trump rebid may be made with a weaker
hand: if your left-hand opponent overcalls your opening bid and
partner then makes a free bid at the two level, depriving you of
your normal rebid. For example:

♠ Q x   ♡ A K x x   ◊ A 10 x x   ♣ x x x

The bidding: One heart by you, two diamonds on your left, two
spades by partner. You may now say two no trump, though you
have only 13 high-card points. You can't rebid your four-card heart
suit, you can't support spades, and you can't pass.

The two no trump rebid in this situation is actually the cheapest
bid available, and therefore guarantees nothing extra. You should be
relatively safe, for partner has shown a strong hand by responding
in such a way that he may be forcing you into the three level on
your next bid.

Which of these hands calls for a two no trump rebid after your
one diamond opening, a one spade overcall, and a two heart response by partner?

♠ K x   ♡ x   ◊ A Q x x x   ♣ A Q x x x **238**

♠ A x x   ♡ J x x x   ◊ A K J x x   ♣ x **256**

♠ K J x x   ♡ x x x   ◊ A K Q x   ♣ x x **264**

(A) ♠ A K J x x   ♥ A x x   ♦ x x x   ♣ x x

(B) ♠ A Q J x x   ♥ Q x x   ♦ x   ♣ A K x x

(C) ♠ A K Q x x   ♥ K x x   ♦ K x x   ♣ x x

You opened with one spade and partner responded two hearts.

YOUR ANSWER: With hand C, I would raise to three hearts.

You are correct. All three hands contain rebiddable spade suits and heart support, but they vary in their over-all strength. Hand A is too weak (13 points) for a heart raise; a rebid in spades will be a better way of showing partner that you have a bare minimum. Hand B is stronger still (18 points; 19 in support of hearts), so you must take stronger action than merely offering a single raise. Hand C is a little stronger (16 points), so you can afford to support partner's suit at the three level.

When your partner responds in clubs or diamonds, it is not nearly so important to give him a raise. It is preferable, as always, to continue to look for a major suit or no trump fit. Even with excellent support for partner's minor suit you may often profit by directing the bidding toward a final no trump contract, provided your distribution is suited to no trump. Eleven-trick game contracts should be avoided if there is a reasonable chance to bring in nine tricks at no trump.

If you opened with one spade and partner responded two diamonds, with which of these hands would you rebid three diamonds?

♠ A K x x   ♥ A J x x   ♦ J x x x   ♣ x   **250**

♠ A Q x x   ♥ K x   ♦ K x x x   ♣ K x x   **254**

♠ A Q J x x   ♥ x x   ♦ A Q J x   ♣ K x   **258**

264

[from 262]

(A) ♠ K x ♡ x ◇ A Q x x x ♣ A Q x x x

(B) ♠ A x x ♡ J x x x ◇ A K J x x ♣ x

(C) ♠ K J x x ♡ x x x ◇ A K Q x ♣ x x

You opened with one diamond, your left-hand opponent bid one spade, and partner bid two hearts.

YOUR ANSWER: With hand C, I will rebid two no trump.

Correct. This will show partner that you have a minimum opening bid. The other hands contain excess strength and besides this, they are unbalanced. With hand A you can say three clubs; with hand B, four hearts.

If partner's initial response is two in a *minor* suit, you need at least 16 points to give him a raise. If partner responds with two in a *major* suit (this would have to be two hearts over your one spade opening because two spades over one heart is a jump shift), however, you need only 14 dummy points to raise him. The reason for this disparity is that it is so important to show a major suit fit. For a minor suit game you need 29 points; for a major suit game, 26. Partner has already shown ten points by his two-level response. Therefore, if you have 14 points in support of his major suit you should announce it at once since you are not far removed from game requirements. He may readily have the extra two points himself.

In order to name a *new* suit at the three level, you must have 17 points. This is more than that required for a raise at the three level because it means that you are willing and able to go this high without a trump suit having been established. This is a drastic step and must be supported by a strong hand.

Go on to **260.**

Answer
Letter

(A) Pass. You have just 15 points, and partner is not encouraging you to go on. Remember, he has at most ten points for his raise.

(B) Jump to three hearts. Even though partner has not supported your suit, you may regard it as self-sustaining. Revalue your hand to 21 rebid points.

(C) Bid three spades. You had 15 points originally, but now that spades have been raised, your hand becomes worth 18 points, and an effort should be made to reach game.

(D) Bid two diamonds. You have 17 points and need not quit just because partner is offering little encouragement. Besides, your hand is not well suited for no trump.

(E) Bid three hearts. You have 16 dummy points and adequate trump support.

(F) Bid three clubs. Your 17-point hand warrants showing a new suit at the three level.

(G) Bid two no trump. You have 17 high-card points and all suits stopped. In fact, we would have preferred a one no trump opening bid with this holding.

(H) Bid two no trump. You have 17 high-card points and two cards in partner's suit. All other suits are well protected.

(I) Raise to three clubs. You have 19 dummy points, more than ample for the raise of the minor suit. However, we prefer a single raise rather than a jump to four clubs, for this will give partner an opportunity to bid three no trump if he so desires.

(J) Raise to three hearts. You have only 14 dummy points, but partner has promised ten points by his takeout at the two level. This puts you close to the requirements for game which partner will bid if he has any excess values.

Go on to **266** to begin Chapter V.

CHAPTER V

REBIDS BY THE RESPONDER

Up till now you have had to acquaint yourself with a great number of bidding rules and point-count requirements. If you are thoroughly familiar with the meanings of all the various opening bids, responses, and opener's rebids, you will find that responder's rebids are largely a matter of common sense. In this particular position the bids are based more upon an understanding of the first three bids than upon a new set of rules.

You have learned that an opening bid of one in a suit may be made with hands containing anywhere from 13 points up and that opener's rebid more narrowly defines his exact strength. Likewise the responder's first bid may be of an indefinite nature, which his rebid serves to describe more precisely.

If his first bid was a single raise or one no trump, responder has already declared a maximum of ten points. But, as you learned in Chapter IV, it may be essential for partner to know whether your moderate response was based on a maximum (nine–ten) or minimum (six–eight) point holding. He may ask you to tell him this on your next bid. Similar second-round clarification may be solicited from you after other limited responses such as two no trump (13–15 high-card points) or a double raise (13–16 dummy points). In sequences such as these the opening bidder is the team captain; responder's function is simply to supply more detailed information so that his partner can visualize the combined resources at his command.

When responder's first bid was of a more indefinite nature, such as a bid of one or more in a new suit, a further exchange of information is required. By naming a new suit you have forced the opener to bid again without having announced your precise strength. And if you choose to name yet another suit on the second round, your partner will be forced to bid once more. Under circumstances such as these the responder has assumed the captain's role and may simply be keeping the bidding alive until he has learned all about the opener's hand.

On 267 is a summary upon which you, as responder, may plan the pattern of your bids.

	Responses	*Rebids*
Minimum hands (6–10 points)	Single raise (7–10 points). 1 NT (6–10 high-card points). 1 in a suit (6 points).	With 6–7 points, pass unless forced to re-bid. With 9–10 points bid once more if urged to do so.
Good hands (10–13 points)	Do not give single raise or bid 1 NT. Make some response which partner can-not pass, (e.g., a new suit takeout).	Rebid own suit, sup-port partner's suit, bid new suit or no trump. (If you wish to insist on a game contract, you must either bid a new suit or make a jump bid.)
Very good hands (13–16 points)	Jump to 2 NT. Game forcing double raise. New suit takeout.	Continue to make forcing bids until game is reached.
Strong hands (16–19 points)	Jump to 3 NT. New suit takeout.	Jump rebid if first re-sponse was simple suit takeout.
Slam hands (19 or more points)	Jump shift.	Investigate slam pos-sibilities.

Rebids, like initial responses, may be specific or temporizing in nature. Weak hands must be described succinctly and quickly. Some strong hands may be as easily defined; others require several rounds of bidding to delineate.

Let's take an example:

♠ J x x   ♡ A K x x x   ◇ x x   ♣ K J x

Partner opens with one spade, you respond two hearts, and he re-bids two spades. What is your best rebid?

Three Hearts **272**   Three Spades **278**   Four Spades **283**

268

[from 285]

♠ K x x   ♥ x x x   ♦ A x x x   ♣ x x x

Partner opens with one heart, you respond one no trump, and he rebids two no trump.

YOUR ANSWER: I would bid three no trump with this hand.

No, you don't have quite enough strength for this.

Partner has indicated 17 or 18 high-card points by his two no trump rebid. He needs to know if your response was nearer the lower or upper limits of its range. You have only seven high-card points, a minimum one no trump response. This would bring the partnership total to 24 or 25 points, and that is not quite enough for game.

The only thing you can do with this hand now is pass.

Please go back to **285** and choose the hand that does call for a three no trump rebid.

269

[from 283]

♠ Q J x   ♥ A x x x x   ♦ x x   ♣ A x x

Partner opens with one diamond, you respond one heart, and he rebids one no trump.

YOUR ANSWER: I should now pass.

Never. You have 11 high-card points. This is a good hand and warrants two bids.

Partner has shown about 13–16 points, you will have enough for game if he is near the upper limit of the minimum range. There is a way to find this out.

Return to **283** and look for a better rebid.

(A)   ♠ Q x x x   ♡ x x   ♢ A Q x x   ♣ x x x

(B)   ♠ K x x   ♡ J x x   ♢ A x x   ♣ Q x x x

(C)   ♠ Q x x x   ♡ x x   ♢ K x x x   ♣ x x x

Opener	Responder
1 ♠	2 ♠
3 ♠	?

YOUR ANSWER: With hand A, my best rebid is four spades.

Quite right. Your raise was based upon ten points. With hand C your raise was based upon only seven points, so you must pass. Since hand B is evenly balanced and contains ten points in high cards, we would favor a three no trump bid; partner can return to spades if his hand is unsuitable for play at no trump.

When the opening bidder tests out his partner's raise by a rebid of two no trump, the same principle applies.

Opener	Responder
1 ♠	2 ♠
2 NT	?

Again you are responder. With a near-maximum raise, if your hand is evenly balanced and most of your points consist of high-card values, you should raise to three no trump. If you have four trumps and your raise is worth nine or more points, you should take your partner to four spades. With a weaker (seven–eight point) holding and a hand unsuited to no trump, return to three in partner's suit. With a minimum raise and relatively balanced distribution, you may pass two no trump.

With the bidding sequence just discussed, which of the three hands shown at the top of this page is best described by a simple return to three spades?

Hand A   **276**

Hand B   **282**

Hand C   **286**

271

[from 288]

♠ K J 9 x   ♡ x x   ◇ x x x   ♣ A Q 10 x

Opener	Responder
1 ♡	1 ♠
2 ♠	?

YOUR ANSWER: I would now bid four spades.

This would not be altogether out of line, but we would not recommend it.

You have 11 points and partner has promised about 14–16, so your game prospects are bright. But you have a balanced hand and another biddable suit. If you now say three clubs you will give yourself more scope. Partner may be in position to bid three no trump if he has a diamond stopper. Or he can go to game in spades with good spades and maximum values. If he says three spades, you may elect to pass.

So please go back to **288** and look for the hand better suited to a four spade bid.

272

[from 267]

♠ J x x   ♡ A K x x x   ◇ x x   ♣ K J x

Partner opens with one spade, you respond with two hearts, and he rebids two spades.

YOUR ANSWER: I should now bid three hearts.

No. This would be too weak a rebid. You have 13 points, so you know game is in sight, but partner doesn't know this and he may very well pass three hearts. Your hearts are rebiddable but partner has denied support for them and you do have adequate support for his spades.

Return to **267** and try one of the other rebids.

♠ x x x   ♡ K 10 x x   ◇ A J x   ♣ x x x

Opener	Responder
1 ♣	1 ♡
1 ♠	?

YOUR ANSWER: I would now pass.

No. With eight points you don't want the bidding to die at the one level. You can afford a more encouraging note than "Pass." You can best show the slight additional values in this hand by saying one no trump. From here on you can pass, for you have done full justice to your hand.

Now return to **300** and pick the proper answer.

♠ x x   ♡ K x x x   ◇ K x x x   ♣ Q x x

Opener	Responder
1 ♡	2 ♡
3 ♣	?

YOUR ANSWER: I should now bid three hearts.

This is the wrong answer. Partner has bid three clubs in order to test the nature of your raise. If it was based upon only seven–eight points he expects you merely to return to his first suit. If it was based upon nine–ten points he wants you to contract for game.

Please go back to **286** for the right answer.

275

[from 306]

♠ K x x x   ♡ A x x   ◊ K x x   ♣ 10 x x

Opener	Responder
1 ◊	1 ♠
2 ♣	?

YOUR ANSWER: As responder with this hand, I would pass.

Oh, no. You certainly don't want to pass and leave partner in clubs—his second choice and your weakest suit. And yet with ten points you should not give up.

You can and should by all means bid. Can you rebid your spades? Should you return to partner's first suit? Is there another choice?

Return to **306** and see if you can pick the best bid.

276

[from 270]

♠ Q x x x   ♡ x x   ◊ A Q x x   ♣ x x x

Opener	Responder
1 ♠	2 ♠
2 NT	?

YOUR ANSWER: I should now bid three spades.

No. You have too strong a hand for a signoff. Partner is simply testing the nature of your original raise. Since it consisted of the maximum ten points and four trumps, a raise to four spades is now in order.

Please return to **270** to find the hand best described by a three spade rebid.

♠ x x x   ♡ A K   ◇ x x x x   ♣ x x x x

Opener	Responder
1 ♠	1 NT
2 ♡	?

YOUR ANSWER: I should now pass.

No. This would show partner that you prefer hearts as trump. You don't. You prefer spades.

It doesn't matter that you have two high hearts. They will take two tricks whether they are trumps or not. You prefer spades because you have more of them and since he bid them first, partner may well have more spades too. Furthermore, he has a better chance of using your small spades to ruff his small hearts than of using your heart ace-king to ruff losing spades.

Remember this hand. It illustrates an important point.

Now return to **296** and select the proper rebid with this hand.

♠ J x x   ♡ A K x x x   ◇ x x   ♣ K J x

Partner opens with one spade, you respond two hearts, and he rebids two spades.

YOUR ANSWER: I should now bid three spades.

No. This would be too weak a rebid. Your partner has at least 13 points and a rebiddable spade suit. You have 13 points and adequate spade support for a rebid suit. So game in spades seems assured, but if you say only three spades partner will pass with a minimum hand. He will assume you have about 11 points and that you are asking him to go to game if he has 15.

Please go back to **267** for the right answer.

279

[from 287]

♠ K x x   ♡ J x x   ◇ A x x   ♣ Q x x x

Opener	Responder
1 ♠	2 ♠
3 ♠	?

YOUR ANSWER: My best rebid with this hand would be four spades.

Not quite. We would not be critical of a four spade rebid here, but there is a better call available.

With ten points you surely wish to reach game when partner invites you to go on. But since the hand is balanced and all your points are in high cards you would do better by saying three no trump. If partner's hand is suited to no trump play, he will pass; otherwise he will say four spades.

Return to the original question on **287** and try again.

280

[from 283]

♠ Q J x   ♡ A x x x x   ◇ x x   ♣ A x x

Partner opens with one diamond, you respond one heart, and partner rebids one no trump.

YOUR ANSWER: I should now bid two hearts.

We don't think so. Your hearts are not quite rebiddable and partner has denied support for them. Furthermore, a simple rebid in hearts is not especially forward going and may merely indicate an inability to play no trump.

You have 11 high-card points and should make a distinct effort to reach game.

Please return to **283** and pick the correct rebid.

♠ J x   ♡ x x x   ◊ x x x x   ♣ A J x x

Opener	Responder
1 ♡	1 NT
2 ♠	?

YOUR ANSWER: I would not bid three hearts.

You should.

It is vitally important to bear in mind the exact sequence of partner's bidding. By naming hearts first and then spades partner has "reversed," thereby advertising a strong (more than 18-point) hand. He has promised the strength to tolerate your return to hearts at the three level.

In addition you know that partner has more hearts than spades, for otherwise he would have bid spades first.

With this knowledge you must realize that you are obligated to show your preference for hearts even though it increases the level of the contract. Partner will not count on you for any additional values for this bid.

Return to **289** and try again.

♠ K x x   ♡ J x x   ◊ A x x   ♣ Q x x x

Opener	Responder
1 ♠	2 ♠
2 NT	?

YOUR ANSWER: I should now bid three spades.

No. Partner wishes to know more about the strength and distribution behind your original raise. Since you have ten points in high cards and no trump distribution, you should raise his two no trump bid to three.

Please return to **270** and find the hand which would be best described by a three spade rebid.

283

[from 267]

♠ J x x   ♡ A K x x x   ◇ x x   ♣ K J x

Partner opens with one spade, you respond two hearts, and partner rebids two spades.

YOUR ANSWER: I should now bid four spades.

Correct. Partner showed a minimum hand by his two spade bid, but you know that he has at least 13 points and a rebiddable suit. You have 13 points and adequate spade support for a rebid suit. So you must jump directly to game. Partner may pass a lesser call.

If, on the other hand, you held

♠ J x x   ♡ A K x x x   ◇ x x   ♣ Q x x

and the first three bids proceeded as above, you would rebid only three spades, for here you have just 11 points and want to reach game only if partner has a few extra values.

Another problem:

♠ Q J x   ♡ A x x x x   ◇ x x   ♣ A x x

Partner opens the bidding with one diamond, you respond one heart, he rebids one no trump. What is your rebid?

Pass **269**   Two Hearts **280**   Two No Trump **287**

284

[from 287]

♠ Q x x x   ♡ x x   ◇ K x x x   ♣ x x x

Opener	Responder
1 ♠	2 ♠
3 ♠	?

YOUR ANSWER: My best rebid with this hand is four spades.

Definitely not. By bidding three spades your partner is asking you to go to game only if you possess nine or ten points. Since you have only the most minimum raise containing a bare seven points you must pass.

Return to the original on **287** and try again.

(A) ♠ K J 9 x   ♡ x x   ◊ x x x   ♣ A Q 10 x

(B) ♠ A Q x x x x   ♡ x x x   ◊ Q x x   ♣ x

(C) ♠ A Q x x x   ♡ x x x   ◊ K x x   ♣ x x

Opener	Responder
1 ♡	1 ♠
2 ♠	?

YOUR ANSWER: I would say four spades with hand B.

This would be correct. Hand B is worth 13 rebid points, so game should be bid, and obviously you prefer spades. Hand C contains only 11 rebid points so you must be content to say three spades and let partner bid four if he has maximum values. And hand A is valued at 11 points, so a game is possible, but by bidding three clubs you will give partner the choice of saying three spades, four spades, or three no trump.

Clarifying the No Trump Response

As you will recall, an initial response of one no trump shows from six–ten high-card points. If opener has 17 or 18 points in high cards and a balanced hand, he may be vitally interested in knowing whether your count is a minimum (six or seven points) or a maximum (nine–ten points). Opener may solicit this information by bidding two no trump. With only six or seven points in your hand, you should pass for game is unlikely. But with eight–ten, you should accept his invitation and bid three no trump.

Partner opens with one heart and you respond one no trump. Partner rebids two no trump, asking you to clarify your response. Which hand calls for a rebid of three no trump?

♠ K x x   ♡ x x x   ◊ A x x x   ♣ x x x   **268**

♠ A x x   ♡ x x x   ◊ Q J x x   ♣ J x x   **294**

286

[*from 270*]

(A)　♠ Q x x x　　♡ x x　　　♢ A Q x x　　♣ x x x

(B)　♠ K x x　　　♡ J x x　　♢ A x x　　　♣ Q x x x

(C)　♠ Q x x x　　♡ x x　　　♢ K x x x　　♣ x x x

	Opener	Responder
	1 ♠	2 ♠
	2 NT	?

YOUR ANSWER: I should rebid three spades with hand C.

Right. This bid would show preference for spades over no trump and no more than minimum values. With hand A you have enough additional strength to jump to four spades. With hand B you also have enough to accept the invitation but the even distribution renders no trump more appealing than spades, so you should rebid three no trump.

When the responder has given a single raise in a *minor* suit and the opener rebids three of the same suit, the responder should try for a game in no trump even with an unstopped suit if he has about eight or nine points in high cards. For example, you hold:

　　♠ K x　　♡ x x x　　♢ A x x x　　♣ Q x x x

Partner opens with one diamond, which you raise to two. Partner rebids three diamonds. You should try for three no trump.

When a single raise has been given in a major suit and opener now bids a new suit, responder is forced to speak once more.

　　♠ x x　　♡ K x x x　　♢ K x x x　　♣ Q x x

The bidding:

	Opener	Responder
	1 ♡	2 ♡
	3 ♣	?

What is your rebid with this hand?

Three Hearts　**274**

Four Hearts　**288**

Pass　**293**

♠ Q J x   ♡ A x x x x   ◇ x x   ♣ A x x

Partner opens with one diamond, you respond one heart, and he rebids one no trump.

YOUR ANSWER: I should now bid two no trump.

Yes, you should. With 11 high-card points your hand is definitely worth two bids. Even ten points is sometimes enough. Furthermore, your hearts are not rebiddable, especially in view of partner's failure to support them. Your strength is well distributed, so you are pleased with the prospects of a no trump contract. If partner has about 15 points he should bid game. With a bare minimum he will pass two no trump.

With a somewhat weaker hand, however, you should not encourage partner to go on. If you held:

♠ x x x   ♡ A x x x x   ◇ x x   ♡ A x x,

you would pass to one no trump.

With a stronger hand (13 points), you would bid three no trump yourself.

Responder Clarifies the Raise

When responder gives a single raise in his partner's major suit he announces possession of seven–ten dummy points. As you saw in Chapter IV, it is sometimes vitally important for the opener to know precisely what your strength is, seven–eight points or nine–ten. He invites a game by bidding once more in the agreed trump suit. Responder either passes or goes to game, depending on the size of his original raise.

Let's assume that the bidding has proceeded:

Opener	Responder
1 ♠	2 ♠
3 ♠	?

With which hand would responder's best rebid be four spades?

♠ Q x x x	♡ x x	◇ A Q x x	♣ x x x	**270**
♠ K x x	♡ J x x	◇ A x x	♣ Q x x x	**279**
♠ Q x x x	♡ x x	◇ K x x x	♣ x x x	**284**

288

[from 286]

♠ x x   ♡ K x x x   ◇ K x x x   ♣ Q x x

Opener	Responder
1 ♡	2 ♡
3 ♣	?

YOUR ANSWER: I should now bid four hearts.

You are so right. Partner has bid three clubs in an effort to get you to clarify your original raise. His three club bid (after the initial major suit opening was raised) is a one-round force. With maximum values such as these you must jump to game. Without the king of diamonds, you would merely return to three hearts.

Rebid by Responder after a Single Raise by Opener

If your response in a new suit is raised by partner you know that he has about 14–16 points and trump support. Now you must reassess your assets in terms of rebid points. With a combined total-point count of 26 you may, of course, bid game. If 26 is out of the question, you pass. And if 26 is possible but not assured, you test your partner's strength by giving him another chance.

These calculations are based upon the supposition that you are dealing with a major suit. For a minor suit you need 29 points for game and hence should endeavor to extend your efforts in the direction of no trump if at all possible.

Opener	Responder
1 ♡	1 ♠
2 ♠	?

With which of these hands would you now bid four spades?

♠ K J 9 x   ♡ x x   ◇ x x x   ♣ A Q 10 x   **271**

♠ A Q x x x x   ♡ x x x   ◇ Q x x   ♣ x   **285**

♠ A Q x x x   ♡ x x x   ◇ K x x   ♣ x x   **290**

176

♠ x x x   ♡ A K   ◊ x x x x   ♣ x x x x

Opener	Responder
1 ♠	1 NT
2 ♡	?

YOUR ANSWER: I should now bid two spades.

Yes. You hold more spades than hearts, so you must return to spades. Partner can take two tricks with your hearts as a side suit and can probably use your spades to ruff a losing heart in his hand.

You can show preference for one of partner's suits by passing or by returning to his first suit. The latter bid requires no additional strength beyond that shown by your initial response. If the bidding goes:

Opener	Responder
1 ♡	1 ♠
2 ◊	2 ♡

partner will not interpret your two heart bid as indicative of strength. As a matter of fact, he knows that your one spade response might have been made with only six points and since your two heart bid shows no additional values he will assume that your hand is very weak. All that partner has the right to infer from such a bid is that you have at least as many hearts as diamonds and that your hearts are Q x or x x x or better.

(A)   ♠ J x   ♡ x x x   ◊ x x x x   ♣ A J x x

Opener	Responder
1 ♡	1 NT
2 ♠	

(B)   ♠ A J x x   ♡ x x   ◊ x x x   ♣ x x x x

Opener	Responder
1 ♡	1 ♠
2 ◊	

(C)   ♠ J x x   ♡ K x x   ◊ A x x x   ♣ x x x

Opener	Responder
1 ♠	1 NT
2 ♡	

With which of these three hands would you not return to partner's first-bid suit?

Hand A **281**   Hand B **299**   Hand C **304**

[from 288]

♠ A Q x x x   ♡ x x x   ◊ K x x   ♣ x x

Opener	Responder
1 ♡	1 ♠
2 ♠	?

YOUR ANSWER: I would now bid four spades.

You shouldn't. You have 11 rebid points (add one for the fifth spade when partner raises your suit) and partner has about 14–16. This should be a familiar theme by now. If partner is near the maximum a game contract will be warranted. So how do you find this out? By bidding three spades. He will pass with a minimum and go to game with a maximum.

Now go back to **288** and find the hand which calls for a four spade bid.

[from 300]

♠ x x x x   ♡ A J x x   ◊ A x   ♣ x x x

Opener	Responder
1 ♣	1 ♡
1 ♠	?

YOUR ANSWER: I would now pass.

How did you get to this page? By mistake, we hope.

Yes, you prefer partner's spade suit, but you are too strong to pass. With ten points you must state your preference more loudly by bidding two spades. If partner has 16 points you should reach four spades or three no trump.

Now return to **300** for the proper answer.

♠ x x x   ♡ A K   ◇ x x x x   ♣ x x x x

Opener	Responder
1 ♠	1 NT
2 ♡	?

YOUR ANSWER: I should now bid three hearts.

We think not. In the first place this hand is worth only seven points in support of hearts, so to show a preference for hearts you should merely pass.

And in the second place you don't want to show preference for hearts with this hand. You would rather have spades as trump. Your heart ace-king will take two tricks whether they are trumps or not. You have more spades than hearts and probably partner has a longer spade holding too. So you must guide him back to the suit in which you hold the most cards.

Please return to **296** now and choose a better rebid with this hand.

♠ x x   ♡ K x x x   ◇ K x x x   ♣ Q x x

Opener	Responder
1 ♡	2 ♡
3 ♣	?

YOUR ANSWER: I should pass.

No, no, no. When opener mentions another suit after his initial bid in a major suit has been raised, responder may not pass. This is just another way for the opener to test the nature of your raise. With a maximum raise you must now proceed to game; with a minimum you must return to his first suit. But you may not pass.

Please go back to **286** for the proper rebid.

(A) ♠ K x x ♡ x x x ◇ A x x x ♣ x x x

(B) ♠ A x x ♡ x x x ◇ Q J x x ♣ J x x

Partner opens with one heart, you respond one no trump, and he rebids two no trump.

YOUR ANSWER: With hand B, I would rebid three no trump.

Yes. Partner has 17 or 18 points in high cards and he wants to know more precisely how strong your hand is. If your response was based on only six or seven high-card points, you should pass (as with hand A above). But with eight–ten high-card points, you should carry on to three no trump.

In the following quiz we have five different bidding situations presented and there are four holdings listed under each bidding sequence. In each case, you are the responder. Study the bidding, and choose the proper rebid with each hand.

				Answer
Opener	*Responder*			*Letter*
1 ♠	2 ♠			

♠ Q x x x ♡ x x ◇ A Q x x ♣ x x x (A)
Opener's rebid: three spades

♠ K x x ♡ A x x ◇ x x x ♣ Q x x x (D)
Opener's rebid: three diamonds

♠ Q x x x ♡ x x ◇ K x x x ♣ J x x (G)
Opener's rebid: three spades

♠ J 10 x x ♡ A x x x ◇ x x x ♣ x x (J)
Opener's rebid: two no trump

Opener *Responder*
1 ◇ 2 ◇

♠ A x x ♡ x x ◇ J x x x ♣ J x x x (M)
Opener's rebid: three clubs

Go on to **295**.

♠ A x x   ♡ x x x x   ◇ J 10 x x   ♣ K Q   (O)
   Opener's rebid: three diamonds

♠ A x x   ♡ x x   ◇ Q x x x   ♣ J x x x   (R)
   Opener's rebid: three diamonds

♠ J x   ♡ x x   ◇ Q x x x x   ♣ K Q x x   (I)
   Opener's rebid: two no trump

Opener   *Responder*
1 ♡   1 NT
2 NT   ?

♠ J x x   ♡ x x x   ◇ A K x x   ♣ J x x   (S)
♠ J x x x   ♡ x x   ◇ A x x x   ♣ Q x x   (Q)
♠ x x x x   ♡ x   ◇ Q J x x   ♣ A x x x   (N)
♠ x x x   ♡ x x   ◇ K J x   ♣ A x x x x   (K)

Opener   *Responder*
1 ♡   1 ♠
2 ♠   ?

♠ A K x x   ♡ x x x   ◇ K x x x   ♣ x x   (B)
♠ K J x x x   ♡ A x   ◇ x x   ♣ Q x x x   (E)
♠ A J x x   ♡ x x   ◇ A Q x x   ♣ x x x   (H)
♠ K Q x x   ♡ Q x   ◇ J x x x   ♣ x x x   (L)

Opener   *Responder*
1 ♠   2 ♣
3 ♣   ?

♠ x x x x   ♡ A x x   ◇ x x   ♣ A Q x x   (P)
♠ x x x   ♡ Q J x   ◇ K x x   ♣ A J x x   (T)
♠ x x   ♡ K 10 x x   ◇ x   ♣ A K x x x x   (F)
♠ x x   ♡ Q J x   ◇ x x x x   ♣ A K J x   (C)

Check your answers on **297**.

Showing Preference When Partner Bids Two Suits

When the opening bidder mentions two suits it often becomes responder's duty to determine which of the two he will trump. This is an obligation not to be lightly regarded.

There are several guiding principles which will help you in this task.

1. You must usually assume that partner has bid his longer suit first.
2. You must evaluate the strength of partner's hand by the sequence in which he mentioned his suits.
3. You must base your preference more on the length than on the strength of your holdings in each suit.

Rules 1 and 3 will help you accomplish the main objective of trump-suit selection; to find the suit in which your partnership possesses the greatest number of cards.

Let us test your understanding of this fundamental principle with this problem.

The bidding:

Opener	Responder
1 ♠	1 NT
2 ♡	?

What is your rebid with this hand?

♠ x x x   ♡ A K   ◊ x x x x   ♣ x x x x

Pass **277**

Two Spades **289**

Three Hearts **292**

Answer
Letter

(A) Bid four spades. Partner is asking you to clarify your initial raise. You have ten points, a maximum raise. You should accept partner's invitation.

(B) Bid three spades. You have 11 points, not enough to go on to game yourself. If partner has a maximum raise, he should bid four spades.

(C) Bid three no trump. You may take a chance on partner having a diamond stopper. Your hand is balanced and an 11-trick contract may be out of reach.

(D) Bid three no trump. You have nine high-card points and a balanced hand. If partner's hand is unsuited for no trump play, he is at liberty to go on to four spades.

(E) Bid four spades. You have 13 rebid points and partner has at least 13 or 14.

(F) Bid five clubs. You have an opening bid and wish to be in game, but your hand is not suited for no trump play.

(G) Pass. This is as far as you can go with eight dummy points.

(H) Bid three diamonds. This may enable partner to say three no trump if he has a club stopper.

(I) Bid three no trump. You have eight high-card points and an established five-card suit. Nine tricks should be easier to take than 11.

(J) Bid three spades. This will show that you had a weak raise but that you prefer spades to no trump.

(K) Bid three no trump. You have eight high-card points and a five-card suit.

(L) Pass. Partner has shown about 14–16 points and you have only eight, so game is out of the question.

Go on to **298**.

298

[from 297]

Answer
Letter

(M) Bid three diamonds. You are merely preferring opener's original suit.

(N) Pass. You have just seven high-card points and poor distribution.

(O) Bid three no trump. You have no trump distribution and ten high-card points. It would have been better strategy to respond with one no trump originally with this hand.

(P) Bid three spades. You were too strong for a single raise of partner's suit on the first round. Now when you give him delayed support he will know that you have about 11 or 12 points.

(Q) Pass. You have just seven high-card points and with a minimum one no trump response, partner wouldn't want you to continue.

(R) Pass. You have a weak raise and have given your all.

(S) Bid three no trump. You have nine high-card points.

(T) Bid three no trump. You have 11 high-card points and protection in the unbid suits.

Go on to **296.**

(A)   ♠ J x   ♡ x x x   ◇ x x x x   ♣ A J x x

Opener	Responder
1 ♡	1 NT
2 ♠	

(B)   ♠ A J x x   ♡ x x   ◇ x x x   ♣ x x x x

Opener	Responder
1 ♡	1 ♠
2 ◇	

(C)   ♠ J x x   ♡ K x x   ◇ A x x x   ♣ x x x

Opener	Responder
1 ♠	1 NT
2 ♡	

YOUR ANSWER: With hand B, I would not return to partner's first-bid suit.

If you arrived here direct from page **289**, you have done very well.

With hand A you must be aware that partner has "reversed," thereby promising a strong hand which will tolerate your return to hearts at the three level.

With hand C you have no actual preference between hearts and spades, but you must return partner to his spade suit because:

(1) he probably has more spades than hearts,
(2) upon hearing of your slight spade support he may be able to contract for game.

But with hand B you have minimum strength and no real support for either suit. Since partner was unable to make a jump bid you may conclude that there is no chance for game. It is preferable to pass with poor support in each of partner's suits rather than to encourage any further action by partner.

Go on to **300**.

300

[from 299]

If you have a hand that is minimum and prefer partner's second suit you should pass. When your partner shows his second suit at the one level, however, you should strain to keep the bidding open for one more round with even slight additional values, even if you are satisfied with partner's second suit.

	Opener	Responder
	1 ♣	1 ♡
	1 ♠	?

With which of these hands would you now pass?

♠ x x x	♡ K 10 x x	◇ A J x	♣ x x x	**273**
♠ x x x x	♡ A J x x	◇ A x	♣ x x x	**291**
♠ x x x	♡ K 10 x x	◇ Q J x	♣ x x x	**306**

301

[from 318]

YOUR ANSWER: In cases 2–5 the new-suit forcing principle is abandoned because responder has already announced weakness.

Right.

In case 2, where responder has originally passed, this explanation is obviously true.

In case 3, where there has been an intervening takeout double, the responder would redouble (as you will learn in Chapter VIII) if he held ten or more points, any bid other than a redouble stems from weakness.

In case 4, where the partners have each bid one suit twice and responder then names another suit, it must be reasoned that he would have mentioned this second suit sooner if he had any real strength.

In case 5, where responder names a new suit over a no trump overcall, the same reasoning applies: with a stronger hand he would have doubled instead.

Go on to **309.**

Answer
Letter

(A) Bid two hearts. You have only seven points but must show a preference. The three-card length of your heart suit is more important than the two high diamond honors.

(B) Pass. You have only seven points and no preference between hearts and clubs. You might be tempted to take partner back into his first suit, but with only two trumps to contribute, your hand isn't worth it.

(C) Bid three hearts. You lacked the necessary four trumps to make this jump on the first round but should do so now.

(D) Bid two hearts. When you have three cards in each suit, you should take partner back to his first suit. It is probably his best one.

(E) Bid three clubs. You have 11 dummy points and excellent support for clubs. If partner has some control in the diamond suit, he may want to try three no trump.

(F) Rebid two spades. You have ten points, so you are strong enough to bid on your own at the two level. You might as well let partner know you have a rebiddable spade suit.

(G) Bid two no trump. You have ten high-card points and protection in diamonds.

Go on to **305**.

303

[from 306]

♠ K x x x   ♡ A x x   ◇ K x x   ♣ 10 x x

Opener	Responder
1 ◇	1 ♠
2 ♣	?

YOUR ANSWER: As responder with this hand, I would rebid two diamonds.

Well, you could return to two diamonds, but this would merely announce a preference and therefore would seem discouraging to your partner. He would have no way of knowing that you have more than a minimum hand and a dislike for clubs.

Actually, you have ten points, and you should make certain that partner gets to know this. It might be all he needs for a game contract.

Please go back to **306** and pick the rebid that will properly describe your hand.

304

[from 289]

♠ J x x   ♡ K x x   ◇ A x x x   ♣ x x x

Opener	Responder
1 ♠	1 NT
2 ♡	?

YOUR ANSWER: I would not bid two spades.

You should. Partner probably bid his longer suit first and your spades and hearts are of equal length. The fact that you have a king in hearts and only a jack in spades is much less important. And furthermore, you don't choose to let the bidding die, for your slight spade support may be all partner needs to bid and make game.

Return to **289** and try again.

It is imperative that responder completely understands the forcing principle. He must be able to differentiate the cases in which he is obliged to rebid, the cases in which he is urged to rebid, and the cases in which he is at liberty to pass.

The responder is given much more leeway in this regard than the opening bidder. He may pass most of partner's rebids. The reason for this is obvious: the opening bidder has already declared possession of a better-than-average hand. Responder, on the other hand, may base his reply on six points or as many as 19. With weak hands responder has accomplished his purpose by bidding once and is therefore allowed to pass most rebids by his partner. With strong hands, however, responder may use the new-suit forcing principle to gain further information from partner before committing himself to a final contract.

Nonjump new-suit bids, jump bids in the same suit, and jump bids in no trump—all of these bids are forcing upon the opener when made by the responder. None of them is forcing upon the responder when made by the opener. Responder may pass them all if he chooses to.

The only rebid by opener which is absolutely forcing upon responder is the jump shift in a new suit. This is absolutely forcing to game.

Suppose your partner opens with one diamond and you respond with one heart, holding:

♠ x x x x   ♡ K Q 10 x   ◇ x x   ♣ x x x

Which of the following rebids is appropriate?

Opener	*Responder*	
1 ◇	1 ♡	
2 NT	3 NT	308
1 ◇	1 ♡	
2 ♣	3 ♣	312
1 ◇	1 ♡	
3 ◇	3 ♡	316
1 ◇	1 ♡	
3 ♣	3 NT	319

306

[*from 300*]

(A) ♠ x x x   ♡ K 10 x x   ◇ A J x   ♣ x x x

(B) ♠ x x x x   ♡ A J x x   ◇ A x   ♣ x x x

(C) ♠ x x x   ♡ K 10 x x   ◇ Q J x   ♣ x x x

Opener	Responder
1 ♣	1 ♡
1 ♠	?

YOUR ANSWER: I would pass with hand C.

We would subscribe to this. Hand C contains only six points, so you have fulfilled your obligation to the opener by bidding one heart. You don't want to encourage partner any further.

Hand B contains an extra two points, however, so you can afford the mild rebid of one no trump, which will serve to show your complete values. You can then pass any rebid by partner.

With hand A you prefer spades, of course, but you are too strong to stop at the one level. Bid two spades; if partner has 16 points you should reach game.

You can see that the responder, like the opener, must plan his bids with economy, safety, and foresight. If, for example, with hand A above, you had chosen to make an initial response of one no trump instead of one heart, partner may never have been able to mention his spade suit and you might have missed the proper contract. On the other hand, no trump bids may be used on the second round of bidding, as with hand B, to indicate a few extra points and some protection in the unbid suits.

Opener	Responder
1 ◇	1 ♠
2 ♣	?

How would you rebid this hand?

    ♠ K x x x   ♡ A x x   ◇ K x x   ♣ 10 x x

Pass **275**

Two Diamonds **303**

Two No Trump **310**

190

♠ K Q J 9 x   ♡ K x x   ◇ x x   ♣ A x x

Opener	Responder
1 ♡	1 ♠
2 ◇	?

YOUR ANSWER: As responder with this hand, I would rebid two hearts.

No. You have good support for partner's hearts but a two heart bid would simply indicate that you prefer hearts to diamonds. If he has a minimum hand, partner will pass, and you are too strong to permit this to happen.

You must somehow keep the bidding open until you learn whether the hand should be played in hearts, spades, or no trump.

So return to **320** and look for the bid which will accomplish this.

♠ x x x x   ♡ K Q 10 x   ◇ x x   ♣ x x x

YOUR ANSWER: As responder with this hand, I would bid the following sequence:

Opener	Responder
1 ◇	1 ♡
2 NT	3 NT

No. You have only five high-card points, and should have no desire to raise the level. Since partner's bid was not forcing, there is no reason for you to bid again. Pass.

Please go back to **305** to pick the correct pair of rebids.

309

[from 301]

The ability to distinguish between an encouraging bid and a discouraging one is very important. Constant repetition of the same suit indicates great length of suit but not very much strength. However, if responder rebids his own suit, this should not necessarily be construed as discouraging. Whenever responder is at liberty to pass and keeps bidding instead (even in the same suit), he is showing willingness to proceed. This is particularly true when opener has indicated a minimum hand. However, if opener shows signs of strength, and responder keeps bidding his own suit, his bids should be then interpreted as discouraging.

In which two of these sequences is responder's bidding discouraging?

	Opener	Responder
(A)	1 ♡	2 ♣
	2 ♡	3 ♣
(B)	1 ♡	2 ♣
	2 NT	3 ♣
(C)	1 ♢	1 ♡
	2 ♣	2 ♡
	2 NT	3 ♡

A and B   **321**

B and C   **323**

A and C   **326**

♠ K x x x   ♡ A x x   ◇ K x x   ♣ 10 x x

Opener	*Responder*
1 ◇	1 ♠
2 ♣	?

YOUR ANSWER: I should now bid two no trump.

Very good.

You could have returned to two diamonds, but this would merely announce a preference. Since you have previously bid only at the level of one, it would promise no more than six card points. Your hand actually has a value of ten points, all in high cards. It is well balanced and its high cards are evenly distributed. Partner's suits are both minors, and game in either one of them could be more difficult to attain than it would in no trump. Therefore, your most informative bid is two no trump.

Responder's rebid of two no trump (after opener has rebid two in a suit) is mildly encouraging. It shows less than normal support for the opener's suit or suits, but it promises a fairly good hand, one that is worth two bids. Responder should have ten or eleven high-card points, including some strength in the unbid suits. With a weaker hand, responder should show preference for one of partner's suits.

What if you make a new-suit response and partner rebids his own suit? This indicates that he opened with just a minimum hand. Therefore, unless your hand is strong enough to enable you to assume the reins, your proper action is to pass.

For instance, if you have this hand:

♠ x   ♡ x x x x   ◇ A J x x x   ♣ K Q x

and partner opens with one spade, you respond two diamonds, and partner rebids two spades, you will have done your full duty by this hand in responding at the two level and should take no further action.

Go on to **311.**

311

[from 310]

With each of the hands below the bidding has been:

Opener	Responder
1 ♡	1 ♠
2 ♣	?

Choose the rebid you should make with each of these hands.

Answer
Letter

♠ J x x x x	♡ x x x	◇ x x x	♣ K Q	(A)
♠ K J x x	♡ x x x	◇ Q x x	♣ J x x	(D)
♠ A K x x x x	♡ x x	◇ J x x	♣ x x	(F)
♠ A J x x x	♡ x x	◇ x x x x	♣ x x	(B)
♠ A Q x x	♡ x x	◇ x x	♣ Q x x x x	(E)
♠ K J x x	♡ x x	◇ A x x x	♣ Q x x	(G)
♠ A Q J x	♡ K x x	◇ x x x	♣ K J x	(C)

Answers are on **302**.

312

[from 305]

    ♠ x x x x   ♡ K Q 10 x   ◇ x x   ♣ x x x

YOUR ANSWER: As responder with this hand, I would bid the following sequence:

Opener	Responder
1 ◇	1 ♡
2 ♣	3 ♣

No. Your hand is not strong enough for a club raise.

Partner has presented you with a choice between diamonds and clubs, but has not made a forcing bid.

You have more clubs than diamonds and therefore prefer clubs, but you should show your preference by passing.

So please return to **305** and pick the one correct pair of rebids.

Opener	Responder
1 ♦	1 ♠
2 ♣	2 ♦

YOUR ANSWER: In this sequence, responder's bidding is encouraging.

Wrong. In this sequence, responder's bidding is somewhat discouraging.

Responder's first bid was at the one level, so his point count could be as low as six. His second bid showed a preference without increasing the contract. Responder has not shown any excess values at all; he has just done his duty with a minimum-strength hand.

Please go back to **323** to pick up the sequence in which responder's bidding is definitely encouraging.

314

[*from 320*]

♠ K Q J 9 x   ♡ K x x   ♦ x x   ♣ A x x

Opener	Responder
1 ♡	1 ♠
2 ♦	?

YOUR ANSWER: As responder with this hand, I would rebid two spades.

No. Your spades are rebiddable, but you have 14 points in this hand, so you know that you and your partner can probably fulfill a game contract. A two spade rebid will not force your partner to bid again. He might—to your common chagrin—decide to pass.

You must keep the bidding open. So please go back to **320** and pick the bid that will do so for you.

315
[from 318]

YOUR ANSWER: In cases 2–5 the new-suit forcing principle is abandoned because it is obvious from one bidding that game is not to be contemplated.

No. If the responder passes originally, his partner bids one club, and he then says one spade, this is not forcing upon opener, but it certainly isn't obvious that game is impossible, for opener may have 20 points.

Nor does an intervening takeout double necessarily rule out the possibility of a game. The doubler's strength may be in the unbid suits.

If there is evidence that partner cannot support responder's suit and responder cannot support his partner's, the chances for game are indeed dim, but not impossible. Three no trump may still be a possibility.

After an intervening overcall of one no trump, game is quite unlikely; however, if opener and responder possess all of the outstanding strength plus some distributional values, a game may be feasible.

So you can hardly regard this as the best answer. Return to **318** and try again.

316
[from 305]

♠ x x x x   ♡ K Q 10 x   ◇ x x   ♣ x x x

YOUR ANSWER: As responder with this hand, I would bid the following sequence:

Opener	Responder
1 ◇	1 ♡
3 ◇	3 ♡

No. A jump rebid in the same suit does not force the responder. You have shown all your values by saying one heart and you must now pass.

Please return to **305** and pick the correct pair of rebids.

196

♠ K Q J 9 x   ♡ K x x   ◇ x x   ♣ A x x

Partner opens with one heart, you respond with one spade, and he rebids two diamonds.

YOUR ANSWER: If I had this hand, I would rebid three clubs.

Right. The best game contract may be in spades, hearts, or no trump. As yet, however, you're not sure which, and you want more information before making a decision. It depends entirely upon the texture of partner's hand. In order to learn more about partner's holding, you make an artificial new-suit bid of three clubs. Opener is forced to bid again (there is no danger of landing in a club contract). He may bid three spades if he has three spades in his hand, three hearts if he has five hearts, or he may try three no trump.

There are some exceptions to the rule that the naming of a new suit by responder forces the opener to speak once more:

1. When opener's rebid is one no trump. For example:

Opener	*Responder*
1 ◇	1 ♠
1 NT	2 ♡
(may pass)	

(But when responder rebids in a suit higher ranking than his first-bid suit he is "reversing" and this indicates such a strong hand that partner must bid again even after having rebid one no trump.)

2. When responder has previously passed. For example:

Opener	*Responder*
1 ♡	Pass
(may pass)	1 ♠

3. When there has been an intervening takeout double by responder's right-hand opponent. For example:

SOUTH	WEST	NORTH	EAST
1 ♣	Double	1 ♠	Pass
(may pass)			

Go on to **318**.

4. When it is evident from the preceding bidding that responder is not trying to go places but is seeking a safe landing place. For example:

Opener	Responder
1 ♡	1 ♠
2 ♡	2 ♠
2 NT	3 ♡

5. When the right-hand opponent overcalls the opening bid with one no trump, the bid of a new suit by responder is not forcing.

SOUTH	WEST	NORTH	EAST
1 ♠	1 NT	2 ♣	Pass
(may pass)			

The reason why responder's new-suit bid is not forcing in case 1 is that opener has already announced weakness and some ability to support other suits.

What is the reason for abandoning the new-suit forcing principle in cases 2–5?

Because responder has already announced weakness. **301**

Because it is obvious from the bidding that game is
not in contemplation. **315**

♠ x x x x   ♡ K Q 10 x   ◇ x x   ♣ x x x

YOUR ANSWER: If I held this hand, bidding sequence **D** would be correct.

(A)	*Opener*	*Responder*
	1 ◇	1 ♡
	2 NT	3 NT
(B)	1 ◇	1 ♡
	2 ♣	3 ♣
(C)	1 ◇	1 ♡
	3 ◇	3 ♡
(D)	1 ◇	1 ♡
	3 ♣	3 NT

Yes. Very good.

After partner's three club bid, a jump takeout to a new suit, you would have no choice but to bid again (and keep bidding until game is reached). You cannot rebid hearts and you cannot support diamonds. So there is only one call left for you—three no trump.

The point count of the hand is just six. Since none of opener's other rebids is forcing, your correct move in each case would be to pass.

In addition to knowing when he is forced to bid, responder should have a clear idea of how he can force his partner to bid.

Go on to **320.**

320

[from 319]

The rule that the naming of a new suit by responder forces opener to bid once more applies not only to the first round but also to subsequent rounds of bidding. For example, suppose you hold:

♠ A K J x x   ♡ A Q J x   ◇ x   ♣ x x x

Partner opens with one diamond. You respond with one spade. Partner bids two diamonds. With this hand you are quite set on going to game, but it is neither necessary nor wise for you to make a jump bid to game, for you don't yet know whether the contract should be hearts, spades, or no trump. You may force another bid from partner merely by naming a new suit, so you bid two hearts. On the next round you will be in a better position to judge where the hand should be played.

If you use it to best advantage, you can find the new-suit forcing principle extremely useful. It can be used to find the best suit or no trump fit, to explore the possibilities of game or slam, or to temporize when you need more information about your partner's hand.

Let's say you have this hand:

♠ K Q J 9 x   ♡ K x x   ◇ x x   ♣ A x x

Partner opens one heart, you respond one spade, and he rebids two diamonds. What should your next bid be?

Two Hearts   **307**

Two Spades   **314**

Three Clubs   **317**

Three No Trump   **324**

	Opener	Responder
(A)	1 ♡	2 ♣
	2 ♡	3 ♣
(B)	1 ♡	2 ♣
	2 NT	3 ♣

YOUR ANSWER: Responder's bidding is discouraging in both of these sequences.

No. Remember that when opener indicates a minimum hand, and responder is free to pass but continues to bid instead, he is encouraging his partner.

In sequence A, opener has shown a minimum hand by rebidding his own suit. If responder also had a weak hand, he would give up and pass instead of rebidding on the second round.

In sequence B, opener has shown a strong hand with his two no trump rebid. If responder also had a strong hand, he would raise partner to three no trump. Instead, he has rebid his own club suit, saying "Sorry, partner, I don't have enough strength to help you out in no trump. Even my clubs would not be very useful."

So, in sequence A, responder's bidding is encouraging, while in sequence B, it is discouraging.

Please go back to **309** for the two sequences in which responder's bidding is discouraging.

322

[*from 328*]

Opener	Responder
1 ♡	2 ◇
2 NT	3 ♡

YOUR ANSWER: In this sequence, responder's bidding is encouraging.

Correct. He has increased the contract twice. His first takeout to the two level promises ten or more points, and his raise of partner's hearts to the three level shows trump support and a desire to go to game. With a poor hand, responder would have given partner a single raise to two hearts instead of bidding a new suit at the level of two.

As a matter of fact, the three heart call in this sequence is regarded as forcing to game.

Responder doesn't necessarily have to raise the contract to be encouraging. For instance:

Opener	Responder
1 ♡	1 ♠
3 ♡	3 ♠

Responder isn't forced to rebid after opener's jump, but any rebid after the jump is considered somewhat encouraging. Responder isn't trying to rescue partner; opener has jumped in his own suit and should be able to take care of himself. With a poor hand, responder could pass. As it is, his rebid invites partner to go to game.

The three heart jump bid is highly encouraging. Whenever (as in this case) a strong rebid is accepted by partner, both players are committed to reach a game contract.

When you are trying to decide whether to proceed further, you should consider how many points your partner has indicated, and how eager he has been to bid new suits and/or increase the contract. If, in view of these questions, game is possible, and a convenient contract is available, game should be searched for.

Go on to **327.**

	Opener	*Responder*
(A)	1 ♡	2 ♣
	2 ♡	3 ♣
(B)	1 ♡	2 ♣
	2 NT	3 ♣
(C)	1 ◇	1 ♡
	2 ♣	2 ♡
	2 NT	3 ♡

YOUR ANSWER: Responder's bidding in sequences B and C is somewhat discouraging.

Quite right. In both cases, opener has indicated a strong hand and a desire to go to game. If responder had a strong hand too, he should have bid three no trump at least. Instead, he has continued to bid his own suit, telling partner that his hand is not strong, that he feels it would not be useful in no trump, and that even his one long suit is not very strong. In the case of sequence C, he might also have bid four hearts if his suit was really strong.

By continuing to bid despite opener's discouraging bidding in sequence A, responder is plainly indicating a desire to go on. Here his bidding is encouraging.

When partner opens and later bids two no trump, he has a good hand. If you have a good hand too, you must not merely repeat your suit at the three level. You should either respond in no trump or jump in your own suit.

Look at these bidding sequences. In one, the responder's bidding is encouraging; in the other, it is not. See if you can figure out which sequence is encouraging.

Opener	*Responder*	
1 ◇	1 ♠	
2 ♣	2 ◇	**313**

Opener	*Responder*	
1 ♠	2 ♣	
2 ◇	2 ♠	**328**

324

[from 320]

♠ K Q J 9 x   ♡ K x x   ◇ x x   ♣ A x x

Opener	Responder
1 ♡	1 ♠
2 ◇	?

YOUR ANSWER: As responder with this hand, I would rebid three no trump.

A game contract in no trump would definitely be a good possibility. Partner has hearts and diamonds, you have good spades and a stopper in clubs. But you don't know as yet if this would be the best contract.

You have good support for partner's hearts, so maybe a game contract in hearts would be better. Also, you have five good spades and partner might have three, so perhaps a game contract in spades would be best.

You must keep the bidding open until you can decide which is the proper game contract. A three no trump bid may bring the bidding to an abrupt close.

Please return to **320** and pick the bid that will force partner to bid again.

325

[from 328]

Opener	Responder
1 ♡	2 ◇
2 NT	3 ♡

YOUR ANSWER: In this sequence, responder's bidding is not encouraging.

Not so fast. Responder has increased the contract twice, and his first bid at the two level promised ten or more points. Furthermore, by raising partner's hearts to the three level, he has shown trump support and a willingness to go to game.

With a similar but weaker hand, responder would have made a single raise to two hearts right away.

Please go on to **322** and continue with the correct answer.

	Opener	Responder
(A)	1 ♡	2 ♣
	2 ♡	3 ♣
(C)	1 ◇	1 ♡
	2 ♣	2 ♡
	2 NT	3 ♡

YOUR ANSWER: Responder's bidding is discouraging in both of these sequences.

No. Remember that when opener indicates a minimum hand, and responder is free to pass but continues to bid instead, he is encouraging his partner.

In sequence A, opener has shown a minimum hand by rebidding his own suit. If responder also had a weak hand, he would give up and pass instead of rebidding on the second round.

In sequence C, opener has shown a strong hand. He has bid two suits and then gone to two no trump. If responder also had a strong hand he would raise partner to three no trump, or, if he had really strong hearts he would bid game in hearts at this point.

So, in sequence A, responder's bidding is encouraging, while in sequence C, it is discouraging.

Please go back to **309** for the two sequences in which responder's bidding is discouraging.

327

[from 322]

How would you interpret the final bid in each of the following sequences?

	Opener	Responder			Opener	Responder
(1)	1 ♠	3 ♠?	(9)	1 ♡	1 ♠
				2 NT?	
(17)	1 ♡	2 ◊	(25)	1 ♡	1 NT
	3 ♣?			2 ♠?	
(5)	Pass	1 ♠	(13)	1 ♠	2 ◊
	2 ♡?			2 ♠	3 ♣?
(21)	1 ♡	1 ♠	(32)	Pass	1 ♡
	1 NT?			2 ♠?	
(3)	1 ♠	2 ♣?	(11)	1 ♡	1 ♠
				3 ♡	3 ♠?
(19)	1 ◊	1 ♠	(30)	1 ♣	1 ♠
	2 ♣	2 ◊?		1 NT	3 ♠?
(7)	1 ♡	1 ♠	(15)	1 NT	2 ♣
	3 ♠?			2 ◊	2 ♡?
(23)	1 ♠	2 ◊	(2)	1 ♠	1 NT?
	2 ♠	3 ◊?		2 ?	
(10)	1 ♠	2 ♠	(18)	1 ♠	2 ♠
	3 ◊?			2 NT	3 ♠?
(26)	1 ♠	2 ♣	(6)	1 ♣	1 ◊
	3 ♠?			1 ♡?	
(14)	1 ♡	1 ♠	(22)	1 ♠	2 ♣
	1 NT	2 ♣?		2 NT?	
(4)	Pass	1 ♠	(12)	1 ♡	1 ♠
	3 ♠?			2 ♣?	
(20)	1 ♠	2 ♡	(31)	1 ♣	1 ◊
	2 ♠?			1 ♡	3 ♣?
(8)	1 ♡	1 NT?	(16)	1 NT	2 ♠?

Go on to **329**.

206

	Opener	Responder
(A)	1 ◇	1 ♠
	2 ♣	2 ◇
(B)	1 ♠	2 ♣
	2 ◇	2 ♠

YOUR ANSWER: In sequence B, responder's bidding is encouraging.

Very good.

In both sequences, responder is showing preference for his partner's first-bid suit. In sequence A, he promised no more than six points by his first response and he showed no additional values by his rebid, so the opener should be cautious about carrying on.

In sequence B, however, he elected to bid at the two level on the first round, thereby indicating at least ten points. He then showed his spade support on the second round. Obviously, with a weak hand he could have supported spades immediately and neglected to mention the clubs. So opener should appreciate his partner's encouragement and not give up if he has 14 or more points.

In this bidding situation:

Opener	Responder
1 ♡	2 ◇
2 NT	3 ♡

obviously, the opening bidder has a good hand; but is responder being encouraging?

Yes **322**

No **325**

329

[*from 327*]

		Opener	Responder
(24)		1 ♠	2 ◇
		2 NT	3 ♠?

		Opener	Adversary	Responder
(29)		1 ◇	1 NT	2 ♠?
(27)		1 ♣	1 ♡	1 NT?
(28)		1 ◇	Double	1 ♠?

Check your answers below.

Quiz Answers

1. Game-forcing. 13–16 dummy points.
2. Game-forcing. 13–15 high-card points.
3. One-round-force. Ten or more points. New-suit forcing principle.
4. Not forcing. Strongly invitational. 12–14 dummy points.
5. Not forcing. Ten–12 points. New-suit bid not forcing after a previous pass.
6. Not forcing. 13–16 points. Opener can't force responder by new-suit bid.
7. Semi-forcing. 17–19 dummy points. Responder may pass any rebid by opener except jump shift.
8. Weak bid. Six–ten high-card points.
9. Semi-forcing. 19–20 high-card points. Strongly invitational.
10. One-round-forcing. 16–18 rebid points. New-suit bid after first suit support.
11. Game-forcing. Ten–12 points. Responder has accepted opener's semi-force.
12. Not forcing. 13–16 points. Opener can't force partner with non-jump new-suit bid.
13. One-round-force. 12 or more points. New-suit bid by responder.

Go on to **330**.

14. Not forcing. Responder's hand not suited for no trump play. New-suit bid not forcing after opener's one no trump rebid.
15. Not forcing. Eight points and five-card heart suit. The two club and two diamond bids were artificial.
16. Not forcing. Weak bid. Long spades and less than eight points.
17. One-round-force. At least 17 points to reach three level without establishing trump suit.
18. Signoff. Weak hand suitable only for spade contract.
19. Signoff. Weak hand with diamond support, nonrebiddable spades, and no heart stopper.
20. Not forcing. 13–15 points. Rebiddable spades and no desire to go on.
21. Not forcing. 13–15 high-card points. A discouraging rebid.
22. Semi-forcing. 15–18 high-card points.
23. Not forcing, but mildly encouraging. Opener has shown weak hand with rebiddable spades, but responder has gone to three level.
24. Game-forcing. At least ten dummy points and good spade support. Responder has accepted opener's semi-force.
25. Semi-forcing. At least 21 points. Opener has "reversed."
26. Game-forcing. 19–21 rebid points. This jump in opener's original suit is forcing only after a two level takeout.
27. Not forcing, but encouraging. Ten–12 high-card points required to say one no trump after an overcall.
28. Not forcing. Weak hand (otherwise would redouble) with distributional values.
29. Not forcing. Weak hand (otherwise would double) with distributional values.
30. Game-forcing. At least 13 points and rebiddable spades. All jump bids by responder are forcing to game.
31. Game-forcing. At least 15 dummy points. With weak hand, responder could have supported clubs on the first round.
32. One-round-force. At least 13 dummy points. Jump shift after previous pass is forcing for one round.

Go on to Chapter VI on **331.**

CHAPTER VI

SLAM BIDDING

Slam bidding is basically no different from any other type of bidding. There are a variety of special slam-bidding conventions and techniques designed to improve the accuracy of the slam approach, but fundamental to all of them is the need to recognize possibilities of slam when they exist. And this basic problem of slam suspicion rests quite simply upon the ABC's of point-count requirements.

Slam Approach

Knowing that 33 or more points are needed for a small slam and 37 or more for a grand slam, how does one first suspect that his partner and he possess this much power? Usually, this is merely a matter of thoroughly understanding the requirements for the various basic opening bids, responses, and rebids dealt with previously.

If you make an opening bid (13 or more points) and partner responds with a jump shift (19 or more points), you suspect that a slam may be possible. Or if partner makes an opening two bid (21 or more points) and you have ten or more points, slam may be possible. Or if you open with one of a suit and partner jumps to three no trump (16 to 18 points), slam may be possible if you have more than a minimum.

There are, of course, many other bidding combinations which should turn your thoughts slamwards. Sometimes it is the opening bidder who first becomes aware of a hand's slam potential, on other occasions it is the responder. The partner who first suspects the slam possibility should guide the bidding accordingly.

Let's start with a problem in simple point-count arithmetic. Your partner opens with one club and you respond one heart. Partner's rebid is two no trump. What is your rebid?

♠ Q J 10   ♡ A K J x   ◊ A 10 9   ♣ x x x

Three No Trump **335**   Four No Trump **339**
Six No Trump **344**

♠ x x   ♡ A K J x x   ◇ K x x x   ♣ A x

You open one heart, and partner responds three hearts.

YOUR ANSWER: I would rebid four clubs.

Right. And this bid will serve several purposes: It will proclaim
your interest in slam, it will show your ace of clubs, and it will solicit further information about partner's point count and aces. Don't
worry lest he leave you in clubs; hearts have been established as
trump. Any bid in a new suit after a double raise must be construed
as a slam try and partner is expected to give whatever information
he may possess.

If partner had the minimum requirements for his jump response
he will now say four hearts. But if he has some extra values he will
now show his aces in logical order. If you show the ace of clubs
and partner bids four spades, you are reasonably safe in assuming
that he lacks the ace of diamonds for he would bid four diamonds
(holding the ace) over your four club ace bid, thus affording himself
the opportunity to show the spade ace as well.

And the success of many slams depends upon not only the *exact
number* of aces possessed by the partnership but also their *precise
location*. Heading toward a slam in spades while holding a void in
clubs, for example, your partner's possession of the red aces will be
more valuable than, say, the aces of diamonds and clubs, for otherwise the opponents can take a trick right off the bat.

Holding the hand at the top of this page, which ace would you
prefer your partner to have?

The ace of spades   **338**

The ace of diamonds   **342**

♠ K Q x x   ♡ A J x x x   ◊ x   ♣ A Q x

Your partner opens with one spade and there is a two club overcall on your right.

YOUR ANSWER: I would now bid two hearts.

So would we. This would force partner to bid again and at the same time conserve bidding room so that you will be able to describe the rest of your hand later on in the auction. Right now it is important to show your good heart suit. The club control and spade support can be proclaimed later.

It has been emphasized that cue bids should be used only with the intention of reaching slam. There is one exception: belated cue bids may be employed in the course of otherwise nonaggressive bidding in an effort to reach game in no trump.

The Importance of Position

Oftentimes a slam can be made by one partner and not by the other simply because of his position at the table relative to that of the opening leader. Holding K x or a tenace in a side suit, for example, every effort should be made to be the declarer, not the dummy. On the other hand, holding a worthless doubleton in an unbid suit, one should try to permit partner to play the hand in the hope that he has K x or a tenace in that suit.

Here is a case in point: The bidding has gone:

SOUTH	WEST	NORTH	EAST
1 ♣	Pass	1 ♠	Pass
4 ♠	Pass	5 ♡	Pass
?			

Sitting South you hold:

♠ K Q x x   ♡ Q   ◊ K x   ♣ A K Q J x x

What do you bid now?

Five Spades **337**   Six Spades **346**   Six Clubs **354**

♠ K Q x x x   ♡ x   ◇ K Q x x x   ♣ K x

SOUTH	WEST	NORTH	EAST
1 ♠	Pass	2 ◇	3 ♣
3 ♡	Pass	4 ♠	Pass
5 ◇	Pass	?	

YOUR ANSWER: As North, I should now bid six spades.

No. Although this is the stronger of the two hands presented with this problem, it fails to satisfy the requirement for this bid. Spades have been agreed upon as trump and your partner has exceeded the game level by showing the diamond ace at the five level. This bid specifically requests you to go to slam only if you have first or second-round control of the opponents' suit, clubs.

As it is, you cannot prevent the loss of two club tricks and so you must settle for a bid of five spades. Partner will get the message.

Return to **341** for the proper hand upon which to bid six spades.

♠ Q J 10   ♡ A K J x   ◇ A 10 9   ♣ x x x

Partner opens with one club and you respond one heart with this hand. His rebid is two no trump.

YOUR ANSWER: I would rebid three no trump.

This is the kind of mistake that would be made by an overcautious beginner. You have 15 high-card points and partners rebid promises 19 or 20. This adds up to 34 or 35 points—enough for a small slam. A three no trump rebid would tell partner you have minimum-strength hand, worth only 7–11 high-card points. Partner would pass and an almost certain slam would be missed.

Only you, as responder, know the partnership's true strength in this case, so it's your duty to carry the contract to its proper level.

Return to **331** and do so.

336

[from 344]

♠ x x ♡ A K J x x ◇ K x x x ♣ A x

You open one heart, and partner responds three hearts.

YOUR ANSWER: I would rebid four diamonds with this hand.

No. Four diamonds would not be proper. Your diamonds would be biddable at a lower level in search of a suit fit, but here you have already found a suit fit, so mentioning diamonds at the four level would mislead your partner. When you bid a new suit after trump is agreed upon and slam is a definite possibility, you are telling partner that you have the ace of that suit.

Now return to **344** and choose the correct answer.

337

[from 333]

♠ K Q x x ♡ Q ◇ K x ♣ A K Q J x x

SOUTH	WEST	NORTH	EAST
1 ♣	Pass	1 ♠	Pass
4 ♠	Pass	5 ♡	Pass
?			

YOUR ANSWER: As South, I should now bid five spades.

Where will this get you? Partner's first bid announced spade strength and six or more points. His second bid showed the ace of hearts and sufficient power to warrant slam interest. Your four spade bid assured a game contract (three spades might, of course, have been passed), but now that you have this extra information about partner's hand, aren't you also interested in slam? Of course you are, but a five spade bid would be a peculiar way of showing your interest. This might very well talk your partner out of his slam hopes.

Go back to **333** and try again.

214

♠ x x   ♡ A K J x x   ◇ K x x x   ♣ A x

SOUTH	NORTH
1 ♡	3 ♡
4 ♣	

YOUR ANSWER: I would prefer that partner hold the ace of spades.

Most assuredly you would, for without the spade ace you might very well lose two spade tricks immediately. Lacking the ace of diamonds, however, you are at least sure of second-round control in that suit.

Bear in mind that if partner now bids four diamonds he may still possess the ace of spades as well. You could ascertain this by further probing, if you like, for with a minimum 31 points you need not fear ending up in a five-level contract. Since the partnership possesses a maximum 34 points, a grand slam should, of course, be avoided.

Doubletons and Singletons

The above hand illustrates a rather common pitfall in slam biddings: the danger of the worthless doubleton. Note that this danger is lessened by bids which name specific aces and not by bids which simply indicate the number of aces held.

Just as important as fear of the worthless doubleton is appreciation of the singleton in slam bidding. Often a singleton in the right suit means the difference between a makable and unmakable slam. For instance:

♠ A K Q x x   ♡ x x x   ◇ K x x   ♣ J x

SOUTH	NORTH
1 ♠	2 ◇
2 ♠	3 ♣
3 ◇	4 ♠

Do you sense a slam here?

Yes **341**
No **352**

339

[*from 331*]

♠ Q J 10   ♡ A K J x   ◇ A 10 9   ♣ x x x

Partner opens with one club and you respond one heart. Partner's rebid is two no trump.

YOUR ANSWER: I would rebid four no trump.

By jumping to two no trump your partner has promised 19 or 20 high-card points and stoppers in spades, diamonds, and clubs. You are correct in suspecting that a slam is possible, but isn't this fact more or less certain? Your 15 points in high cards plus partner's minimum of 19 points place the hand well within the slam range.

Return to **331** and pick the correct answer.

340

[*from 348*]

(A)   ♠ x x x   ♡ A Q x x x x   ◇ x   ♣ A K x
(B)   ♠ A K x   ♡ A Q x x x x   ◇ x   ♣ x x x

You open with one heart, your left-hand opponent overcalls with one spade, and your partner bids two spades.

YOUR ANSWER: I would expect to reach slam with hand A.

Correct. In hand B, your spade strength is nullified by partner's void; you will expect to lose too many tricks in the minor suits. With hand A, however, you have first-round control of both black suits.

When you have the choice between making an immediate cue bid and showing a genuine suit of your own, the latter course should be preferred. While it is very difficult to describe a good suit late in the bidding, it is never too late to show control of an adverse suit.

Your partner opens with one spade and there is a two club overcall on your right. You hold:

♠ K Q x x   ♡ A J x x x   ◇ x   ♣ A Q x

What do you bid?

Two Hearts **333**   Three Hearts **343**   Three Clubs **359**

♠ A K Q x x   ♡ x x x   ◇ K x x   ♣ J x

SOUTH	NORTH
1 ♠	2 ◇
2 ♠	3 ♣
3 ◇	4 ♠

YOUR ANSWER: I sense a slam here.

So do we. With this bidding your partner cannot have more than one heart. This is the crux of the matter. You should picture his hand as something like this:

♠ J x x x   ♡ x   ◇ A Q J x   ♣ A Q x x

With any luck you should make six spades.

It may be stated as a general principle of bidding that when a player names three suits and incorporates a jump in his sequence of bids he shows a singleton or void in the fourth suit. If North held a doubleton heart he might bid three suits but he then would not be justified in jumping to four spades; over your three diamond bid he should say only three spades.

If, in the above problem, your diamond and heart holdings had been reversed, you would not be interested in slam, for your king of hearts would be less valuable opposite a singleton and your diamonds would not be solid.

This singleton business is so vital to slam bidding that another rule is based upon it. A bid beyond the game level in the face of opposition bidding should be interpreted as a request for partner to contract for slam if he has no more than one loser in the adverse suit.

You are sitting North. The bidding:

SOUTH	WEST	NORTH	EAST
1 ♠	Pass	2 ◇	3 ♣
3 ♡	Pass	4 ♠	Pass
5 ◇	Pass	?	

With which of these hands would you now bid six spades?

♠ K Q x x x   ♡ x   ◇ K Q x x x   ♣ K x   **334**

♠ K Q x x x   ♡ x x   ◇ K Q x x x   ♣ x   **348**

342

[from 332]

♠ x x　　♡ A K J x x　　◇ K x x x　　♣ A x

SOUTH	NORTH
1 ♡	3 ♡
4 ♣	

YOUR ANSWER: I would prefer that partner held the ace of diamonds.

You haven't thought this out thoroughly. If partner now bids four diamonds and you reach a six heart contract without the ace of spades, what suit do you expect West to lead? Spades, of course—the only unbid suit. And even if your partner has the king of spades, the chances are fairly good that the enemy will take two spade tricks.

Possession of the ace of spades would at least prevent the opponents' taking the first two tricks.

Return to **332** and try again.

343

[from 340]

♠ K Q x x　　♡ A J x x x　　◇ x　　♣ A Q x

Your partner opens with one spade and there is a two club overcall on your right.

YOUR ANSWER: I would bid three hearts with this hand.

This would be ill-advised. Admittedly you have the power for this jump shift (19 points in support of spades), but it would use up so much bidding space that you may never get the chance to show the many features of this hand.

If you do say three hearts and partner then bids four diamonds, where are you? You are already at the four level and you haven't announced your trump support or your club control. Even in slam bidding it is important to be economical with bidding space.

So return to **340** and look for a better response.

♠ Q J 10   ♡ A K J x   ◇ A 10 9   ♣ x x x

Partner opens with one club and you respond one heart with this hand. His rebid is two no trump.

YOUR ANSWER: I would rebid six no trump.

Correct. Opener's rebid of two no trump promises 19 or 20 high-card points. The partnership has at least 34 points (virtually assuring six no trump) and no more than 35 points (making a grand slam very risky).

This hand illustrates another sequence of bids which usually spells slam: an opening bid facing an opening bid and followed by a jump.

If you make an opening bid and partner gives you a double raise (e.g., one spade—three spades), you know that he has 14–16 points in support of your suit. With 13–16 points in your hand, you simply contract for game. With 17, 18, or 19 points (don't forget to calculate in rebid points now), you will have slam strength if partner has 16, 15, or 14 respectively. With 20 points, you know you are in the slam zone.

Ace-Showing Bids

But aside from being sure of the proper point count and a suit or no trump fit, it is vital in slam bidding to know how many aces (and, quite often, precisely which aces) are in enemy hands. After having discovered that the potential of the hand is in the slam zone, a bid in a new suit is ace-showing (cue bid). In the quest for what may be vital controlling cards, the proper procedure is to bid each ace individually in ascending order. For example:

You open with one heart, and partner responds three hearts. Since your hand is worth 18 points, and partner has indicated a range of 13–16 points, you acknowledge that there may be some possibility to the hand. What is your next bid with this hand?

♠ x x   ♡ A K J x x   ◇ K x x x   ♣ A x

Four Clubs **332**
Four Diamonds **336**
Four Hearts **353**

345

[*from 369*]

♠ A K x x x   ♥ Q x x   ♦ Q J 10 x x   ♣ void

Partner opens with one heart, vigorously supports your diamonds, and then bids four no trump.

YOUR ANSWER: I would now pass.

This would be very poor strategy. Partner has proclaimed a good hand and a diamond fit. Now he wants to know how many aces you have. You should not pass a Blackwood four no trump bid.

Hurry back to **369** and try again.

346

[*from 333*]

♠ K Q x x   ♥ Q   ♦ K x   ♣ A K Q J x x

SOUTH	WEST	NORTH	EAST
1 ♣	Pass	1 ♠	Pass
4 ♠	Pass	5 ♥	Pass
?			

YOUR ANSWER: As South, I would now bid six spades.

This would be poor technique. You were willing to let partner play a spade contract because you felt that at most he should lose three tricks in the red suits. But now that he has announced his desire to proceed to slam, do you want him to play the hand? Can he handle a diamond lead as well as you can?

Go back to **333** and try again.

347

[*from 358*]

NORTH	EAST	SOUTH	WEST
1 ♥	Pass	3 ♥	Pass
4 NT	Pass	?	

YOUR ANSWER: With one ace, I would now bid five hearts.

Certainly not. This situation calls for the standard response of five diamonds to indicate one ace.

Please return to **358** and find the right answer.

220

SOUTH	WEST	NORTH	EAST
1 ♠	Pass	2 ♦	3 ♣
3 ♡	Pass	4 ♠	Pass
5 ♦	Pass	?	

(A) ♠ K Q x x x   ♡ x   ♦ K Q x x x   ♣ K x

(B) ♠ K Q x x x   ♡ x x   ♦ K Q x x x   ♣ x

YOUR ANSWER: As North, I should now bid six spades with hand B.

Quite right. Although hand A contains 17 points and hand B only 13, hand B meets the requirements for this bid. By exceeding game level in the agreed-upon suit (spades), partner has asked specifically whether you have first- or second-round control of the opponents' suit. With a singleton club you can contract for slam.

This same bidding technique can be used to investigate first- or second-round control of an unmentioned suit. After vigorous bidding in spades and ace-showing bids in the red suits, for example, a bid of five spades will now request partner to say six if he has a singleton club. Otherwise, with every other trick in the book, the partnership may lose two quick club tricks.

The Cue Bid

Another bid with slam overtones is the cue bid in the opponents' suit. This shows first-round control in that suit—either the ace or a void—and definite slam aspirations. Agreement on the trump suit, expressed or implied, must precede the use of this bidding device.

Cue bids can be very helpful. Don't abuse them. Remember the prerequisites:

1. Agreement on the trump suit.
2. An ace or a void in the opponents' suit, and
3. Sufficient strength to suggest slam.

Now suppose you open with one heart, the opponent on your left overcalls with one spade, and your partner responds two spades. With which of these hands would you expect to reach a slam?

♠ x x x   ♡ A Q x x x x   ♦ x   ♣ A K x **340**

♠ A K x   ♡ A Q x x x x   ♦ x   ♣ x x x **355**

221

349

[from 374]

♠ A K Q x x x   ♥ x   ♦ Q x x   ♣ x x x

Partner opens with one heart and then rebids two no trump after your one spade response.

YOUR ANSWER: With this hand, I would now bid six no trump.

Never. Partner has promised 19–20 high-card points and you have only 11 more. This does not add up to 33. Moreover, your spade suit is self-sustaining, so you should plan on a spade slam.

Now please return to **374** and be more careful with your addition.

350

[from 354]

♠ x x   ♥ A K J x x   ♦ K Q x   ♣ x x x

Your partner opens with one spade and then raises your two heart response to four.

YOUR ANSWER: I would now pass.

Coward. You have 15 rebid points and partner has promised 16 to 19. If you ignore slam possibilities in this sort of situation you will miss out on a lot of big scoring opportunities.

Go back to **354** and think it over.

351

[from 369]

♠ A K x x x   ♥ Q x x   ♦ Q J 10 x x   ♣ void

Partner opens with one heart, vigorously supports your diamonds, and then bids four no trump.

YOUR ANSWER: I would now bid five diamonds.

This would be the stereotyped answer to Blackwood, showing one ace. However, you have a valuable void in clubs which you haven't mentioned. If you say five diamonds, partner may be forced to pass, fearing one or two club losers. You can't lie about your aces, but you can jump directly to slam.

Return to **369** and jump to slam.

♠ A K Q x x   ♡ x x x   ◇ K x x   ♣ J x

SOUTH	NORTH
1 ♠	2 ◇
2 ♠	3 ♣
3 ◇	4 ♠

YOUR ANSWER: I do not sense a slam here.

Well, you should. Your partner has shown some strength and length in three suits and incorporated a jump in his bidding. Even with your minimum-strength opening you seem to have a fine fit with partner's hand.

The main point here is that your partner, by naming the three other suits, has virtually assured you that he has no more than one heart. This, together with his aggressive bidding, should awaken you to the likelihood of slam.

Now return to **338** and try again.

♠ x x   ♡ A K J x x   ◇ K x x x   ♣ A x

You open one heart, and partner responds three hearts.

YOUR ANSWER: I would rebid four hearts with this hand.

No. Four hearts would show no interest at all in a slam. By jumping to three hearts, partner has asked you to say four hearts with 13–16 points and to bid something else if you have more. With your 18 rebid points you can hope for slam if partner has about 15 points, including an ace. You can proclaim your interest in slam, show your ace of clubs, and at the same time, inquire about partner's precise point count and aces by making the correct rebid now.

Return to **344** and choose the correct answer.

♠ K Q x x ♡ Q ◇ K x ♣ A K Q J x x

SOUTH	WEST	NORTH	EAST
1 ♣	Pass	1 ♠	Pass
4 ♠	Pass	5 ♡	Pass
?			

YOUR ANSWER: As South, I would now bid six clubs.

Very good. Knowing of partner's spade strength, heart ace, and slam interest, you want to bid six of something, but you realize that if the diamond ace is on your left you should be declarer. In six spades, with your hand as dummy, the contract would be doomed from the outset if the diamond ace is off side and a diamond is led through your king. As a game contract, four spades is superior; in slam, however, you want the opening lead to come up to you.

The Cautious Approach

Sometimes the enumeration of specific aces and voids is impractical or impossible. In these cases, slam may be approached by exceeding the game level and letting partner decide on the basis of his over-all strength. This is the same principle used in reaching many game bids, i.e., making a bid which asks partner to proceed if he has maximum values for his previous bids.

Suppose you hold:

♠ x x ♡ A K J x x ◇ K Q x ♣ x x x

Your partner opens with one spade and raises your two heart response to four. What call do you now make?

Pass **350**

Five Diamonds **363**

Five Hearts **368**

Six Hearts **370**

♠ A K x   ♡ A Q x x x x   ◇ x   ♣ x x x

You open with one heart, your left-hand opponent overcalls with one spade, and your partner bids two spades.

YOUR ANSWER: I would now expect to reach a slam with this hand.

This would be wishful thinking. Your partner has announced heart support, a void in spades, and slam aspirations. But with your side strength in the same suit as his void, you cannot share these aspirations. You have too many losers in the unbid suits. In other words, your strength and his strength duplicate rather than supplement each other, a condition to be avoided whenever possible, especially at the slam level.

Please return to **348** and study the other hand.

♠ A Q J x x x   ♡ K Q x x x   ◇ void   ♣ Q x

Partner opens with one heart and then bids two hearts over your one spade response.

YOUR ANSWER: I would now say four hearts.

Go to the bottom of the class. You have a powerhouse. Four hearts would be the meekest bid you could make. Partner would surely pass and type you as a Caspar Milquetoast if, as is not unlikely, he made six.

Go back to **368** and try again.

357

[from 362]

♠ x x   ♡ K J x   ◇ K Q x   ♣ A Q x x x

You open with one club, which partner raises to three?

YOUR ANSWER: The Blackwood convention will help to determine slam safety here.

No, it won't. If you say four no trump and partner has one ace, you are in trouble. He will respond five diamonds and you will have to bid six clubs with two aces out against you. You should anticipate partner's probable response and avoid this trap.

Return to **362** and try again.

358

[from 369]

♠ A K x x x   ♡ Q x x   ◇ Q J 10 x x   ♣ void

Partner opens with one heart, vigorously supports your diamonds, and then bids four no trump.

YOUR ANSWER: I would now bid six diamonds.

So would we. If you give the literal response of five diamonds, partner may pass, not knowing about your club void.

Blackwood after Interference Bids

Responses to Blackwood after an intervening overcall begin with the suit in which the overcall was made. For example, if the intervening overcall was five diamonds, a pass shows no aces, five hearts shows one ace, five spades shows two aces, five no trump shows three aces, and six clubs shows all four.

Sitting South with one ace in your hand, in which of these problems would you bid five hearts?

NORTH	EAST	SOUTH	WEST	
1 ♡	Pass	3 ♡	Pass '	
4 NT	Pass	?		347
1 ♡	Pass	3 ♡	Pass	
4 NT	5 ◇	?		374

♠ K Q x x   ♡ A J x x x   ◇ x   ♣ A Q x

Your partner opens with one spade and there is a two club over-call on your right.

YOUR ANSWER: I would now bid three clubs.

No. You have a heart suit worth showing. True, you hope to reach slam with this hand sitting opposite a one spade opening, but if you show your club control now and mention your hearts later, partner will have no way of knowing whether you have a genuine heart suit or are merely showing the ace. If he holds A x x x in spades and K Q x x in hearts, you may arrive at slam in the wrong suit.

So return to **340** and look for a better response.

♠ A Q J x x x   ♡ K Q x x x   ◇ void   ♣ Q x

Partner opens with one heart and then bids two hearts over your one spade response.

YOUR ANSWER: I would now bid five hearts.

Where would this get you? This type of bid is reserved for probing for extra values from partner in cases where his previous bids have covered a rather wide range of possible point-count holdings. Here he has already proclaimed a minimum by rebidding hearts. If you want to go to slam, it's up to you; he's probably told you all he can.

So go back to **368** and look for a more independent bid.

361

[*from 374*]

(A) ♠ A K Q x x x   ♥ x   ♦ Q x x ♣ x x x

(B) ♠ A K J x x   ♥ J x   ♦ x x x ♣ K Q x

(C) ♠ A x x x x   ♥ Q x x x x   ♦ K x   ♣ x

Partner opens with one heart and then rebids two no trump after your one spade response.

YOUR ANSWER: I would now bid six no trump with hand B.

Correct. Partner's two no trump bid promises 19–20 high-card points and you have 14 more, making a total of 33–34. You can't support his hearts and he has not shown support for your spades, so you should take the bull by the horns and bid six no trump straightaway. Hands A and C are better suited to slams in spades and hearts respectively.

Similar mathematical predications may be made after all opening bids, responses, and rebids in no trump, for each is precisely defined in point count.

With a good five-card suit you may bid a slam with one point less than usual; with a six-card suit, with two or three points less. But in these cases it is wise to check first on the number of aces out against you.

Say, for example, you hold:

♠ x x   ♥ x x   ♦ x x x   ♣ K Q J x x x

Partner opens with three no trump (25–27 points).

Would you consider slam possibilities to be:

Poor **364**

Dependent upon the number of partner's aces. **367**

Assured **371**

♠ A Q J x x x   ♡ K Q x x x   ◇ void   ♣ Q x

Partner opens with one heart and then rebids two hearts over your one spade response.

YOUR ANSWER: I should now bid six hearts.

Very good. It's not a scientific bid, but scientific bids may not be effective with this hand. Partner has already announced a minimum. You have a very good hand and trump support, so you wish to get to slam. But if you bid your diamond void now, you will surely get a club lead, which you don't desire. If you jump directly to six hearts, the enemy will have to guess whether to lead diamonds or clubs. Of course, partner just may hold the club king or ace; but, if he doesn't, blasting to six hearts might lead the enemy astray.

The Blackwood Convention

The Blackwood convention is known to almost everybody who plays bridge. Far fewer players know precisely how and when to use it. First of all, a trump suit must have been previously agreed upon. Secondly, at least 11 tricks must be already assured. Thirdly, the bidder must need to know how many aces partner has, not specifically which ones. And there is more to it than this, as you will see below. Once a trump suit has been established, either player may ask for aces by bidding four no trump. The responses are as follows:

With no aces, bid five clubs.
With one ace, bid five diamonds.
With two aces, bid five hearts.
With three aces, bid five spades.
With four aces, bid five clubs.

Note that five clubs indicates no aces and all four aces. No confusion is apt to result here because partner will readily distinguish between the two meanings.

After your one club opening and partner's double raise to three clubs, will the Blackwood convention help you assess slam possibilities with this hand?

♠ x x   ♡ K J x   ◇ K Q x   ♣ A Q x x x

Yes **357**
No **369**

363

[from 354]

♠ x x ♡ A K J x x ◇ K Q x ♣ x x x

Your partner opens with one spade and then raises your two heart response to four.

YOUR ANSWER: I would now bid five diamonds.

You should not do this. Granted that hearts have been agreed upon as trump, so you will not be stuck with a diamond bid, nevertheless such a bid would be misleading for it would promise the diamond ace. It is acceptable to show a king in a side suit if partner has already shown the ace in that suit, but you cannot start off by showing a king.

Return to **354** and think it over.

364

[from 361]

♠ x x ♡ x x ◇ x x x ♣ K Q J x x x

Partner opens with three no trump.

YOUR ANSWER: I would consider slam possibilities to be poor with this hand.

How can you say this? Partner has promised 25–27 high-card points, balanced distribution, and stoppers in every suit. Therefore he must have the club ace, at least one other club, and 21–23 high-card points in the other three suits. He can almost certainly take six club tricks and five or six more in the other suits.

Now return to **361** and pick the most accurate statement.

♠ A x x x x   ♡ Q x x x x   ◇ K x   ♣ x

Partner opens with one heart and then rebids two no trump after your one spade response.

YOUR ANSWER: With this hand I would now bid six no trump.

Never. Partner's two no trump bid promises 19–20 high-card points. You have only nine more. This does not add up to 33. But you do have 14 dummy points in support of hearts, so a heart slam is virtually assured if you are not off two aces to begin with. Bid three hearts. If partner raises to four, employ the Blackwood four no trump convention.

Now please return to **374** and be more careful with your addition.

♠ A Q J x x x   ♡ K Q x x x   ◇ void   ♣ Q x

Partner opens with one heart and then bids two hearts over your one spade response.

YOUR ANSWER: I would now say three diamonds.

This answer would seem to follow the advice on the ace-showing slam approach in bidding. If partner can now show the ace of clubs, your heart slam is virtually assured.

But there are two major defects to this bid:

1. Your partner is as yet unaware of your heart support and so may interpret your bid as representing possession of a diamond suit and denial of heart support. Hence, with K x x in clubs he may bid three no trump and you will find yourself in an awkward position. And,

2. This diamond bid tells the enemy all too much. It practically invites them to lead clubs, your only unbid suit.

So here is a case where an ace-showing bid may do more harm than good.

Return to **368** and select another bid.

♠ x x   ♡ x x   ◇ x x x   ♣ K Q J x x x

Partner opens with three no trump.

YOUR ANSWER: I would consider slam possibilities dependent upon the number of partner's aces.

True. You have a partnership total of 31–33 high-card points, which should be enough for slam with this six-card suit, but it is still possible that there are two aces missing.

The Gerber Four Club Convention

A response of four clubs over an opening bid of one, two, or three no trump is artificial and is treated in the Blackwood manner as a request for aces. The responses are as follows:

With no aces, bid four diamonds.

With one ace, bid four hearts.

With two aces, bid four spades.

With three aces, bid four no trump.

With four aces, bid five clubs.

When the four club bidder wishes to probe for kings he employs five clubs as his asking bid.

This convention is most useful when the responder to a no trump opening possesses a very long suit. Figuring that declarer can take six or seven tricks with his suit the responder shaves the requirements for a slam by several points, but in order to be sure that the enemy cannot immediately defeat the hand with aces he uses the Gerber convention.

You open one no trump with this hand:

♠ A x x x   ♡ A K x x   ◇ A x   ♣ K x x

Partner responds four clubs. What do you bid?

YOUR ANSWER: I would rebid four no trump.

Correct. This rebid shows three aces.
Go to **372.**

♠ x x   ♡ A K J x x   ◊ K Q x   ♣ x x x

Partner opens with one spade and then raises your two heart response to four.

YOUR ANSWER: I would now bid five hearts.

We are with you. Partner has between 16 and 19 points for his double raise. You wish to find out if he has 16–17 or 18–19. You have no aces to show, so the simplest way to learn more about partner's strength is to sound him out with the slam exploring bid of five hearts. With a maximum holding he will bid six; with a minimum he will pass.

Blasting

Occasionally, the scientific approach to a slam is ill-advised, for there appears to be no clear-cut way for eliciting the necessary information. In these instances, the slam should be bid with bravado. This is especially true when the success of a slam depends largely upon the opening lead. If you blast your way directly to slam without mentioning the side suits in these cases, the opponents will have to probe for your weakness. A bit of old-fashioned gambling is involved here, but since the maximum loss should be limited to less than the potential gain, the odds are at least favorable.

If, for example, your partner opens with one heart and then bids two hearts over your one spade response, what do you now bid with this holding?

♠ A Q J x x x   ♡ K Q x x x   ◊ void   ♣ Q x

Four Hearts **356**

Five Hearts **360**

Six Hearts **362**

Three Diamonds **366**

369

[from 362]

♠ x x   ♥ K J x   ♦ K Q x   ♣ A Q x x x

You open with one club, which partner raises to three.

YOUR ANSWER: The Blackwood convention may be useless here.

Right. If you say four no trump and partner responds five diamonds, showing one ace, you're in over your head. You will have to say six clubs with two aces out against you.

Not every four no trump bid is Blackwood, of course. A suit has to have been mentioned on the way up. You will remember that the immediate raise of an opening one no trump to the four level simply signifies 15 or 16 high-card points. Likewise, four no trump may occasionally be used as a refuge in obvious cases of misfit.

After asking for aces, the Blackwood bidder may proceed to ask for kings by bidding five no trump. The answers are the same, only at the six level. It is an unwritten law that you can't ask for kings unless the partnership possesses all four aces.

As for who initiates the convention, this is variable, but usually it is more useful for the player with the distributional hand (one with long suits and a singleton) to know how many aces the partnership has. Whoever starts it must set the final contract.

There are three exceptions to this:

1. When the bidding has shown that the partnership has all four aces, the responder may exercise his own judgment as to the final contract.

2. The responder may ignore the ace issue altogether and jump directly to slam if he has a void.

3. When the four no trump bidder mentions an unbid suit at the five level after partner's response, he indicates that the partnership is missing two aces, and the responder is required to say five no trump, which becomes the final contract.

♠ A K x x x   ♥ Q x x   ♦ Q J 10 x x   ♣ void

Partner opens with one heart, vigorously supports your diamonds, and then bids four no trump. What would you now bid with this hand?

Pass   **345**
Five Diamonds   **351**
Six Diamonds   **358**

♠ x x   ♡ A K J x x   ◇ K Q x   ♣ x x x

Your partner opens with one spade and then raises your two heart response to four.

YOUR ANSWER: I would now bid six hearts.

Courageous, but unwise. You have 15 rebid points and partner has shown 16–19 more. This will add up to 33 only if partner has a maximum. Why not find out rather than leap into the dark?

Return to **354** and think it over.

♠ x x   ♡ x x   ◇ x x x   ♣ K Q J x x x

Partner opens with three no trump.

YOUR ANSWER: I would consider slam assured with this hand.

Hold on now. It is true that partner has promised 25–27 high-card points and stoppers in every suit. It is also true that you can count six more points in your hand and this adds up to 31–33 points, which may be enough for slam with a six-card suit. And it is almost certain that partner will be able to run six club tricks. But what if he lacks two aces?

Partner's holding may be something like this:

♠ A K Q   ♡ K Q J   ◇ K Q J x   ♣ A x x

If so, he can't avoid losing two tricks in the red suit aces.

Now return to **361** and pick the most accurate statement.

372

[from 367]

Now, let's have some practice in slam bidding. In each of the following cases you are South. What is your bid?

(1)
♠ A K J x x
♡ K Q J
◇ void
♣ A K Q x x

SOUTH	NORTH
2 ♠	3 ♠
?	

(2)
♠ A Q J 9
♡ K 10 9
◇ Q J x x
♣ x x

NORTH	SOUTH
1 ♡	1 ♠
3 ♡	?

(3)
♠ A x
♡ K Q 9 x x x x
◇ K x
♣ K x

NORTH	SOUTH
1 NT	?

(4)
♠ A K x x x
♡ A J 10 x
◇ A x
♣ x x

SOUTH	NORTH
1 ♠	2 ◇
2 ♡	4 ♡
?	

(5)
♠ x
♡ K Q 10 x
◇ J x x x x
♣ x x x

NORTH	SOUTH
2 ♠	2 NT
3 ♡	?

(6)
♠ A Q 10 9
♡ K J x
◇ 10 x x
♣ A J x

NORTH	SOUTH
1 ◇	1 ♠
2 NT	?

(7)
♠ A J 10 x x x
♡ void
◇ K x x
♣ Q J 9 x

SOUTH	NORTH
1 ♠	3 ◇
3 ♠	4 NT
?	

(8)
♠ K x x x
♡ A 9 x x
◇ x x
♣ Q J x

WEST	NORTH
1 ◇	2 ◇
EAST	SOUTH
Pass	?

Please go on to **373** and check your answers.

QUIZ ANSWERS

1. Bid four clubs to show your ace. Blackwood would be useless because partner may have only one ace and you wouldn't know which one it is. If he bids four hearts (showing the ace), you should contract for seven spades.
2. Five hearts. An opening bid faced by an opening bid followed by a jump suggests slam. You must let partner know about your strength by a bid beyond game.
3. Bid four clubs (Gerber). This is the ideal hand for such a bid. If partner shows one ace, you avoid slam; if he shows three aces, bid seven no trump.
4. Five diamonds. Blackwood would be pointless here, for partner may have no aces yet may still have second-round club control. The five diamond bid specifically asks partner to bid slam if he has second-round control of this unbid suit.
5. Bid five hearts. The leap over game will inform partner of excellent heart support and no controls to show on the side.
6. Six no trump. You have 15 points; partner's jump rebid promises 19 or 20.
7. Six diamonds. There is a risk that the normal five diamond response may be passed. True, you don't know which suit the hand belongs in, but if partner's jump shift was predicated on a spade fit, he can still bid six spades.
8. Three diamonds. This is a tremendous hand opposite an immediate cue bid. This will tell partner that you are prepared to offer excellent support for suit he bids.

Now go on to Chapter VII on **375**.

	NORTH	EAST	SOUTH	WEST
(A)	1 ♡	Pass	3 ♡	Pass
	4 NT	Pass	?	
(B)	1 ♡	Pass	3 ♡	Pass
	4 NT	5 ◊	?	

YOUR ANSWER: With one ace, I would now bid five hearts with hand B.

Right. After an intervening bid of five diamonds, you show no aces by passing, one ace by bidding five hearts. The proper response with hand A is five diamonds.

No Trump Slams

Slams in no trump are generally easier to bid than slams in a suit since they involve simple arithmetic. Usually you don't even have to check for aces. If you know that the partnership possesses 33 or more high-card points, you know that the opponents can't hold more than an ace and a king or queen-jack between them. And if you know that the partnership possesses 37 or more points, you can bid a grand slam knowing that there cannot be an ace outstanding.

Herein lies the advantages of precisely defined no trump bids. Once partner has made such a bid, you know his high-card count within one or two points. All you have to do is to add your total to his to know the potential of the hand.

Let us say that your partner opens with one heart and then rebids two no trump after your one spade response.

With which of these hands should you now bid six no trump?

♠ A K Q x x x   ♡ x   ◊ Q x x   ♣ x x x   **349**

♠ A K J x x   ♡ J x   ◊ x x x   ♣ K Q x   **361**

♠ A x x x x   ♡ Q x x x x   ◊ K x   ♣ x   **365**

CHAPTER VII

OVERCALLS

An overcall is a competitive bid made after an opponent has opened the bidding. An overcall is usually a defensive bid. The opening bidder has already announced possession of at least 13 points. If the remaining 27 points are equally divided, each player will have nine. If this is so, the opponents will have 22 points to your 18.

You can already sense that overcalling can be fraught with danger. Since the overcaller is on the defensive, his motives for bidding are necessarily different from those of the opening bidder.

There are several reasons for making an overcall. Your primary objective is the hope of reaching a successful contract of your own. Another purpose is to suggest an opening lead to partner in case the opponents eventually buy the contract. For example, you hold:

♠ K Q J x x   ♡ A x x   ♢ x x x   ♣ x x

Your right-hand opponent opens with one club. You should overcall the spade. You probably will not end up playing a spade contract, but you may be defending against a no trump or suit contract of the opponents. If so, you would dearly love a spade lead from partner, who may hardly be expected to choose such a lead on his own.

Finally, an overcall can be of some slight pre-emptive value, if it consumes bidding space which may be vital to the opposition for discovering their best contract. In the above example, when you overcall one club with one spade, you are depriving the enemy of some bidding room. If your left-hand opponent has eight–nine points and a heart suit, he will be unable to show it at the level of one, and he may hesitate to bid two hearts since a response in a new suit is forcing on the opening bidder and might in this case force his partner into the three level on the next round.

Your right-hand opponent opens the bidding with one diamond. What purpose would be served here by an overcall of one heart?

♠ x x   ♡ A x x x   ♢ K x x   ♣ A x x x

376

[from 394]

♠ J x x   ♡ A x   ◇ K J 8 x x   ♣ K x x

You are vulnerable and your right-hand opponent opens with one spade.

YOUR ANSWER: I would make a two diamond overcall with this hand.

We would not advise it. In the first place, your diamond suit is broken, and you may readily lose more than two trump tricks. Furthermore, if you are doubled, it is quite possible the loss might be as much as 1100 points if partner's hand proves to be trickless.

Go back to **394** and look for a better hand with which to make this bid.

377

[from 382]

♠ x x   ♡ x x x   ◇ K Q x   ♣ Q J x x x

West opens with one spade and both North and East pass.

YOUR ANSWER: Sitting South, I would now bid two clubs.

With the black suits reversed in this hand, we advised you to make a fourth-position competitive bid of one spade over one club, but we cannot recommend bidding two clubs over one spade. Your suit is too weak to warrant a competitive overcall at the two level despite the fact that your opponents seem to be indifferent about this hand.

Please return to **382**.

WEST	NORTH	EAST	SOUTH
1 ♡	3 ◊	4 ♡	?

♠ J x x x x   ♡ void   ◊ A 10 x x x   ♣ x x x

YOUR ANSWER: I would bid five diamonds with this hand.

We would suggest that you pass instead. The opponents are already in a game contract, and your length in diamonds, a suit which partner has at least six or seven cards, suggests that your defensive values are practically nonexistent. Don't goad the enemy into any aggressive action.

Return to **393** and try again.

♠ A Q 10 9 x x   ♡ K x   ◊ x x x   ♣ x x

East opens the bidding with one diamond. You are South, non-vulnerable.

YOUR ANSWER: I would bid two spades with this hand.

One spade would be preferable. Jump overcalls should be avoided on hands containing any significant defensive strength. This hand has two quick tricks and will be better described by a simple overcall.

If you return to **400** you will find a better hand suited for a jump overcall.

380
[from 387]

♠ A Q x x   ♥ K Q x x   ♦ K x   ♣ J 10 x

Your right-hand opponent opens with one club.

YOUR ANSWER: I would make a one no trump overcall with this hand.

You should not.

In the first place, you have only 15 high-card points, and 16–19 are required for a direct one no trump overcall.

Secondly, your club stopper is rather poor.

Finally, you have two good four-card major suits.

In anticipation of Chapter VIII: The correct bid with this hand is a takeout double. Even though you may not know this, you should know enough already not to bid one no trump.

Back on **387** you will find a better no trump hand.

381
[from 375]

♠ x x   ♥ A x x x   ♦ K x x   ♣ A x x x

Your right-hand opponent opens with one diamond.

YOUR ANSWER: An overcall of one heart could be made in the hope of reaching a heart contract.

No. This is most unlikely and it would probably be suicidal to try it. Your heart suit is biddable by opening-bid standards, but the standards for overcalling are more strict. With 13 or more points already announced by one of your opponents and no knowledge as to the location of the remaining nine hearts, an ultimate heart contract is too much to hope for.

Please return to **375** and try again.

(A)	♠ J x x	♡ A x	◇ K J 8 x x	♣ K x x
(B)	♠ K x	♡ x x x	◇ A Q J 10 x	♣ A x x
(C)	♠ Q x x x	♡ x x	◇ A K J x	♣ A x x

You are vulnerable and your right-hand opponent opens with one spade.

YOUR ANSWER: I would make a two diamond overcall with hand B.

Right. The diamond suit in hand A is a little too weak, and it is always unwise to overcall with a four-card suit such as in hand C. With both hands A and C you would be risking the loss of more than 500 points.

Reopening the Bidding

When an opponent opens the bidding and his partner passes him out at the one level, you may take greater liberties in making an overcall. You know that one of your opponents has less than six points and that the other could not open with a demand bid. It follows, therefore, that your partnership probably possess about half of the points in the deck, and may well be able to score offensively. Therefore, you may enter the bidding by overcalling with mediocre values, especially if your suit outranks the suit of the opponents. For example, you are sitting South and hold:

♠ Q J x x x   ♡ x x x   ◇ K Q x   ♣ x x

If West opened with one club and both North and East passed, you may contest the auction with one spade. Your partner should not expect too much from your bid in such a situation.

As South, you hold:

♠ x x   ♡ x x x   ◇ K Q x   ♣ Q J x x

West opens with one spade and both North and East pass. Would you bid two clubs?

Yes **377**
No **387**

383

[from 397]

♠ x x   ♡ 10 x x   ◇ K Q x   ♣ A K x x x

WEST	NORTH	EAST	SOUTH
1 ♠	2 ♡	Pass	?

YOUR ANSWER: As South, with this hand I would bid three hearts.

You have good support for partner's major suit overcall, and you should by all means make a raise.

However, you can do better than three hearts. Partner has promised to take six tricks, and you can probably contribute four more. So what should your bid be?

Please go back to **397**.

384

[from 401]

♠ A Q J 10 x x   ♡ A x   ◇ K J x x   ♣ x

You are sitting South, nonvulnerable. East opens with one heart.

YOUR ANSWER: I would overcall with three spades on this hand.

No, this hand is too strong for such a bid. It contains 15 high-card points (plus three more for distribution) and will probably take three tricks on defense. The purpose of pre-emption is defeated if it is based on strength.

As you will see in the next chapter, hands with this much power are best described by a takeout double. You will compete in spades later, and you might have a good play for game if North, not West, has the balance of power.

Now look at the other hands on **401** and try again.

♠ x x   ♡ A x x x   ◇ K x x   ♣ A x x x

Your right-hand opponent opens with one diamond.

YOUR ANSWER: An overcall of one heart would be useful in suggesting an opening lead to partner.

Why? If partner is to lead, the opposition will either be playing a spade or a no trump contract. Since you have no preference in either of the remaining suits, it would seem best to permit partner to make the opening that suits his hand best. To overcall in hearts would tend to sway him in his choice of leads, and this might prove to be disastrous.

Now turn to **375** and try again.

♠ Q x x x   ♡ x x   ◇ A K J x   ♣ A x x

You are vulnerable and your right-hand opponent opens with one spade.

YOUR ANSWER: I would make a two diamond overcall with this hand.

Let's hope not. Let's hope you never make an overcall at the two level on a four-card suit, for in doing so, you are contracting for eight tricks in a suit in which the opponents may have a numerical superiority. We agree that you have a goood 15-point hand, but you can't enter the auction safely at the present time. If you overcalled two diamonds, and were doubled, you might easily lose 1100 or more points.

Go back to **394** and look for a better answer.

387

[from 382]

♠ x x   ♡ x x x   ◊ K Q x   ♣ Q J x x x

West opens with one spade and both North and East pass.

YOUR ANSWER: Sitting South, I would not bid two clubs.

Neither would we. With the black suits reversed in this hand we advised you to make a fourth-position competitive overcall of one spade over one club, but we cannot recommend bidding two clubs over one spade.

The One No Trump Overcall

For an immediate overcall of one no trump you should have a hand which is equivalent to a one no trump opening. Two differences: You may have 16–19 high-card points rather than 16–18, and, of course, you *must* have the adverse suit stopped.

If an opening bid has been passed around to you, in fourth position you may make an overcall of one no trump on reduced values.

For example, if your left-hand opponent bid one spade and both other players passed, you could say one no trump with this hand:

♠ A Q x   ♡ Q x x   ◊ K J x   ♣ J x x x

Partner again must recognize this as competitive action rather than a show of strength on your part, for with a stronger hand, you would be inclined to make a takeout double.

Your right-hand opponent opens with one club. With which of these hands would you bid one no trump?

♠ A Q x x   ♡ K Q x x   ◊ K x   ♣ J 10 x   **380**

♠ K x x   ♡ K x   ◊ A Q J x x   ♣ Q x x   **395**

♠ A Q x   ♡ Q x x   ◊ K Q x   ♣ K J x x   **400**

WEST	NORTH	EAST	SOUTH
1 ♣	2 ◇	2 ♠	?

♠ K J x x   ♡ Q J 10 x   ◇ A x   ♣ K Q 9

YOUR ANSWER: I would now bid five diamonds with this hand.

We would prefer to hear you pass.

You obviously can't make five diamonds and there is no need to sacrifice when the enemy is headed for trouble on its own steam. East has just made a response which will force his partner to rebid at the three level (it's unlikely he can stop the diamonds well enough to bid no trump). Your silence, combined with partner's announced weakness, may induce the enemy to overreach themselves.

Return to **393** and try again.

♠ x x   ♡ A x x x   ◇ K x x   ♣ A x x x

Your right-hand opponent opens with one diamond.

YOUR ANSWER: An overcall of one heart would pre-empt some of the opponent's bidding room.

You must have reached this page by mistake.

Since hearts are next in rank to diamonds, there is no consumption of bidding space unless the responder desired to call hearts himself. In that case he might be chagrined enough to take exception to your call and double for penalties.

Return to **375** and choose the correct answer.

390

[from 401]

♠ Q J 10 x x x   ♡ x x   ◇ Q J 9 x   ♣ x

You are sitting South, nonvulnerable. East opens with one heart.

YOUR ANSWER: I would overcall with three spades on this hand.

How many tricks can you take if you play this hand at three spades? Five. With luck you'll take four spades and one diamond, four tricks short of your bid. Down four, doubled and nonvulnerable, is 700. This will be too costly. You should not risk going down more than 500.

Look at the other hands on **401** and try again.

391

[from 397]

♠ x x   ♡ 10 x x   ◇ K Q x   ♣ A K x x x

WEST	NORTH	EAST	SOUTH
1 ♠	2 ♡	Pass	?

YOUR ANSWER: As South, I would pass with this hand.

No, you certainly shouldn't do that.

You have an excellent hand no matter how you analyze it: 13 points, heart support, and three quick tricks. Bid you must.

Go back to **397** and decide which bid would be best.

392

[from 407]

♠ K 9 x x   ♡ x   ◇ A 10 x x   ♣ Q 10 x x

WEST	NORTH	EAST	SOUTH
1 ◇	1 ♠	Pass	3 ♠

YOUR ANSWER: With this hand the three spade bid would be incorrect.

No, this bid is correct.

Partner has bid a major suit, and you have fine support for him.

Partner has promised to take five tricks and you can contribute four more. He should go on to game if he has any extra values.

Please go back to **407** to pick the incorrect bid.

(A)   ♠ A J 10 x x x   ♡ K x   ◇ x x x   ♣ x x

(B)   ♠ K Q J 9 8 x   ♡ x   ◇ x x   ♣ J x x x

(C)   ♠ K Q J x x x   ♡ J 10 9 x x   ◇ x x   ♣ void

East opens the bidding with one diamond. You are South, non-vulnerable.

YOUR ANSWER: I would bid two spades with hand B.

So would we. Jump overcalls should be avoided with the defensive strength of hand A or with two-suited hands such as C.

When your partner makes a jump overcall, he announces: (*a*) defensive weakness and (*b*) willingness to sacrifice against an adverse contract because of his trump length. Do not plan on a plus score unless your hand can supply the high-card strength necessary to bring the combined assets of the partnership to the game or part-score level.

With which of the following hands would you, sitting South, bid five diamonds?

WEST	NORTH	EAST	SOUTH
1 ♡	3 ◇	4 ♡	?

♠ J x x x x   ♡ void   ◇ A 10 x x x   ♣ x x x   **378**

WEST	NORTH	EAST	SOUTH
1 ♣	2 ◇	2 ♠	?

♠ K J x x   ♡ Q J 10 x   ◇ A x   ♣ K Q 9ı   **388**

WEST	NORTH	EAST	SOUTH
1 ♡	3 ◇	Pass	?

♠ x   ♡ x x   ◇ K J 9 x x   ♣ A x x x x   **401**

♠ x x   ♡ A x x x   ◇ K x x   ♣ A x x x
Your right-hand opponent opens with one diamond.

YOUR ANSWER: An overcall of one heart would serve no purpose at all.

Right. A heart contract is unlikely. You have no preference for a particular lead, and a one heart overcall would not use up any bidding space. Such an overcall would even be dangerous if you were doubled for penalties and it might aid your opponents in bidding and play since you have notified them that your hand has some merit, and your action would help them to place the outstanding strength.

The only correct action with the above hand is a pass. Though your hand contains 12 points, the point count is of secondary importance. Primarily, you should have a good trump suit, and your possible loss, if doubled, should be held within safe limits.

The trump suit for an overcall should be at least five cards long and of fairly solid texture. Intermediate spots such as tens and nines help in this respect. While you might open the bidding with a five-card suit such as A Q 9 4 2 or K J 7 3 2, for an overcall you would infinitely prefer A Q 10 9 8 or K J 10 9 3. These suits contain no more high-card points, but they are deeper in reserves and furnish better protection against a bad adverse trump break.

Whereas you may stretch a point to suggest a lead or a possible part score by overcalling at the one level, you should be increasingly more cautious when your overcall requires entry at the two level. Your trump suit should be able to stand on its own feet.

The safety of an overcall is calculated not in terms of point count, but in terms of possible loss. You should seldom risk incurring a set of more than 500 points. The wise overcaller assumes that he is going to be doubled and that he is going to face a very anemic dummy. So this means he will avoid a set exceeding three tricks when nonvulnerable or two tricks when vulnerable.

You are vulnerable and your right-hand opponent opens with one spade. With which hand would you overcall two diamonds?

♠ J x x   ♡ A x   ◇ K J 8 x x   ♣ K x x   **376**
♠ K x   ♡ x x x   ◇ A Q J 10 x   ♣ A x x   **382**
♠ Q x x x   ♡ x x   ◇ A K J x   ♣ A x x   **386**

♠ K x x   ♡ K x   ◇ A Q J x x   ♣ Q x x

Your right-hand opponent opens with one club.

YOUR ANSWER: I would make a one no trump overcall with this hand.

We would not.

You have only 15 high-card points instead of the 16–19 required for this bid.

Your club stopper is poor.

You have a perfectly good suit of your own.

Bid one diamond.

On **387** you will find a better no trump hand.

(A)   ♠ A Q J 10 x x   ♡ A x   ◇ K J x x   ♣ x

(B)   ♠ Q J 10 x x x   ♡ x x   ◇ Q J 9 x   ♣ x

(C)   ♠ Q J 10 x x x x   ♡ x   ◇ Q J 9 x   ♣ x

You are sitting South, nonvulnerable. East opens with one heart.

YOUR ANSWER: I would overcall with three spades on hand C.

Correct. Hand C is defensively weak, yet should take six tricks if spades are trump. More important, such a bid might prevent the opponents from reaching an easy four heart contract.

Hand B is a little shy of the requirements for a double jump; two spades would be a better bid. And hand A is too strong for preemptive action.

Go on to **397**.

Action by Partner of Overcaller

The partner of an overcaller is often in position to judge the overall possibilities of the hand. Everyone else has bid at least once. The approximate strength of the opponents can be estimated from their bids. And partner has promised that he can make within two or three tricks of his bid.

There is seldom any purpose in raising an overcall unless there is a chance for game. But when such a chance exists, a raise may be based on less trump support than is required in response to an opening bid, for the overcaller can be counted on for a fairly good suit of at least five cards. Three small trump or Q x will do, especially if the overcaller's side is vulnerable. It therefore follows that there is little use in naming a suit of your own unless you would have overcalled independently of your partner, and you have no support for his suit. Remember that partner's strength is largely concentrated in his suit, and he may have little or no interest in yours.

Remember, too, that you cannot in this position force partner to bid again by a change in suit or even by a jump raise. You may well be stuck with whatever bid you make.

Don't be tempted to bid no trump just to show stoppers in the enemy's suit. In contrast to the no trump response to an opening bid, such a bid in this position shows strength and a desire to go on.

Suppose that both sides are vulnerable and you, as South, hold this hand:

♠ x x   ♡ 10 x x   ◇ K Q x   ♣ A K x x x

The bidding:

WEST	NORTH	EAST	SOUTH
1 ♠	2 ♡	Pass	?

What action would you take?

Three Hearts **383**

Pass **391**

Four Hearts **407**

Three Clubs **409**

252

♠ x x x   ♡ Q 10   ◇ K J 9 x x   ♣ K Q x

SOUTH	WEST	NORTH	EAST
Pass	1 ♠	2 ♡	Pass
3 ♡			

YOUR ANSWER: With this hand the three heart bid would be incorrect.

No, this bid is correct.

Remember that you should always give preference to a major suit when you can. Your own long suit is a minor. Also remember that when partner has overcalled you can raise him with less support than you would need had he opened. Your Q 10 doubleton is adequate support for a raise.

Therefore, with roughly three winners in your hand it is entirely correct for you to raise partner's bid to three hearts. If he has a little extra, he will proceed to game.

Please go back to **407** to pick the incorrect bid.

♠ x x   ♡ none   ◇ A J 10 9 x x   ♣ A Q 10 x x

WEST	NORTH	EAST	SOUTH
Pass	Pass	1 ♡	?

YOUR ANSWER: As South, I would make an unusual no trump overcall with his hand.

No. It is not normal to make an unusual no trump overcall immediately after an opening bid. In this position an overcall in no trump would have a natural meaning (16–19 points for one no trump; 22–24 points for two no trump; and denote a balanced hand plus protection in the adverse suit).

Your best action is to overcall with two diamonds now, and show the clubs later if it is expedient to do so.

Please go back to **408** and pick the hand and bidding sequence where the unusual no trump bid is appropriate.

400

[from 387]

(A) ♠ A Q x x   ♥ K Q x x   ♦ K x   ♣ J 10 x
(B) ♠ K x x   ♥ K x   ♦ A Q J x x   ♣ Q x x
(C) ♠ A Q x   ♥ Q x x   ♦ K Q x   ♣ K J x x

Your right-hand opponent opens with one club.

YOUR ANSWER: I would make a one no trump overcall with hand C.

Good. Hands A and B contain only 15 high-card points and their club stoppers are poor. Furthermore, hand A has sufficient major suit strength to warrant a takeout double (Chapter VIII) and hand B contains a diamond suit worth showing.

The Jump Overcall

Jump overcalls used to be based upon very strong hands containing a long suit, but since strong hands of this type are rare following an adverse opening bid, this important type of overcall was seldom used. Nowadays such defensive power is signified by using other strength-showing bids. Jump overcalls are reserved for weak hands with good long suits.

The purpose of the weak jump overcall is similar to that of the opening three bid: pre-emption of the bidding space and preparation for a possible sacrifice. Partner is forewarned that defensive values are lacking.

It is not surprising, therefore, that the prerequisites for such a bid are also similar to those for the opening three bid: (a) a fairly good suit, at least six cards long; (b) no more than nine high-card points, regardless of vulnerability; and (c) high-card strength concentrated in the bid suit.

As always, the bidder should expect to limit his losses to 500 points (down two vulnerable or down three nonvulnerable).

With which of these three hands would you, as South, make a nonvulnerable jump to two spades over East's opening bid of one diamond?

♠ A Q 10 9 x x   ♥ K x   ♦ x x x   ♣ x x **379**
♠ K Q J 9 8 x   ♥ x   ♦ x x   ♣ J x x x **393**
♠ K Q J x x x   ♥ J 10 9 x x   ♦ x x   ♣ void **404**

	WEST	NORTH	EAST	SOUTH	
	1 ♡	3 ◊	4 ♡	?	
(A)	♠ J x x x x	♡ void	◊ A 10 x x x	♣ x x x

	WEST	NORTH	EAST	SOUTH	
	1 ♣	2 ◊	2 ♠	?	
(B)	♠ K J x x	♡ Q J 10 x	◊ A x	♣ K Q 9

	WEST	NORTH	EAST	SOUTH	
	1 ♡	3 ◊	Pass	?	
(C)	♠ x	♡ x x	◊ K J 9 x x	♣ A x x x x

YOUR ANSWER: I would now bid five diamonds with hand C.

Very, very good. In this deal, since partner has already proclaimed defensive weakness, the opposition is assuredly spread for at least a game in one or both of the majors. If you bid five diamonds now, they will have difficulty deciding what to do; even if they double, your losses will be moderate.

With hand A, we would recommend a pass. Further action might push the enemy into a makable slam. With hand B, we would also prefer a pass; West must bid again and you can probably set any three level contract.

Double Jump Overcall

A double jump overcall is based upon the same type of hand as that described for a single jump except that the former should be expected to take one more trick. No additional high-card strength is required. The purpose of pre-emption is preserved. If, for example, you want to pre-empt in spades over an adverse one diamond bid and your hand will take six tricks, you can say two spades, if you are vulnerable, or three spades, nonvulnerable.

Let us say that you are sitting South and nonvulnerable. The opening bid by East is one heart. With which of these hands would you make a three spade bid?

♠ A Q J 10 x x	♡ A x	◊ K J x x	♣ x	**384**
♠ Q J 10 x x x	♡ x x	◊ Q J 9 x	♣ x	**390**
♠ Q J 10 x x x x	♡ x	◊ Q J 9 x	♣ x	**396**

255

402

[from 406]

♠ x ♡ x x x ♦ A K 10 9 x ♣ J x x x

WEST	NORTH	EAST	SOUTH
1 ♡	1 ♠	Double	?

YOUR ANSWER: I would now bid two diamonds with this hand.

No. This temptation must be resisted for several reasons. In the first place, you have no way of knowing that two diamonds will be a better contract than one spade. Secondly, you would have to take eight tricks in diamonds instead of seven in spades. And finally, your hand as dummy will produce two tricks for your partner, which is as many as he has a right to expect.

Return to **406** for a better rescuing situation.

403

[from 408]

♠ A ♡ x ♦ A 10 x x x x ♣ J x x x x

WEST	NORTH	EAST	SOUTH
Pass	Pass	3 ♡	?

YOUR ANSWER: As South, I would make an unusual no trump overcall with this hand.

No. You can't make an unusual no trump overcall immediately after a pre-emptive opening bid. A three no trump overcall in this position would be a natural bid, indicating a desire to play the hand in no trump. Therefore, you should pass with this hand.

Please go back to **408** and pick the hand and bidding sequence where the unusual no trump bid is appropriate.

♠ K Q J x x x   ♡ J 10 9 x x   ◇ x x   ♣ void

East opens the bidding with one diamond. You are South, non-vulnerable.

YOUR ANSWER: I would bid two spades with this hand.

One spade would be preferable. As is the case with opening three bids, jump overcalls should be avoided with two-suited hands, especially if both suits are majors. Partner may have a fit for hearts but not spades. A pre-emptive spade bid would greatly reduce the chances of finding a possible heart fit.

If you return to **400** you will find a better hand for this bid.

(A)   ♠ K 9 x x   ♡ x   ◇ A 10 x x   ♣ Q 10 x x

WEST	NORTH	EAST	SOUTH
1 ◇	1 ♠	Pass	3 ♠

(B)   ♠ x x x   ♡ Q 10   ◇ K J 9 x x   ♣ K Q x

SOUTH	WEST	NORTH	EAST
Pass	1 ♠	2 ♡	Pass
3 ♡			

(C)   ♠ A Q J x x   ♡ x x   ◇ Q x x   ♣ x x x

WEST	NORTH	EAST	SOUTH
1 ♡	2 ◇	2 ♡	3 ◇

YOUR ANSWER: South's bid in example C would be wrong.

Right. Although hand C has support for partner's diamonds, it also has a very good major suit. A bid of two spades would be preferable to a diamond raise. As an added safety factor, you will be able to help if partner insists on a diamond contract.

But if partner's overcall were in a major suit, and you had a choice of supporting it or naming a good minor suit, your proper response would be to raise partner's bid. Hence the bids by South in examples A and B are correct.

Go on to **406**.

Rescuing

When partner has overcalled and you have little or no support for his suit, do not rescue him by naming a suit of your own unless you have a very good reason. One such reason would be possession of a magnificent suit of your own. If, for example, partner makes a one heart overcall and you hold

♠ A K J x x x   ♡ x   ♢ K x x   ♣ x x x

naturally you will bid one spade.

Another good reason would be if partner's bid is doubled and you have a hand which will take tricks only if played in your suit.

As a general rule, however, you must refrain from rescuing if partner's bid has not been doubled.

Under which of the following circumstances would you consider it wise to make a rescuing bid in diamonds?

♠ x   ♡ x x x   ♢ A K 10 9 x   ♣ J x x x

WEST	NORTH	EAST	SOUTH	
1 ♡	1 ♠	Double	?	**402**

♠ x x   ♡ x x x   ♢ Q J 10 9 x x   ♣ x x

WEST	NORTH	EAST	SOUTH	
1 ♠	2 ♣	Double	?	**410**

♠ x x   ♡ x   ♢ K 10 9 x x x x   ♣ 10 x x

WEST	NORTH	EAST	SOUTH	
1 ♠	2 ♡	Pass	?	**413**

♠ x x   ♡ 10 x x   ◊ K Q x   ♣ A K x x x

WEST	NORTH	EAST	SOUTH
1 ♠	2 ♡	Pass	?

YOUR ANSWER: As South, with both sides vulnerable, I would bid four hearts in the above sequence.

Very good. Since you are vulnerable, partner's overcall promises at least six tricks. Your hand contains sufficient heart support and it may well contribute four more tricks. If you said three hearts or three clubs, you risk partner's passing.

As always, even in defensive bidding, you want to stick with the major suits. If partner mentions a major, bend over backwards to support him, even at the cost of hiding a good minor suit of your own.

In the following sequences, both sides are again vulnerable. Which of the bids indicated for you, as South, would be incorrect?

♠ K 9 x x   ♡ x   ◊ A 10 x x   ♣ Q 10 x x

WEST	NORTH	EAST	SOUTH	
1 ◊	1 ♠	Pass	3 ♠	**392**

♠ x x x   ♡ A 10   ◊ K J 9 x x   ♣ K Q x

SOUTH	WEST	NORTH	EAST	
Pass	1 ♠	2 ♡	Pass	**398**
3 ♡				

♠ A Q J x x   ♡ x x   ◊ Q x x   ♣ x x x

WEST	NORTH	EAST	SOUTH	
1 ♡	2 ◊	2 ♡	3 ◊	**405**

The Unusual No Trump Convention

Among the more recent developments in contract bridge is the Unusual No Trump Convention which provides that where a player makes a bid of any number of no trump which could not possibly mean what it says because of the implications of the auction up to that point, then the no trump bid is construed to be a takeout double, and partner is expected to respond in his better minor suit. The common sense of the situation is this: If a player makes a takeout double of a major suit, it is reasonable to suppose that he would like to hear partner respond in the other major. But where doubler is not prepared for the other major, he obtains the effect of doubling for a minor suit response by using an unnatural overcall in no trump.

It is important to emphasize that overcalls in no trump have not lost their natural significance. If the bidding has proceeded:

EAST	SOUTH
1 ♡	1 NT

South's bid is a good old-fashioned overcall describing a balanced hand with 16–19 high-card points and sound protection in hearts.

EAST	SOUTH
1 ♡	2 NT

South's bid is natural, implying a balanced hand with from 22–24 high-card points and adequate stoppers in the heart suit.

With which of these hands would you, as South, make an unusual no trump overcall:

♠ x x   ♡ none   ◇ A J 10 9 x x   ♣ A Q 10 x x

WEST	NORTH	EAST	SOUTH	
Pass	Pass	1 ♡	?	**399**

♠ A   ♡ x   ◇ A 10 x x x x   ♣ J x x x x

WEST	NORTH	EAST	SOUTH	
Pass	Pass	3 ♡	?	**403**

♠ Q 10 x   ♡ x   ◇ A Q J x x   ♣ K Q J x

WEST	NORTH	EAST	SOUTH	
1 ♠	Pass	2 ♠	?	**411**

♠ K Q x   ♡ A K x   ◇ A Q J x   ♣ 10 x x

WEST	NORTH	EAST	SOUTH	
Pass	Pass	1 ♠	?	**414**

♠ x x   ♡ 10 x x   ◇ K Q x   ♣ A K x x x

WEST	NORTH	EAST	SOUTH
1 ♠	2 ♡	Pass	?

YOUR ANSWER: As South, with this hand I would bid three clubs.

You should by all means bid, but certainly not clubs.

With three hearts including the ten, you have good support for partner's major suit overcall. Your clubs will produce at least two winners in any case.

If you bid three clubs, partner might pass. (As an overcaller, he is not obligated to make any further bids.)

So please return to **397** and pick the correct bid.

(A)   ♠ x   ♡ x x x   ◇ A K 10 9 x   ♣ J x x x

WEST	NORTH	EAST	SOUTH
1 ♡	1 ♠	Double	?

(B)   ♠ x x   ♡ x x x   ◇ Q J 10 9 x x   ♣ x x

WEST	NORTH	EAST	SOUTH
1 ♠	2 ♣	Double	?

(C)   ♠ x x   ♡ x   ◇ K 10 9 x x x x   ♣ 10 x x

WEST	NORTH	EAST	SOUTH
1 ♠	2 ♡	Pass	?

YOUR ANSWER: With situation B, I would make a rescuing bid in diamonds.

Right. Hand B offers little or no trick-taking power in support of partner's club suit, yet it can take four tricks with diamonds as trump. Partner's bid has been doubled and your rescue won't increase the level of the contract.

Hand A will take two tricks as dummy and a diamond rescue will necessitate taking eight tricks instead of seven. Hand C would justify a rescue only if partner's bid were doubled.

Go on to **408**.

411

[from 408]

(A) ♠ x x ♡ None ◇ A J 10 9 x x ♣ A Q 10 x x

WEST	NORTH	EAST	SOUTH
Pass	Pass	1 ♡	2 ◇

(B) ♠ A ♡ x ◇ A 10 x x x x ♣ J x x x x

WEST	NORTH	EAST	SOUTH
Pass	Pass	3 ♡	Pass

(C) ♠ Q 10 x ♡ x ◇ A Q J x x ♣ K Q J x

WEST	NORTH	EAST	SOUTH
1 ♠	Pass	2 ♠	2 NT

(D) ♠ K Q x ♡ A K x ◇ A Q J x ♣ 10 x x

WEST	NORTH	EAST	SOUTH
Pass	Pass	1 ♠	1 NT

YOUR ANSWER: As South, I would make an unusual no trump overcall with hand C.

Correct. Hand C provides a nearly classic example for an unusual no trump overcall. The hand contains two excellent minor suits and no support for the unmentioned major.

In examples A and B, you have fine minor suits, but only one opponent has bid. Any no trump overcall you might make would be interpreted as a natural bid; partner would assume you were prepared to play the hand in no trump. You could make a two diamond overcall with hand A, but you should pass with hand B. Hand D calls for a natural one no trump overcall.

Go on to **412.**

It is not always easy to determine whether a no trump overcall is unusual or not. This can best be decided on a logical basis. Normally, any overcall in no trump at the level of two or higher made after the opener and his partner have both bid, is unusual and asks for the better minor. To delve into the matter further and to clarify this definition, it is best to deal in terms of specific cases. Let us examine the following sequences:

	EAST	SOUTH	WEST	NORTH
(1)	1 ♠	Pass	2 ♠	2 NT
(2)	1 ♠	Pass	2 ♡	2 NT

The first example suggests that North has a good minor suit holding but with no tolerance for the other major (hearts), for otherwise he would have employed a takeout double to insist upon hearing from partner.

In the second illustration, the opposition has indicated the possession of about 23 points (13 for the opener and the ten points required for responder to bid a new suit at the level of two). In each case, North is requesting South to bid his better minor suit.

Go on to **415**.

413

[from 406]

♠ x x   ♡ x   ◊ K 10 9 x x x x   ♣ 10 x x

WEST	NORTH	EAST	SOUTH
1 ♠	2 ♡	Pass	?

YOUR ANSWER: I would now bid three diamonds with this hand.

Heavens, no! Just pass and be thankful there has been no double. With any luck, West will rescue partner for you. If the two heart contract is doubled, however, you would be justified in bidding three diamonds.

Return to **406** for a better rescuing situation.

414

[from 408]

♠ K Q x   ♡ A K x   ◊ A Q J x   ♣ 10 x x

WEST	NORTH	EAST	SOUTH
Pass	Pass	1 ♠	?

YOUR ANSWER: As South, I would make an unusual no trump overcall with this hand.

No. You should bid one no trump, but this will not be an *unusual* no trump overcall.

You have 19 high-card points, a balanced hand, with positive protection in the opponent's suit, thereby fulfilling all the requirements for a natural one no trump overcall. There is nothing unnatural in this bidding sequence or in the message you desire to convey to partner.

Please go back to **408** and pick the hand and bidding sequence where the unusual no trump bid is appropriate.

Here are some more advance no trump situations. Let's see if you can figure them out. How would you, as South, bid each of the following hands:

(A) ♠ 10 9 x x   ♡ K x x   ◊ Q 10 x x   ♣ x x

EAST	SOUTH	WEST	NORTH
1 ♡	Pass	Pass	1 NT
Pass	?		

(B) ♠ x x x   ♡ J 10 x x x   ◊ x x   ♣ K x x

EAST	SOUTH	WEST	NORTH
1 ♠	Pass	2 ◊	Pass
2 ♠	Pass	Pass	2 NT
Pass	?		

(C) ♠ J 9 x x x   ♡ x x   ◊ A K Q x   ♣ Q x

WEST	NORTH	EAST	SOUTH
1 ♡	Pass	2 ♡	Pass
Pass	2 NT	Pass	?

(D) ♠ x x x   ♡ 10 9 x x x   ◊ Q x x   ♣ x x

WEST	NORTH	EAST	SOUTH
4 ♠	4 NT	Pass	?

(E) ♠ 10 9 x x x   ♡ x x x x   ◊ Q   ♣ A x x

WEST	NORTH	EAST	SOUTH
1 ♡	Pass	2 ♡	Pass
4 ♡	4 NT	Double	?

Check your answers on **416**.

416

[from 415]

Answer
Letter

(A) Pass. Partner's one no trump overcall in this situation designates a hand of moderate strength. His purpose in making the bid is to keep the opponents from purchasing the hand too cheaply, for since East did not open the bidding with a demand bid, and West has indicated a holding of less than six points, it is quite likely that the point count is divided evenly among the partnerships.

(B) Bid three hearts. While the unusual no trump overcall is conventionally employed to ask partner for his better minor suit, there are occasions where the common sense of the situation makes it apparent that the no trump bidder has an interest in the unbid suits but not a hand strong enough in high cards to risk a double. In this example, the opponents have bid spades and diamonds. North must be interested in the remaining two suits.

(C) Bid four diamonds. Partner's unusual no trump has requested you to bid your better minor suit, but you have a fine hand with a very good fit for partner (your Q x in clubs should be priceless since partner has implied strength in this suit). You, therefore, should make some effort to reach a possible game. A mere three diamond bid would sound forced and might easily be passed out.

(D) Bid five hearts, not five diamonds. The four no trump overcall of a pre-emptive opening of four spades is not treated as an unusual no trump, but rather as a "super" takeout double, and asks for your best suit which is, of course, hearts.

(E) Five clubs. Partner has asked you to name your better minor suit and you have a distinct preference for clubs. A pass would be courting disaster after East's double, for left to his own devices, partner might elect to bid diamonds. You would then have to bid clubs at the six level.

Go on to Chapter VIII on **417**.

CHAPTER VIII

THE TAKEOUT DOUBLE

At times, you will find yourself holding a good hand when the opposition has opened the bidding. When the chances that your side may have a game are not too good, there is no reason why you should not offer some contest. You may bid defensively by over-calling, provided you have a good suit, or you may make a takeout double. But if you double, how is partner to decipher if your double is intended primarily for penalties or for takeout? Here's how!

If your partner has never bid (a pass is not considered a bid), and you double an opponent's bid at your first opportunity to speak, it is considered a takeout double and requests partner to name his best suit. However, the double of two no trump is always for pen-alties. The double of one no trump is intended primarily for pen-alties, but partner is permitted a wide exercise of judgment and may refuse to leave the double in if his hand contains a long suit and has little defensive values.

A double, in order to be construed as takeout, must be made at the player's first opportunity to double that suit. For example:

SOUTH	WEST	NORTH	EAST
1 ♡	Pass	1 NT	Pass
2 ♡	Double		

This double is for penalties. The logic of the situation is this: If West wanted to hear from partner, he would have doubled the one heart opening, which is a request to his partner to bid.

After partner has bid, all doubles are for penalties. For example:

SOUTH	WEST	NORTH	EAST
1 ◇	1 ♠	Double	

This is a penalty double, since North's partner has already bid.

Go on to **418**.

418

[from 417]

The prerequisites for a takeout double are very simple: Your hand must be the equivalent of an opening bid. You may double an opening bid of one in a suit with 13 or more high-card and distributional points; you may double an opening bid of one no trump with 16 or more high-card points. And, just as important, in doubling an opening bid of one of a suit you must have strength in the unbid major or majors. In other words, if an opponent opens with one heart you must have spades and vice versa; and if he opens with a minor suit you must have good cards in both majors.

Your right-hand opponent has opened with one diamond. With which of these hands would you make a takeout double?

♠ K x   ♡ A K J 10 x x   ◇ x   ♣ A J 10 x   **425**

♠ A K J 10 x   ♡ K x x x   ◇ x x   ♣ A x   **428**

♠ K 10 x x   ♡ K 10 x x   ◇ x   ♣ A Q x x   **433**

I would make a takeout double with all three hands.   **439**

419

[from 438]

♠ 10 x x   ♡ J x x   ◇ Q x x x   ♣ x x x

Partner has doubled a bid of one diamond.

YOUR ANSWER: I would respond with one no trump.

No, this would be misleading. Partner would expect you to have a stronger hand and a better diamond stopper. Such a bid might lead to your reaching a highly unsound game contract in no trump.

This is not an easy hand to manage. We must rule out a bid of one no trump and obviously you may not pass. The logical choice therefore, is to make the most economic bid by showing your three-card suit—one heart.

If you go back to **438** you will find a better hand for the one no trump response.

	SOUTH	WEST	NORTH	EAST
(A)	1 ♠	Pass	1 NT	Pass
	2 ♠	Double		
(B)	4 ♡	Double		
(C)	1 ◇	Pass	1 NT	Double
(D)	1 ♠	Pass	2 ♠	Double

YOUR ANSWER: The double in example A is for penalties.

Right. The others are for takeout. If West, in example A, had wanted to double spades for takeout, he would have done so in the first round of bidding.

A Double to Reopen the Bidding

There is one instance in which a takeout double may be made with less than 13 points and that is when you wish to prevent the bidding from dying out when the adversaries have quit at a low level. Since the responder has failed to act and the opener did not deem his hand strong enough to make a game forcing bid, it is quite possible that a part score may be available for your side. A takeout double, when the opponents have permitted the bidding to die, may be made with a hand containing only ten high-card points provided there is support for the unbid suits.

You are sitting South and the bidding has proceeded:

WEST	NORTH	EAST	SOUTH
1 ♣	Pass	Pass	?

With which of these hands would you make a takeout double?

♠ x	♡ K Q x x x	◇ A J x x	♣ x x x	**426**
♠ A J x x	♡ K x x x	◇ K x x	♣ x x	**430**
♠ J x x x	♡ Q x x	◇ A Q x	♣ K J x	**434**

421

[*from 448*]

♠ J x x x x x   ♡ x   ◊ Q x x   ♣ x x x

WEST	NORTH	EAST	SOUTH
1 ♡	Double	2 ♡	?

YOUR ANSWER: I would now pass with this hand.

You shouldn't. Partner wants to know your best suit. He is especially interested in spades. Even though your hand is worth only five points you should bid two spades, for this may be the last opportunity you will have to speak.

If you return to **448**, you will find a better answer.

422

[*from 441*]

♠ A K 10   ♡ x x   ◊ K 10 x   ♣ A K J 10 x

WEST	NORTH	EAST	SOUTH
1 ♡	Pass	Pass	Double
Pass	2 ♣	Pass	?

YOUR ANSWER: My bid should now be four clubs.

No. Partner has dutifully named his best suit in response to your takeout double, but he may not have a point in his hand. Even with your powerful hand as dummy he may be unable to fulfill a ten-trick contract.

Furthermore, a four club bid would dismiss the possibility of playing the hand in three no trump.

Return to **441** and choose the other answer.

♠ Q 10 x x   ♡ K J x   ◇ Q x x   ♣ x x x

Partner has doubled a bid of one diamond.

YOUR ANSWER: I would respond with one no trump.

We would not recommend this. For all intents and purposes a one no trump response denies possession of a four-card major. Presumably, partner doubled because he has spade and heart strength. So do you. Bid one spade.

If you go back to **438** you will find a better hand for the one no trump response.

♠ x x   ♡ J x x x   ◇ Q J x x x   ♣ x x

Partner has doubled a bid of one club.

YOUR ANSWER: With this hand I would now bid one heart.

No. Both your hand and your heart suit are too weak. It would be wiser to bid one diamond and take no further action.

Please return to **430** for the right answer.

♠ K x   ♡ A K J 10 x x   ◇ x   ♣ A J 10 x

Your right-hand opponent has opened with one diamond.

YOUR ANSWER: I would make a takeout double with this hand.

Your answer is right but requires amplification.

This is a powerful hand. In the days of strong jump overcalls it would have prompted a two heart bid in this position. But nowadays the jump overcall is based on weak hands and long suits. Strong hands like this are announced by an immediate takeout double. You may show your hearts later.

For a more complete discussion, return to **418** and find the best answer.

426

[from 420]

♠ x   ♡ K Q x x x   ◇ A J x x   ♣ x x x

WEST	NORTH	EAST	SOUTH
1 ♣	Pass	Pass	?

YOUR ANSWER: Sitting South, I would double with this hand.

No. You aren't prepared for a spade response from partner. Make a simple one heart overcall.

Before you make a takeout double, you should anticipate your partner's most likely response. Most often he will respond in your shortest suit. You should not double if a particular response from partner will prove to be embarrassing.

Please return to **420** and choose another hand for a fourth position takeout double.

427

[from 440]

♠ Q J 10   ♡ J x x   ◇ K J x   ♣ K J x x

YOUR ANSWER: After partner's double of a one diamond bid, a response of three clubs would be correct with this hand.

You certainly should make a jump bid to let partner know that you have more than ten points. However, your clubs are not good enough to justify a jump to the three level. Since you have a stopper in the adverse suit, you should bid two no trump rather than three clubs.

Remember, a major suit response is preferable to no trump, but no trump is preferable to a minor suit response, if you have a stopper in opponents' suit.

Please go back to **440** to pick the correct answer.

♠ A K J 10 x   ♡ K x x x   ◇ x x   ♣ A x

Your right-hand opponent has opened with one diamond.

YOUR ANSWER: I would make a takeout double with this hand.

Your answer is right, but requires amplification.

With 17 points, you are too strong for an overcall in spades. You have strength in both majors. If partner has four hearts, you have a fit. If not you can bid your spades with the reasonable hope that he has at least two little spades.

For a more complete discussion, return to **418** and find the best answer.

♠ Q J x x   ♡ x   ◇ K Q x x   ♣ K J x x

WEST	NORTH	EAST	SOUTH
1 ♡	Double	Pass	?

YOUR ANSWER: As South, I would pass with this hand.

This would be a grievous error. Granted, you might very well set the one heart contract. You might not, too. If West holds something like this:

♠ x x   ♡ A K Q x x x   ◇ x x   ♣ A x x

you will suffer the indignity of watching him rake in seven tricks. This is all the more painful when it is observed that you could have scored a game in one of the other suits.

With such a strong hand as this, having good support for all three unbid suits, you should insist upon a game contract. The proper way to get this message to partner is to cue-bid two hearts. Partner must now name his best suit, which you will, of course, raise.

Now go back to **445** and try again.

430

[*from 420*]

(A) ♠ x   ♡ K Q x x x   ◇ A J x x   ♣ x x x

(B) ♠ A J x x   ♡ K x x x   ◇ K x x   ♣ x x

(C) ♠ J x x x   ♡ Q x x   ◇ A Q x   ♣ K J x

YOUR ANSWER: Sitting South, I would double with hand B.

Right. Holding a 12-point hand you are more than justified in making a takeout double to prevent the bidding from dying. If it is suggested that your requirements for a takeout double have not been met, this can be adjusted by a pass at your next turn to bid. With hand A, overcall with one heart; with hand C, bid one no trump.

Responding to the Takeout Double

When partner makes a takeout double, it is your absolute duty to respond unless (*a*) there has been an intervening bid or (*b*) you can guarantee that the opponents' contract will be set. You must not pass because your hand is weak. Partner is quite aware that you may hold a very poor hand, and he has assumed full responsibility. If you suffer a loss, the blame can be pinned on him.

If your response can be made at the one level, a four-card major suit should be shown in preference to a five-card minor, provided the four-card major is headed by a high honor. Prudence may, of course, dictate exceptions to this advice if your hand is especially weak.

With two-suited hands, show the higher-ranking suit first and then show the other suit on the next round.

In which of the following situations would you make a response of one heart:

♠ x x   ♡ J x x x   ◇ Q J x x x   ♣ x x
Partner has doubled a bid of one club.   **424**

♠ K 10 x x   ♡ A J x x   ◇ x x x   ♣ x x
Partner has doubled a bid of one diamond.   **435**

♠ x x x   ♡ Q x x x   ◇ x   ♣ K x x x x
Partner has doubled a bid of one diamond.   **438**

274

SOUTH	WEST	NORTH	EAST
4 ♡	Double		

YOUR ANSWER: This is a penalty double.

No, it isn't. South has a rather weak hand with a long heart suit. West has a strong hand and is willing to play at the five level if he must, though he most especially hopes that East can bid spades. Of course, East may pass if he feels there would be more profit in playing against four hearts doubled.

Return to **439** and study the other bidding sequences.

♠ x x x x	♡ x x x	◇ x x x	♣ x x x

WEST	NORTH	EAST	SOUTH
1 ♡	Double	Pass	?

YOUR ANSWER: As South, I would pass with this hand.

We must confess we didn't expect you to turn to this page. If you got here directly from **445,** you should read this chapter over from the beginning.

The takeout double is, for all practical purposes, a demand bid. You must not pass unless you have sufficient strength in the adverse suit to be sure of defeating the contract.

You should bid one spade with this hand and then pass thereafter. If you end up in an unmakable contract, it's not your fault; partner knows that he has forced you to bid even though you may have a "bust."

Now go back to **445** and try again.

433

[from 418]

♠ K 10 x x   ♡ K 10 x x   ◇ x   ♣ A Q x x

Your right-hand opponent has opened with one diamond.

YOUR ANSWER: I would make a takeout double with this hand.

Your answer is right, but requires amplification.

Although it contains only 12 points in high cards, your hand will be worth 15–16 points in support of any of the unbid suits. (Your singleton counts three, and the king of your major suit promotes to four if partner responds in one of the majors.)

For a more complete discussion, return to **418** and find the best answer.

434

[from 420]

♠ J x x x   ♡ Q x x   ◇ A Q x   ♣ K J x

WEST	NORTH	EAST	SOUTH
1 ♣	Pass	Pass	?

YOUR ANSWER: Sitting South, I would double with this hand.

While this bid is acceptable, we prefer another action. With most of your strength concentrated in the minor suits you can describe this hand better by a fourth-position overcall of one no trump.

Go back to **420** and choose the best hand for a double.

435

[from 430]

♠ K 10 x x   ♡ A J x x   ◇ x x x   ♣ x x

Partner has doubled a bid of one diamond.

YOUR ANSWER: With this hand, I would now bid one heart.

No. This hand is worth nine points and therefore two bids. Show your spades first and plan to bid the hearts on the next round unless the spades are vigorously supported. This technique follows the principles of bidding economy as outlined in Chapter I.

Please return to **430** for the right answer.

♠ A K 10   ♡ x x   ◇ K 10 x   ♣ A K J 10 x

WEST	NORTH	EAST	SOUTH
1 ♡	Pass	Pass	Double
Pass	2 ♣	Pass	?

YOUR ANSWER: No, as South in this sequence, I would not bid four clubs with the above hand.

Very good. Partner may have no high-card points at all, and the opposing team has at least 13. So you shouldn't jump. Your correct bid is three clubs. If partner has a stopper in hearts, the eventual contract might be three no trump.

Again, you are South and hold this hand:

♠ A Q x x   ♡ x x   ◇ A 10 x   ♣ K J x x

The bidding has proceeded:

EAST	SOUTH	WEST	NORTH
1 ♡	Double	Pass	2 ◇
Pass	?		

What should you do?

Bid Two Spades **443**
Pass **449**
Bid Three Diamonds **452**

SOUTH	WEST	NORTH	EAST
1 ◇	Pass	1 NT	Double

YOUR ANSWER: This is a penalty double.

No, it isn't.
The double of an opening bid of one no trump is primarily intended for penalties; but the double of a one no trump response is for takeout. Partner can support the unbid suits and has the equivalent of an opening bid.

Return to **439** and study the other bidding sequences.

(A)   ♠ x x   ♡ J x x x   ◊ Q J x x x   ♣ x x

Partner has doubled a bid of one club.

(B)   ♠ K 10 x x   ♡ A J x x   ◊ x x x   ♣ x x

Partner has doubled a bid of one diamond.

(C)   ♠ x x x   ♡ Q x x x   ◊ K   ♣ K x x x x

Partner has doubled a bid of one diamond.

YOUR ANSWER: In situation C, I would respond one heart.

So would we. You have a four-card major suit headed by a high honor, hence one heart is preferable to two clubs. With hand A, however, you can say one diamond. With hand B, you should bid spades on the first round and then show your heart suit later unless spades are vigorously supported.

There is an apparent choice in the following example:

♠ K 10 x x   ♡ x x   ◊ x x   ♣ A x x x x

When partner doubles one heart, do you bid clubs or spades? We recommend showing the spades first for the simple reason that a club response is more apt to be passed out. The odds are in favor of your partner being able to assist your spades, and a minor suit response is less apt to induce him to act.

The one no trump response to a takeout double is generally misunderstood. It is not a "negative response," such as the one no trump response to an opening bid of one in a suit. It is based upon at least eight or nine high-card points and a stopper in the adverse suit.

If your hand contains a four-card major and a stopper in the suit adversely bid, it is usually preferable to bid the major. With eight–nine points, a stopper in the opposing suit, and a four-card minor, however, you should bid one no trump.

Which of these hands calls for a one no trump response after partner has doubled a bid of one diamond?

♠ 10 x x   ♡ J x x   ◊ Q x x x   ♣ x x x **419**

♠ Q 10 x x   ♡ K J x   ◊ Q x x   ♣ x x x **423**

♠ x x x   ♡ J x x   ◊ K J x   ♣ K J x x **440**

♠ K x   ♡ A K J 10 x x   ◇ x   ♣ A J 10 x

♠ A K J 10 x   ♡ K x x x   ◇ x x   ♣ A x

♠ K 10 x x   ♡ K 10 x x   ◇ x   ♣ A Q x x

Your right-hand opponent has opened with one diamond.

YOUR ANSWER: I would make a takeout double with any of these hands.

This is 100 per cent right. All three hands meet the requirements —the equivalent of an opening bid, with strength in the majors. Overcalls would not do justice to them.

How do you distinguish between takeout and penalty doubles? These few rules of thumb will help:

The double of two no trump is always for penalties.

The double of an opening one no trump bid is intended primarily for penalties, but partner may take it out if his hand contains a long suit and little defensive value.

The double of an opening three bid is primarily for takeout, though, of course, at so high a bidding level, partner may pass if he deems it more advisable to play for penalties.

A takeout double must be made at the player's first opportunity to double that suit.

After partner has made a bid of any kind, all doubles are for penalties.

Which of the following doubles is for penalties?

SOUTH	WEST	NORTH	EAST	
1 ♠	Pass	1 NT	Pass	
2 ♠	Double			**420**
4 ♡	Double			**431**
1 ◇	Pass	1 NT	Double	**437**
1 ♠	Pass	2 ♠	Double	**442**

440

[from 438]

(A)	♠ 10 x x	♡ J x x	◇ Q x x x	♣ x x x
(B)	♠ Q 10 x x	♡ K J x	◇ Q x x	♣ x x x
(C)	♠ x x x	♡ J x x	◇ K J x	♣ K J x x

Partner has doubled a one diamond bid.

YOUR ANSWER: I would respond one no trump with hand C.

Good. Hand C contains nine high-card points and a diamond stopper, and its strength lies in the minor suits. This makes it ideal for such a response.

With hand A, you are stuck; you must bid your cheapest three-card suit, hearts. With hand B, you should respond with one spade since its high-card strength is concentrated in the majors.

Most players tend to underestimate the value of their hands when partner has made a takeout double. Actually, if partner has doubled and you have six points, you have a fair hand; if you have nine points, you have a good hand. If you have eleven points, you have a probable game. With more than eleven points, your hand is excellent and game is virtually assured provided you arrive at the correct contract.

When you have as many as eleven points and partner has doubled an adverse opening, you should disclose this information immediately. You do this by bidding one more than necessary in your best suit (a single jump), even though the suit is not particularly strong in itself. This holds true for both major and minor suit bids. However, if it is a minor suit and your jump shift response takes you to the three level, then it ought to be a fairly good suit. If you hold minor suit strength and have the opponent's suit guarded, you should make your jump in no trump.

Partner doubles an opening bid of one diamond. Here are three hands followed by the responses. In which case is the response correct?

♠ Q J 10   ♡ J x x   ◇ K J x   ♣ K J x x
       Your Response: three clubs   **427**

♠ A 10 x   ♡ Q J 10   ◇ x x   ♣ K Q J x x
       Your Response: three clubs   **445**

♠ Q J x x   ♡ A J x   ◇ x x x   ♣ K J x
       Your Response: one spade   **454**

♠ x x x   ♡ K J x x   ◇ x x x   ♣ x x x

	WEST	NORTH	EAST	SOUTH
(A)	1 ◇	Double	Redouble	?
(B)	1 ♣	Double	Redouble	?

YOUR ANSWER: With this hand, I would bid in sequence **A**.

Right. Your best suit is hearts, and in sequence A you may show them without using up any bidding space. Partner can bid spades or clubs at the same level just as if you had passed.

If you bid one heart in sequence B, you would deprive partner of the opportunity to bid diamonds at the one level. Your suit is not good enough to justify the assumption of that risk.

Action by Doubler after Partner Responds

In determining action after partner has responded to your takeout double, you must bear in mind that you have forced him to speak. Unless he showed definite values by making a jump bid or bidding no trump, you must assume that he may be broke.

Thus it may be reasoned that if your double was based upon a minimum 13–15 points and partner was unable to jump, game is highly unlikely. Even if your double was based upon a much stronger hand, you should proceed with caution until you have further assessed the nature of partner's response.

For example, let's say that you are South and hold this hand:

♠ A Q x x   ♡ x x   ◇ K x x   ♣ K x x x

East opens with one heart, you double, and North responds with one spade. Since you have in effect shown your point count and your support by making a takeout double, you should pass. Only if partner jumps can you consider further action.

Now consider a stronger hand:

♠ A K 10   ♡ x x   ◇ K 10 x   ♣ A K J 10 x

The bidding:	WEST	NORTH	EAST	SOUTH
	1 ♡	Pass	Pass	Double
	Pass	2 ♣	Pass	?

Would you bid four clubs?

Yes **422**   No **436**

442

[*from* 439]

SOUTH	WEST	NORTH	EAST
1 ♠	Pass	2 ♠	Double

YOUR ANSWER: This is a penalty double.

No, it isn't. East has doubled spades at his first opportunity. He is announcing a good hand with some strength in hearts, for the take-out double of one major suit suggests support for the other major. His hand must be better than that required for the usual takeout double, for he is willing to play at the three level.

Return to **439** and study the other bidding sequences.

443

[*from* 436]

♠ A Q x x	♡ x x	◊ A 10 x	♣ K J x x
EAST	SOUTH	WEST	NORTH
1 ♡	Double	Pass	2 ◊
Pass	?		

YOUR ANSWER: I would bid two spades.

No. You have only moderate strength in your hand and partner may have nothing. You can't afford further exploring, and since partner did not bid spades, you can assume that he has less than four cards in that suit. Besides, you have good support for diamonds.

Please go back to **436** to pick out the right answer.

444

[*from* 456]

♠ J x x x   ♡ x   ◊ x x x   ♣ Q x x x x

YOUR ANSWER: If partner's one spade opening is doubled, I should pass.

No. You have a very weak hand, of course, but it contains sufficient trump support to justify a two spade bid. This will force the opponents to the three level to investigate each other's hands. Yet if they choose to make a penalty double, your distribution alone will give partner a play for two spades.

Return to **456** and choose another answer.

(A) ♠ Q J 10   ♡ J x x   ◇ K J x   ♣ K J x x   3 ♣

(B) ♠ A 10 x   ♡ Q J 10   ◇ x x   ♣ K Q J x x   3 ♣

(C) ♠ Q J x x   ♡ A J x   ◇ x x x   ♣ K J x   1 ♠

YOUR ANSWER: After partner's double of a one diamond bid, the response of three clubs with hand B would be correct.

Yes. The over-all strength of this hand and the caliber of its clubs call for a jump to the three level. With hand C, the proper response is two spades; with hand A, two no trump.

The Penalty Pass of
Partner's Takeout Double

When partner doubles an opening-suit bid and the next opponent passes, you are permitted to pass only if you are sure you can defeat the contract.

With what kind of a hand can you do this? Certainly not a weak hand; here you must bid your best suit and let partner assume the responsibility. And certainly not with a good hand whose strength lies in the unbid suits; here your hopes lie in offense, not defense. This leaves only the good hand whose strength happens to lie in the opponent's suit, for here your hand will be of more value in defense.

Hence, you should never pass the double of one of a suit with less than three sure tricks. Indeed, the type of hand required for the penalty pass is so specific that it carries with it a demand for a trump lead from partner.

In keeping with this important principle, with which of these hands would you pass partner's double of a one heart bid?

♠ Q J x x   ♡ x   ◇ K Q x x   ♣ K J x x   **429**

♠ x x x x   ♡ x x x   ◇ x x x   ♣ x x x   **432**

♠ x   ♡ K Q J x x   ◇ Q x x   ♣ x x x x   **448**

446

[from 458]

♠ x x x   ♡ K J x x   ◇ x x x   ♣ x x x

WEST	NORTH	EAST	SOUTH
1 ♣	Double	Redouble	?

YOUR ANSWER: With this hand I would bid one heart in this sequence.

No, you should pass.

A one heart bid from you may prove awkward if partner's suit is diamonds, for it will force him to name his suit at the two level. Four points and a four-card suit are not worth showing at this level. Pass and let partner rescue himself from the redouble at the one level.

Please go back to **458** and pick out the sequence which will allow you to show your hearts.

447

[from 457]

♠ J x x x   ♡ A x x   ◇ x x x   ♣ K J x

WEST	NORTH	EAST	SOUTH
1 ◇	Double	Pass	1 ♠
Pass	2 ♠	Pass	?

YOUR ANSWER: I would bid four spades with this hand.

No, not quite. Partner raised your bid to the two level, so you can be certain of only 16 points in his hand. You have nine points, and that brings the total to 25—one short of the 26 points required for a game commitment in a major suit.

Your proper bid is three spades. If partner has maximum values for his raise, he will carry on to game.

Please return to **457** and select the right answer.

(A)	♠ Q J x x ♡ x		◊ K Q x x ♣ K J x x
(B)	♠ x x x x ♡ x x x		◊ x x x ♣ x x x
(C)	♠ x ♡ K Q J x x		◊ Q x x ♣ x x x x

WEST	NORTH	EAST	SOUTH
1 ♡	Double	Pass	?

YOUR ANSWER: I would pass with hand C.

Yes, you should. With no strength outside of hearts, your hand will not make a very good dummy, but in combination with partner's strength it should assure defeat of the one heart contract. Since, in effect, you are playing the contract at hearts (for you need seven tricks to defeat the contract), partner will lead a trump to keep declarer from making any of his little trumps by ruffing.

With hand A, you should bid two hearts. This will announce a strong hand, good support for all three unbid suits, and a desire to reach game. With hand B, you must say one spade.

Responding after an Intervening Bid

When your right-hand opponent makes a bid after your partner's takeout double, you are no longer obliged to bid. But, as you will soon learn, such intervening bids are (except for the redouble) based upon weak hands and intended primarily to obstruct your lines of communication. You should resolve all doubts in favor of bidding.

In other words, the usual requirements for a free response do not hold here. Seven or eight points will suffice—even less if you have a long major suit.

The bidding has proceeded:

WEST	NORTH	EAST	SOUTH
1 ♡	Double	2 ♡	?

As South with which of these hands would you now pass?

♠ J x x x x x	♡ x	◊ Q x x	♣ x x x	421
♠ x x	♡ Q x x	◊ Q J x	♣ Q x x x x	458
♠ J x x	♡ x x	◊ A Q x x x	♣ Q x x	461

449
[from 436]

♠ A Q x x   ♡ x x   ◊ A 10 x   ♣ K J x x

EAST	SOUTH	WEST	NORTH
1 ♡	Double	Pass	2 ◊
Pass	?		

YOUR ANSWER: I would pass.

Correct. Since partner was unable to jump, game is remote. There's no point in mentioning your spades; for if partner had four of them he would probably have told you so. And it would be highly optimistic to raise his diamonds and thereby encourage partner when you have no more than a minimum double.

You should exercise the same caution in giving partner a major suit raise. Having forced him to bid, you must not jump to any contract which you cannot reasonably expect to fulfill in your own hand.

Here's a guide for you:

Don't raise to the two level unless you have at least 16 points.
Don't raise to the three level unless you have at least 19 points.
Don't raise to the four level unless you have at least 22 points.

When a doubler follows up his original double with a free bid (after his right-hand opponent has rebid), he asserts that he has a strong hand, with game-going possibilities. With a lesser holding, he should leave any further action up to his partner.

With which of these hands should you raise partner's bid? In each case the bidding has proceeded:

EAST	SOUTH	WEST	NORTH
1 ♠	Double	Pass	2 ♡
2 ♠	?		

♠ x   ♡ K Q x x   ◊ A J x   ♣ A 9 x x x   **455**

♠ K x   ♡ A Q J x x   ◊ A Q x   ♣ K x x   **457**

♠ x x   ♡ A K x x   ◊ A J x x   ♣ K x x   **462**

♠ x x x   ♡ K J x x   ◇ x x x   ♣ x x x

	WEST	NORTH	EAST	SOUTH
(A)	1 ◇	Double	Redouble	?
(B)	1 ♣	Double	Redouble	?

YOUR ANSWER: I would bid one heart in either case.

No, you should pass in sequence B. A heart bid takes up bidding space. If partner's suit is diamonds, it would force him to speak at the two level in order to show it. Pass instead and let partner rescue himself from the redouble at the one level.

Please go back to **458** and pick out the sequence which will allow you to show your hearts.

(A)   ♠ J x x x   ♡ A x x   ◇ x x x   ♣ K J x

(B)   ♠ J x x x   ♡ K Q x   ◇ x x   ♣ Q J x x

WEST	NORTH	EAST	SOUTH
1 ◇	Double	Pass	1 ♠
Pass	2 ♠	Pass	?

YOUR ANSWER: I would bid four spades with hand B.

Yes, indeed. Partner has promised 16 points with his raise. In hand B you have ten points and since this brings the count to at least 26, you should be willing to contract for game.

Hand A, with nine points, is not quite strong enough for a game bid, but you can suggest game possibilities by bidding three spades. If partner has a maximum raise, he will contract for the game.

Go on to **456**.

452

[from 436]

♠ A Q x x   ♡ x x   ◇ A 10 x   ♣ K J x x

EAST	SOUTH	WEST	NORTH
1 ♡	Double	Pass	2 ◇
Pass	?		

YOUR ANSWER: I would bid three diamonds.

You have support for partner's diamonds, but you don't have enough strength in your hand to raise his bid.

Since partner did not make a jump bid, you know that he has less than eleven points. He did not bid one no trump, and you also know that he lacks either a heart stopper or the necessary eight or nine points. Partner may have nothing at all.

Any bid you make, therefore, will have to be based entirely on your own hand, and you certainly don't have enough strength to assume responsibility for a bid of three diamonds.

Please return to **436** and pick the right answer.

453

[from 456]

♠ x x   ♡ x x x   ◇ Q x x   ♣ K x x x x

YOUR ANSWER: If partner's one spade opening is doubled, I should bid two clubs.

No, you should pass with this hand. It is not strong enough for a new suit bid. You should not name a new suit unless you have about eight–ten points.

Please go back to **456** and pick the hand with the correct bid.

♠ Q J x x   ♡ A J x   ◇ x x x   ♣ K J x

YOUR ANSWER: After partner's double of a one diamond bid, a response of one spade would be correct with this hand.

The suit is correct, but the level of response is wrong. With 12 points you should jump to two spades. Otherwise partner will have no way of knowing that you have more than ten points.

Remember, you could make a bid at the one level with no points at all. To show your strength, you should jump the bidding.

Please return to **440** to pick the correct answer.

♠ x   ♡ K Q x x   ◇ A J x   ♣ A 9 x x x

EAST	SOUTH	WEST	NORTH
1 ♠	Double	Pass	2 ♡
2 ♠			

YOUR ANSWER: I would now bid three hearts with this hand.

That would be highly optimistic. You have only 17 points in support of partner's suit and you should have 19 to raise to the three level. Partner has failed to jump, thereby indicating that he has less than eleven points. For the time being you must rely entirely on your own hand in estimating the number of tricks you might take. Without help from partner this hand might take only five tricks. Hence, even a two heart contract may be difficult to make.

Since East made an intervening bid, partner will have another chance to describe his hand if he so wishes. It would be wiser to pass.

Please return to **449** and select the hand that is right for a raise.

Action by Partner of Opening Bidder

When partner's opening bid has been doubled by the opponent on your right, your choice of response may often determine the success or failure of the hand. Here are the basic rules which should govern your action:

1. With a better-than-average hand—i.e., with more than ten points—you should redouble. It matters not whether you have trump support. Thus, partner is immediately informed of your approximate combined strength. He must then pass at his next turn in order to give you the opportunity to clarify the reason for your redouble.

2. With a weak hand and no significant trump support, you should pass.

3. With a weak hand and good trump support (J x x x or better), you give a single raise; with very good trump support (Q J x x x or x x x x x), a double raise. The purpose here is largely pre-emption. It will make it difficult for the enemy to find their best contract.

4. With a weak hand containing a long suit, you may bid the suit if partner's opening bid was no trump.

5. With an intermediate hand, you usually bid at once. With eight–ten points and a good suit you should show it now, for otherwise partner will never hear about it. With eight–ten points scattered in the unbid suits, you may bid one no trump.

If your partner's opening of one spade has been doubled by the opponent on your right, which one of the following bids would be correct for the corresponding hands?

♠ J x x x	♡ x	◇ x x x	♣ Q x x x x	Pass	**444**
♠ x x	♡ x x x	◇ Q x x	♣ K x x x x	2 ♣	**453**
♠ x	♡ K Q 10 x	◇ A Q x x	♣ A 10 x x	1 NT	**460**
♠ 10 x x	♡ A K J x x	◇ K x x	♣ x x	Redouble	**463**

(A)	♠ x	♡ K Q x x	◇ A J x	♣ A 9 x x x
(B)	♠ K x	♡ A Q J x x	◇ A Q x	♣ K x x
(C)	♠ x x	♡ A K x x	◇ A J x x	♣ K x x

EAST	SOUTH	WEST	NORTH
1 ♠	Double	Pass	2 ♡
2 ♠	?		

YOUR ANSWER: I would now bid three hearts with hand B.

Yes. In hand B you have 21 points in support of partner's hearts. With at least nine trumps between you, and the opposing strength in front of your cards, you can reasonably expect to take nine tricks even though partner's hand is totally indifferent. Therefore, your raise to three hearts would be correct. If partner has any extra values (about six points), he may raise the bid to game.

Hand C is worth 16 points in support of hearts, but without help from partner it may take only five or six tricks. Hand A is no better. With these hands you should pass. Partner will have the chance to contest the auction if his hand warrants such action.

Further Action by Doubler's Partner

If, as doubler's partner, you hold an indifferent hand, you should pass when partner raises your response. With a good hand (about nine points), you should make one more bid. Remember, partner promises at least 16 points when he raises your bid to the two level; with ten points you should jump to game. For a three-level raise, partner promises at least 19 points, so you need only seven points to go to game.

Examine the following sequence:

WEST	NORTH	EAST	SOUTH
1 ◇	Double	Pass	1 ♠
Pass	2 ♠	Pass	?

With which of these hands would you bid four spades?

♠ J x x x	♡ A x x	◇ x x x	♣ K J x	**447**
♠ J x x x	♡ K Q x	◇ x x	♣ Q J x x	**451**
Neither hand	**459**			

291

458

[from 448]

(A) ♠ J x x x x x   ♣ x   ♦ Q x x   ♣ x x x

(B) ♠ x x   ♥ Q x x   ♦ Q J x   ♣ Q x x x x

(C) ♠ J x x   ♥ x x   ♦ A Q x x x   ♣ Q x x

WEST	NORTH	EAST	SOUTH
1 ♡	Double	2 ♡	?

YOUR ANSWER: I would now pass with hand B.

This would be correct. Hand B contains eight points, but this can hardly justify a three-level response in a minor suit. Yet hand A, with only five points, calls for a two spade bid. With hand C, you should say three diamonds.

You are also relieved of the obligation to bid when opener's partner redoubles.

If your adversary redoubles partner's takeout double, he indicates a holding of ten or more points. Since opener and partner have announced holdings of 13 or more points, clearly, you cannot have too much in the way of high-card strength. A pass by you indicates, in most cases, that you have nothing to say at the present time and that you would prefer your partner to bid a suit to get you out of the effect of the redouble. It implies that you are more or less willing to have him select any of the suits, that you have no special choice. However, a bid at this point does not promise strength, and should not be regarded as a free bid. If you have a five-card suit, it is generally good practice to show it regardless of its texture. Even a four-card suit may be shown if it does not consume any bidding space.

Suppose you are South and you hold:

♠ x x x   ♥ K J x x   ♦ x x x   ♣ x x x

In which of these sequences should you bid rather than pass?

WEST	NORTH	EAST	SOUTH	
1 ◇	Double	Redouble	?	**441**
1 ♣	Double	Redouble	?	**446**

Both of them   **450**

292

(A)   ♠ J x x x   ♡ A x x   ◇ x x x   ♣ K J x

(B)   ♠ J x x x   ♡ K Q x   ◇ x x   ♣ Q J x x

WEST	NORTH	EAST	SOUTH
1 ◇	Double	Pass	1 ♠
Pass	2 ♠	Pass	?

YOUR ANSWER: I can't bid four spades with either of these hands.

As a matter of fact, you should bid four spades with one of these hands.

Partner raised your bid to the two level, so you can expect 16 points from him. Hand A has nine points, bringing the total to 25, which is one point short of what you would require for a game-level bid in spades. Hand B, however, has ten points, which brings the total point count to 26—enough for you to bid four spades.

Please turn to **451** which proceeds with the right answer.

♠ x   ♡ K Q 10 x   ◇ A Q x x   ♣ A 10 x x

YOUR ANSWER: If partner's one spade opening is doubled, I should bid one no trump.

No indeed. One no trump in this position is used to show scattered strength but not enough for a redouble. This hand contains 15 high-card points.

You should immediately redouble to announce your strength. You don't like partner's spades, but your other three suits are very good. If there is no further bidding, you can feel confident of partner's making one spade redoubled. If your opponents bid again, you will be in a position to make a very profitable penalty double in any suit they select.

Please return to **456** and pick the hand with the correct bid.

461

[from 448]

♠ J x x   ♡ x x   ◇ A Q x x x   ♣ Q x x

WEST	NORTH	EAST	SOUTH
1 ♡	Double	2 ♡	?

YOUR ANSWER: I would now pass with this hand.

You shouldn't. This hand is worth ten points. Partner has already promised 13 or more. It is safe to say three diamonds. An added safety feature here is your spade holding. If partner elects to bid three spades, you have suitable support. If, on the other hand, you held:

♠ x   ♡ Q x x   ◇ A x x x x   ♣ Q x x x,

here you would also have ten points, but a three diamond bid would appear less attractive.

If you return to **448**, you will find a better answer.

462

[from 449]

♠ x x   ♡ A K x x   ◇ A J x x   ♣ K x x

EAST	SOUTH	WEST	NORTH
1 ♠	Double	Pass	2 ♡
2 ♠	?		

YOUR ANSWER: I would now bid three hearts with this hand.

No, not with this hand. Partner has told you that his longest suit is hearts and that he has less than eleven points (he didn't jump). Since he may be trickless, you are still on your own as far as winning tricks is concerned. And without assistance from partner, you may take only five or six tricks.

East's intervening bid has given partner another chance to speak if he wishes. You should pass.

Please return to **449** and select the hand that is right for a raise.

(A)	♠ J x x x	♡ x	◊ x x x	♣ Q x x x x	Pass
(B)	♠ x x	♡ x x x	◊ Q x x	♣ K x x x x	2 ♣
(C)	♠ x	♡ K Q 10 x	◊ A Q x x	♣ A 10 x x	1 NT
(D)	♠ 10 x x	♡ A K J x x	◊ K x x	♣ x x	Redouble

YOUR ANSWER: After opponent's double of partner's spade opening, the response with hand D would be correct.

Yes. Hand D is very good for a redouble. This tells partner you have a stronger-than-average hand. You may show your hearts later if you wish.

With hand A, the correct response would be two spades; this is intended for pre-emptive purposes. With hand B, you should pass; your hand is not strong enough to bid a new suit. With hand C, you should redouble to let partner know you have a strong hand; the one no trump bid in this position is reserved for hands with scattered strength but not enough point count to redouble.

Use of the Takeout Double by Opening Bidder

The takeout double may also be used by the opening bidder to force a partner who has previously passed. For example, as South you hold:

♠ K J x x   ♡ A K x x   ◊ x   ♣ K Q x x

The bidding has proceeded:

SOUTH	WEST	NORTH	EAST
1 ♣	1 ◊	Pass	Pass
?			

What should you do?

Naturally you are going to carry on the fight, and it would be pointless for you to guess whether to rebid in hearts or spades. So you double. Partner may express a preference for either major suit; he may return to two clubs; or, with great length in diamonds, he may elect to pass.

Such a double, after partner has passed, is obviously for takeout. However, if partner has bid, a double is for penalties.

Now try your hand at the bidding problems on the next page.

464

[*from 463*]

(A) ♠ x   ♡ A x   ◇ x x x   ♣ Q J 10 9 x x x

| | EAST | SOUTH |
| | 1 ◇ | ? |

(B) ♠ A K 10 9 x x x   ♡ x x x   ◇ A Q   ♣ x

| | EAST | SOUTH |
| | 1 ◇ | ? |

(C) ♠ x x x   ♡ x x   ◇ K Q 10 x   ♣ K x x x

| NORTH | EAST | SOUTH |
| 1 ♡ | Double | ? |

(D) ♠ x x x   ♡ K J 9 x x x   ◇ K x x   ♣ x

| WEST | NORTH | EAST | SOUTH |
| 1 ♣ | Pass | 1 ♠ | ? |

(E) ♠ x x   ♡ A Q 10 x x   ◇ K Q x   ♣ K x x

| SOUTH | WEST | NORTH | EAST |
| 1 ♡ | Double | 3 ♡ | Pass |
| ? |

(F) ♠ K x x x   ♡ x x   ◇ Q 10 x x   ♣ x x x

WEST	NORTH	EAST	SOUTH
1 ♣	Double	Pass	1 ♠
Pass	3 ♠	Pass	?

(G) ♠ x x x   ♡ A J   ◇ A Q x   ♣ Q 10 8 x x

| | EAST | SOUTH |
| | 1 ◇ | ? |

(H) ♠ A J 10 x   ♡ J x x x   ◇ A Q x   ♣ x x

| WEST | NORTH | EAST | SOUTH |
| 1 ♣ | Double | Pass | ? |

Go on to **465**.

296

(I)   ♠ x   ♡ A K Q 10 x   ◇ A K J x x   ♣ x x

	EAST	SOUTH
	1 ♠	?

(J)   ♠ A   ♡ x x   ◇ Q J 9 x x   ♣ K 10 x x x

EAST	SOUTH	WEST	NORTH
1 ♡	Pass	2 ♡	Pass
Pass	?		

(K)   ♠ x x x   ♡ x x x   ◇ J x x   ♣ K 10 x x

WEST	NORTH	EAST	SOUTH
1 ♣	Double	Pass	?

(L)   ♠ Q J   ♡ x x x   ◇ A K J x   ♣ x x x x

WEST	NORTH	EAST	SOUTH
1 ♡	1 ♠	Pass	?

(M)   ♠ x x   ♡ K x x   ◇ x x   ♣ A K J 10 x x

WEST	NORTH	EAST	SOUTH
1 ♠	2 ♡	2 ♠	?

(N)   ♠ K 10 9 x   ♡ x   ◇ A 10 x x   ♣ Q 9 8 x

NORTH	EAST	SOUTH
1 ♡	Double	?

(O)   ♠ x x   ♡ K Q 10 9   ◇ A J x x   ♣ Q 10 x

WEST	NORTH	EAST	SOUTH
1 ♡	2 ♠	Pass	?

(P)   ♠ K x x x x   ♡ A K Q 10   ◇ x   ♣ A J x

SOUTH	WEST	NORTH	EAST
1 ♠	2 ◇	Pass	Pass
?			

Check your answers on **466**.

466

[from 465]

Answer
Letter

(L) Two spades. Since you have 11 high-card points, game is a distinct possibility; and Q J is adequate trump support for a sound overcall.

(D) Pass. This hand does not offer sufficient playing power for any kind of overcall, even nonvulnerable.

(P) Double. You are prepared for any response by partner. A two heart bid might not produce the best result, especially if partner happens to have considerable strength in clubs.

(H) Two clubs. This hand should produce game in combination with even a minimum takeout double. Why guess at partner's best suit?

(I) Double. This hand is too strong for an overcall. You can jump in hearts later.

(A) Three clubs, if nonvulnerable. Your hand is defensively almost worthless and can play well only in clubs. This bid robs the opponents of two full levels of bidding.

(M) Four hearts. There is no point in bidding clubs. You have enormous playing strength for partner and his two-level overcall indicates a very good heart suit.

(E) Pass. Partner's jump was based upon trump length and a weak hand.

(K) One diamond. With this weak a hand you must make the cheapest available bid, even though it requires replying in a three-card suit.

(C) One no trump. With eight or nine points and a balanced hand, it is best to describe your strength immediately. Thus fortified, partner may be able to carry on the fight.

(O) Pass. Don't bid two no trump. Partner's jump overcall indicates a bad hand with long spades, so game is not in prospect.

(G) Pass. Your majors are too weak for a double; your clubs are too weak for an overcall. Pass and await developments.

(J) Two no trump. Since you previously passed, partner will know that this is an unusual no trump bid.

Go on to **467.**

(B) Double, with the intention of jumping in spades on the next round.

(N) Pass. A redouble is not recommended here. You will probably profit more by waiting in ambush for further enemy action.

(F) Four spades. Partner has promised 19 points and you have six more of which he is as yet unaware.

Now go on to Chapter IX on **468.**

CHAPTER IX

THE PENALTY DOUBLE

The penalty double is an outstanding source of unrealized wealth, especially when an opponent overcalls at the level of one or two. The average player never contemplates penalizing the opponents until they reach the upper levels, and seems completely oblivious of the fact that by far the most profitable penalties are exacted at the very low levels. The reason for this seems clear.

When your opponents eventually reach a contract of four, five, or six, they have had an opportunity to exchange information, and although they may have misjudged their strength, they usually have found a reasonably good trump suit. However, at the early levels, there has been no exchange of information, and more often than not, an overcaller has merely tested his luck with what he considers a "nuisance bid." Penalties at this point can be devastating.

It is important to differentiate between a penalty and a takeout double. As a general rule, if partner opens the bidding and your right-hand opponent overcalls in the same suit in which you were anxious to respond, you should double.

If the bidding has proceeded:

NORTH	EAST	SOUTH
1 ♡	1 ♠	?

with which of these hands should you double?

♠ K J x x   ♡ x x x   ◇ K x x   ♣ x x x **472**

♠ K J 9 x   ♡ J 10   ◇ A J 10 x   ♣ x x x **475**

Both hands **478**

♠ x x   ♡ K J x x x x   ◊ A x   ♣ Q x x

EAST	SOUTH
1 ♡	?

YOUR ANSWER: As South, I would double with this hand.

Heavens, no! This would be regarded by partner as a takeout double. A takeout double, you will recall, requires 13 or more points (which you do not have) and strength in the unbid suits (which you also do not have). You must pass and await developments.

Return to **476** for the right answer.

SOUTH	WEST	NORTH	EAST
1 ♡	1 ♠	2 ♡	Pass
3 ◊	Pass	3 ♡	Pass
6 ♡	Pass	Pass	Double
Pass	Pass	Pass	

YOUR ANSWER: As West, I would lead a club.

No, the double of a slam contract by the partner of the player who will make the opening lead is a signal calling for an unusual lead. You seem to have your signals mixed up.

Here are the leads requested by the double:

If dummy has bid any suit or suits (other than trump), lead the first suit bid by the dummy.

If dummy has not bid a side suit but declarer has bid in another suit, lead the first side suit bid by the declarer.

If neither declarer nor dummy has bid a side suit but the defensive side has, lead one of the unbid suits.

Look over these rules and see which one applies here. Then return to **486** and choose the correct lead.

471

[from 485]

Doubling Slam Contracts

Doubling slam bids in the vague hope of a one- or two-trick set is a bad practice. This is so for three main reasons: (1) Simple arithmetic: a one-trick set will net you only 100 or 200 points, whereas it will cost you 170–230 points if the contract is fulfilled. (2) Slam bids are usually based upon such strong hand combinations that even your aces cannot be counted upon as sure defensive tricks. (3) More often than not, your double will pinpoint the outstanding strength for the opposing player so that he can play the hand to his advantage. Consequently, you must double an enemy slam for conventional purposes only when you are almost positive that they have overreached themselves.

And since the success of a slam double can rarely be assumed on the basis of strength alone, this bid has acquired a new meaning: The double of a slam contract by the defender who does not have the opening lead demands an unnatural lead from the partner.

Go on to **486**.

472

[from 468]

♠ K J x x   ♡ x x x   ◇ K x x   ♣ x x x

NORTH	EAST	SOUTH
1 ♡	1 ♠	?

YOUR ANSWER: I would double with this hand.

No, this wouldn't be a very sound business double. To be sure, you would have responded with one spade if East had passed, but you wouldn't have been very enthusiastic about it. You have only seven points. You would have just kept the bidding open out of a sense of duty to your partner. This could be a case where the opponents hold the balance of power, so you should not be eager to double for penalties.

Now return to **468** and choose the correct answer.

♠ x ♡ K J x x x x ◊ x x x ♣ Q x x

NORTH	EAST	SOUTH
1 ◊	1 ♡	?

YOUR ANSWER: As South, I would double with this hand.

No, for two reasons. In the first place, you have insufficient high-card strength to double a one bid. And secondly, someone—West, North, or East—will almost certainly bid one spade, which you would not like. You should prefer to pass with this hand.

Return to **476** for the right answer.

SOUTH	WEST	NORTH	EAST
1 ♡	1 ♠	2 ♡	Pass
3 ◊	Pass	3 ♡	Pass
6 ♡	Pass	Pass	Double
Pass	Pass	Pass	

YOUR ANSWER: As West, I would lead a heart.

No, the double of a slam contract by the partner of the player who will make the opening lead is a signal calling for an unusual lead. You seem to have your signals mixed up.

Here are the leads requested by the double:

If dummy has bid any suit or suits (other than trump), lead the first side suit bid by the dummy.

If dummy has not bid a side suit but declarer has bid in another suit, lead the first side suit bid by the declarer.

If neither declarer nor dummy has bid a side suit but the defensive side has, lead one of the unbid suits.

Look over these rules and see which one applies here. Then return to **486** and choose the correct lead.

475

[from 468]

(A)   ♠ K J x x   ♡ x x x   ◊ K x x   ♣ x x x

(B)   ♠ K J 9 x   ♡ J 10   ◊ A J 10 x   ♣ x x x

YOUR ANSWER: After partner's one heart opening bid, and opponent's one spade overcall, I would double with hand B.

Correct. Had the second player passed instead of bidding, you would have been happy to respond with spades with hand B. However, with hand A you would have bid spades to fulfill your obligation to keep the bidding open with six or seven points. This difference should prompt you to double East's overcall with hand B but not with hand A.

Note that this is a penalty double—not a takeout double. You are not asking partner to name a suit, for he has already done so.

Another instance in which you should consider a penalty double is when you are tempted to respond two no trump after partner has opened in one suit and opponent has overcalled at the two level. For instance, you hold this hand:

♠ J x   ♡ A x x   ◊ Q 10 x x   ♣ K x x x

Partner opens one spade and the next hand overcalls with two diamonds. Because of his bid, you can expect partner to take three tricks. You can reasonably expect to take four more (heart ace, club king, and two trump tricks). This amounts to seven tricks, so you should be able to set the diamond contract by two tricks. Assuming the opponents are not vulnerable, this will amount to a 300-point setback.

You may inquire, "What about the situation in which you will be abandoning game, for which 300 points will not be adequate compensation?" The answer to your question is a matter of simple arithmetic. You have based your prediction of a two trick set upon the assumption that partner has minimum values for his opening bid. With the above hand, you are not going to make a game if partner has 13 or 14 points. Yet if he has more than a minimum and a game is therefore quite possible, it also follows that you will defeat the opponents' contract by more than two tricks. Down three doubled and nonvulnerable is 500 points; vulnerable it is 800. This is more than you can make by scoring a game.

Go on to **476.**

Another important consideration: when the contract which you double will yield a game if fulfilled, you must excercise more caution. You should not double a bid of two or three hearts or spades or three or four diamonds unless you expect to defeat the contract by at least two tricks. Bids of one in a major or two in a minor may, of course, be doubled more promiscuously.

In which of these deals would you, as South, consider doubling?

♠ x x   ♡ K J x x x x   ◊ A x   ♣ Q x x

	EAST	SOUTH	
	1 ♡	?	**469**

♠ x   ♡ K J x x x x   ◊ x x x   ♣ Q x x

NORTH	EAST	SOUTH	
1 ◊	1 ♡	?	**473**

Neither   **482**

SOUTH	WEST	NORTH	EAST
1 ♠	Pass	3 ♣	3 ♡
3 ♠	Pass	4 ♠	Pass
6 ♠	Pass	Pass	?

YOUR ANSWER: I would double with this hand.

♠ Q J 10   ♡ A Q J x x x   ◊ x x   ♣ x x

No, if you double, you signal partner that you want an unusual lead. West will then lead a club (the first side suit bid by the dummy), and this will do you no good at all.

You made an overcall in hearts on the first round of bidding, and West will lead a heart unless you tell him otherwise. Actually, you want a heart lead; it might be your only chance to save your ace. If you double, partner will have instructions *not* to lead a heart, so you would be defeating your own purpose.

Note that you have a sure trump trick. If you get a heart lead and make your ace good, you have defeated the contract.

Now return to **480** and see how the other hand is different.

478

[from 468]

(A) ♠ K J x x   ♥ x x x   ♦ K x x   ♣ x x x

(B) ♠ K J 9 x   ♥ J 10   ♦ A J 10 x   ♣ x x x

NORTH	EAST	SOUTH
1 ♥	1 ♠	?

YOUR ANSWER: I would double with either of these hands.

No, it wouldn't be very wise to do so with hand A. To be sure, you would have responded one spade with hand A if East had not bid, but you would have done so only as a means of keeping the bidding open in case partner had a powerhouse.

With hand B, though, it's a different story. You would have eagerly responded with one spade on this hand. When East denies you this opportunity by overcalling in spades, you may feel you can express your objections in the form of a penalty double.

Now go on to **475**.

479

[from 488]

♠ x x   ♥ K Q J 10 x x   ♦ A x x x   ♣ x

SOUTH	WEST	NORTH	EAST
1 ♥	2 ♣	Double	Pass
?			

YOUR ANSWER: I would let partner's double stand with this hand.

No, that wouldn't be a good idea. Your hand is very weak defensively. Not holding the ace in your suit, you might not win any heart tricks at all. This leaves the ace of diamonds as your only defensive trick. Remember, partner is counting on you for three tricks. Since you won't be able to deliver, you had better warn him with a rebid of two hearts.

Now return to **488** and choose the hand that should be passed after partner's penalty double.

SOUTH	WEST	NORTH	EAST
1 ♡	1 ♠	2 ♡	Pass
3 ◇	Pass	3 ♡	Pass
6 ♡	Pass	Pass	Double
Pass	Pass	Pass	

YOUR ANSWER: Because of partner's double, I would lead a diamond.

Right. Dummy has bid no suit other than trump, but declarer has —diamonds. So that is the suit your partner wants you to lead. He may be void of diamonds which will allow him to trump in and take the first trick. He will expect you to take one more trick with your spades to set the opponents.

If your opponents are obviously out of line in their bidding of a slam, then the opening lead won't make a great deal of difference. When such is the case, you or your partner may go ahead and double for a sure bonus.

Say the bidding has proceeded:

SOUTH	WEST	NORTH	EAST
1 ♠	Pass	3 ♣	3 ♡
3 ♠	Pass	4 ♠	Pass
6 ♠	Pass	Pass	?

With which of the following hands should you, as East, double?

♠ Q J 10   ♡ A Q J x x x   ◇ x x   ♣ x x   **477**

♠ A x x   ♡ K Q J 10 x x   ◇ x x x x   ♣ void   **490**

481

[*from 488*]

♠ x   ♡ A Q J 10 x x   ◊ A K J x x   ♣ x

SOUTH	WEST	NORTH	EAST
1 ♡	2 ♣	Double	Pass
?			

YOUR ANSWER: I would let partner's double stand with this hand.

No, that wouldn't be a good idea.

It is true that your hand has sufficient defensive strength to assure success of partner's double, but you might be missing greater things by passing.

Assume, for the moment, that partner has the ace of clubs for his double. Would it then be difficult to visualize a small slam in hearts or diamonds? And even if a slam is impossible, game your way is as likely as a two-trick set.

You should signal your strength with a jump to three diamonds.

Now return to **488** and choose the hand that should be passed after partner's penalty double.

482

[*from 476*]

(A)   ♠ xx   ♡ K J x x x x   ◊ A x   ♣ Q x x

EAST	SOUTH
1 ♡	?

(B)   ♠ x   ♡ K J x x x x   ◊ x x x   ♣ Q x x

NORTH	EAST	SOUTH
1 ◊	1 ♡	?

YOUR ANSWER: I would not double in either case.

Nor would we. In problem A, a double would be interpreted by partner as a takeout double, so you must pass. In B, you have insufficient high-card strength for a one-level double and, furthermore, one of the players will surely switch to spades.

Go on to **483**.

Counting Defensive Tricks for a Double

In estimating the tricks in your hand for a penalty double, your position at the table and the length of your suits are of greater importance than your point count. Holding a tenace in a suit bid by an opponent on your right is obviously more valuable than holding a tenace in a suit bid on your left since the rotation of play is clockwise, and you therefore play after he does. Likewise, a guarded king can be counted on as a winner in a suit bid strongly on your right, but not so if the suit was bid on your left.

It is seldom sound to count on more than two defensive tricks in one suit, even holding A K Q, and if you have great length in a suit or partner has supported it, your honors may be worthless.

In estimating the tricks in partner's hand, the following round guide may help you:

Partner's bid	His defensive worth
Opening of one no trump	Four tricks
Opening of one of a suit	Three tricks
Takeout double	Three tricks
Overcall	One trick
Raise	One trick
Pre-emptive bid	No tricks

Here are some other valuable tips:

1. Be quick to double when short in partner's suit.
2. Four small cards in opponent's suit are worth one trick.
3. Be wary of doubling if the opponents may escape to a safer suit.
4. Don't double a close contract if your double may cost you a trick—i.e., if your double may give information to the opponent which will permit him to play the hand to his advantage.

Go on to **484.**

484

[*from* 483]

Count the number of defensive tricks probable in each of these situations. You are South and the bidding has been:

NORTH	EAST	SOUTH	WEST	*Answer Letter*
1 ♣	Double	Pass	2 ♡	
3 ♣	3 ♡	?		

♠ x x x x   ♡ x x x x   ◊ K Q x x   ♣ A   (A)

♠ K x x   ♡ x x x x   ◊ x   ♣ J x x x x   (D)

♠ x x x x   ♡ Q x x x x   ◊ x x   ♣ K x   (G)

Again you are South, not vulnerable, and the bidding now is:

WEST	NORTH	EAST	SOUTH
1 ◊	1 ♡	1 ♠	2 ♡
2 ♠	Pass	3 ♠	Pass
4 ♠	Pass	Pass	?

♠ x x x   ♡ Q x   ◊ K Q x   ♣ A x x x x   (I)

♠ void   ♡ J x x x   ◊ A K Q   ♣ Q x x x x x   (B)

♠ x x x x   ♡ K x   ◊ Q J x x   ♣ A K x   (E)

♠ x   ♡ A x x x   ◊ K Q J x x   ♣ K x x   (H)

The bidding:

WEST	NORTH	EAST	SOUTH
Pass	1 ♠	2 ♡	?

♠ A x   ♡ A Q x   ◊ K Q x x   ♣ J x x x   (J)

♠ K x x x   ♡ x x x   ◊ A K   ♣ K x x x   (F)

♠ void   ♡ K Q x   ◊ x x x x x   ♣ A Q x x x   (C)

Check your answers on **487**.

(A) ♠ x x   ♡ K Q J 10 x x   ◇ A x x x   ♣ x

(B) ♠ x   ♡ A Q J 10 x x   ◇ A K J x x   ♣ x

(C) ♠ x   ♡ K Q J x x   ◇ A K x x   ♣ J x x

SOUTH	WEST	NORTH	EAST
1 ♡	2 ♣	Double	Pass
?			

YOUR ANSWER: With hand C, I would let partner's double stand.

Right. Hand C is very well suited for defensive play. You should be able to count on one heart and two diamond tricks. In addition, you have three of West's clubs, headed by the jack, which may be useful. Your partner is counting on you for three tricks and he can supply the rest. Yet you have too many possible losers to aspire to a game contract of your own.

Hand A is very weak defensively. With such a long heart suit, you can't be certain of scoring a trick. In fact, your diamond ace is your only sure defensive winner. Hence, you should reject the penalty double by bidding two hearts.

Hand B is adequate from a defensive point of view (despite its shortage of clubs), but its offensive potential is almost unlimited. Rather than stand for the double, you should flash the slam warning signal with a jump bid to three diamonds.

Please go on to **471**.

486

[from 471]

Here are the cues on doubling a slam bid:

1. If dummy has bid any suit or suits (other than trump), the double demands the lead of the first suit bid by dummy.
2. If dummy has bid no side suit, but declarer has bid another suit, the double demands the lead of the first side suit bid by declarer.
3. If neither dummy nor declarer has bid any side suit, but the defensive side has, the double demands the lead of one of the unbid suits.

In other words, the opening leader must not lead his own or his partner's suit. It follows, therefore, that you must not ordinarily double a slam contract if you are anxious for partner to make his normal lead.

SOUTH	WEST	NORTH	EAST
1 ♡	1 ♠	2 ♡	Pass
3 ◇	Pass	3 ♡	Pass
6 ♡	Pass	Pass	Double
Pass	Pass	Pass	

As West, what would you lead?

A Club **470**

A Heart **474**

A Diamond **480**

A Spade **489**

Answer
Letter

(A) You have six defensive tricks. Count one for the ace, one for the king-queen (you don't know where the ace is), and one for having four trumps. Partner opened the bidding, so his hand should be worth three more tricks.

(B) You have three tricks. You can count on just two in your diamond suit and one from partner.

(C) About six tricks. You'd better count on just one in clubs since it's a long suit. The ace of hearts should be on your right, so both trump honors should win. Count on partners for three, of course.

(D) Four and one-half tricks. Your four small trumps are worth one, and the guarded king may come through. Count at least three for partner's opening bid. Unless the bidding goes higher, you would not double.

(E) You have a total of five tricks. One from partner, one in trumps, one in hearts, and two in clubs.

(F) About five and one-half. Three from partner, two in your diamond suit, and one-half in clubs. It would be unwise to expect much from your king of spades since that is partner's suit and you have some length in it.

(G) You have at least six tricks. Count two in trumps, and the K-x in partner's suit should be worth one. Figure partner for three more.

(H) About three and one-half. Allow just one from the long diamond suit, one-half in clubs, and maybe one from the ace of partner's suit. Partner should be good for one more.

(I) You have at least three tricks. Allow one because partner was strong enough to overcall, one in diamonds, and one in clubs. You may take another heart or diamond.

(J) You may win seven tricks. Both of your high hearts should be good, for the king should be on your right; you have one trick in spades and one in diamonds, and you can figure on three from partner since he opened the bidding.

Now go on to **488.**

Taking Partner out of a Business Double

Usually, taking partner out of a business double is a bad policy, but there are exceptions. If, for example, your hand is worthless at defense, you may refuse to stand for a low-level double. You may have opened the bidding with a hand whose strength is concentrated in a long, strong trump suit. Your partner doubles an adverse over-call on the assumption that you can contribute three defensive tricks. But you know that because of the unusual complexion of your hand, you cannot supply these tricks. In such a case you may rebid your suit.

Occasionally, you will hold another type of hand which will lead you to decline partner's double: you may hold a hand with such great offensive strength that you feel a game or even a slam might be missed if you allow the double to stand. In such a case, you are willing to forego a certain penalty above the line in order to score a larger dividend below the line.

Don't forget that most business doubles should be left alone. If your rescue boomerangs, no one will rise in your defense. Occasionally, the case for a rescue will be clear, but if there is any doubt about it you'd better let the double stand.

SOUTH	WEST	NORTH	EAST
1 ♡	2 ♣	Double	Pass

With which of these hands would you pass in South's seat?

♠ x x   ♡ K Q J 10 x x   ◇ A x x x   ♣ x **479**

♠ x   ♡ A Q J 10 x x   ◇ A K J x x   ♣ x **481**

♠ x   ♡ K Q J x x   ◇ A K x x   ♣ J x x **485**

SOUTH	WEST	NORTH	EAST
1 ♡	1 ♠	2 ♡	Pass
3 ◊	Pass	3 ♡	Pass
6 ♡	Pass	Pass	Double
Pass	Pass	Pass	

YOUR ANSWER: As West, I would lead a spade.

No, the double of a slam contract by the partner of the player who will make the opening lead is a signal calling for an unusual lead. You seem to have your signals mixed up.

Here are the leads requested by the double:

If dummy has bid any suit or suits (other than trump), lead the first side suit bid by the dummy.

If dummy has not bid a side suit but declarer has bid in another suit, lead the first side suit bid by the declarer.

If neither declarer nor dummy has bid a side suit but the defensive side has, lead one of the unbid suits.

Look over these rules and see which one applies here. Then return to **486** and choose the correct lead.

490

[from 480]

(A) ♠ Q J 10   ♥ A Q J x x x   ♦ x x   ♣ x x

(B) ♠ A x x   ♥ K Q J 10 x x   ♦ x x x x   ♣ void

SOUTH	WEST	NORTH	EAST
1 ♠	Pass	3 ♣	3 ♥
3 ♠	Pass	4 ♠	Pass
6 ♠	Pass	Pass	?

YOUR ANSWER: As East, I would double with hand B.

Yes, this demands the lead of dummy's first-bid suit, clubs. Your ruff together with the ace of trumps will defeat your opponent's contract.

With hand A, you should not double because that would request partner not to lead a heart and that is exactly the lead you want.

Doubles of Three No Trump Contracts

The double of a three no trump contract by the player who does not have the opening lead also carries a specific message.

1. If the doubler has bid a suit, his partner must lead that suit, even though he may have only a singleton in it and a very fine suit of his own.
2. If the opening leader has bid a suit, partner's double requests him to lead that suit.
3. When neither the leader nor the doubler has bid, the double is a suggestion to partner to lead the dummy's first bid, unless he has a very fine opening lead of his own.

Go on to **491.**

316

Now test your talents on these doubling situations.

(A)   ♠ A J 10 x x   ♡ J x   ◇ x x x x   ♣ J x

WEST	NORTH	EAST	SOUTH
1 ♡	2 ♣	Pass	Pass
2 ♡	Double	Pass	?

(B)   ♠ K x x x   ♡ x x x   ◇ K x x   ♣ Q x x

WEST	NORTH	EAST	SOUTH
2 NT	Pass	6 NT	?

(C)   ♠ A K Q x x   ♡ A   ◇ A K x   ♣ Q x x

SOUTH	WEST	NORTH	EAST
2 ♠	Pass	2 NT	3 ♣
?			

(D)   ♠ x   ♡ x   ◇ K Q J 10 x x x   ♣ K J 10 x

EAST	SOUTH	WEST	NORTH
1 ♣	1 ◇	1 ♠	2 ◇
2 ♠	3 ◇	4 ♠	Double
Pass	?		

(E)   ♠ A K x x x   ♡ A x x   ◇ void   ♣ A x x x x

SOUTH	WEST	NORTH	EAST
1 ♠	2 ◇	Double	Pass
?			

(F)   ♠ K Q x x x   ♡ x x x x   ◇ K x   ♣ x x

NORTH	EAST	SOUTH	WEST
1 ◇	2 ♣	Pass	Pass
Double	Pass	?	

(G)   ♠ x x x   ♡ K x x x   ◇ A x x   ♣ Q 10 x

NORTH	EAST	SOUTH
1 NT	2 ♣	?

Check your answers on **492.**

492

Answer
Letter

(D) Five diamonds. True, partner's double is for penalties, but it cannot be based on spade strength, with double East and West bidding spades; so it must be based on high cards. If these include two aces, you might well make five diamonds. In any event, you have too little to contribute in defense.

(B) Pass. This would be a rather poor penalty double, for it would locate all the outstanding high cards for declarer.

(F) Three spades. A bid of two spades would be a forced response, which partner would probably pass.

(A) Pass. Had partner wanted you to bid, he would have doubled one heart. Evidently he can set two hearts.

(E) Pass. Though normally reluctant to pass a penalty double at a low level with a void in the adverse suit, here you have four sure defensive tricks and a probable misfit with partner's hand.

(G) Double. You have three defensive tricks and can count on partner for four more; yet you might very well not be able to make a game.

(C) Pass. Having already promised a game-going hand, you must now let partner decide whether to double or continue the bidding.

Go on to Chapter X on **493**.

CHAPTER X

SPECIAL BIDDING SITUATIONS

Misfits

Is there any one who has played bridge without occasionally getting involved in this kind of hassle:

Opener	Responder
1 ♠	2 ♡
2 ♠	3 ♡
3 ♠	4 ♡

Et cetera. An obvious misfit. Opener is overly fond of his spades and hates his partner's hearts; vice versa with the responder. But how to stop this insane merry-go-round?

After two rounds of bidding, if neither partner can support the other's suit and no trump is out of the question, a misfit should be diagnosed and the hand regarded as hopeless.

When a misfit is obvious, the bidding should cease in the higher-ranking suit, for otherwise the bidding level must ascend one more step. It is not always wise in these cases to look for the best possible contract. In case of a storm, an inferior contract undoubled is better than a superior contract which is doubled and defeated.

Let's say, as South, you hold the following cards:

♠ K Q 10 x   ♡ A Q x x x   ◇ void   ♣ A J x x

In which of these bidding sequences should South pass on the third round?

SOUTH	WEST	NORTH	EAST	
1 ♡	Pass	2 ◇	Pass	
2 ♠	Pass	3 ♣	Pass	
?				497

1 ♡	Pass	2 ◇	Pass	
2 ♠	Pass	3 ◇	Pass	
?				499

1 ♡	Pass	2 ◇	Pass	
2 ♠	Pass	3 ♡	Pass	
?				505

494

[*from 500*]

♠ x   ♡ K Q x x x x   ◊ Q x x x   ♣ A x

SOUTH	WEST	NORTH	EAST
1 ♡	Pass	3 ♡	3 ♠

YOUR ANSWER: I would now pass with this hand.

We wouldn't advise it. This hand is of little use in defense. It may well take only one trick against three spades. This would mean that partner, playing behind the declarer, would have to take four more just to set the enemy by one trick. Yet you can probably make four hearts. So you must bid four hearts straightaway.

You will find a better forcing-pass situation on **500**.

495

[*from 507*]

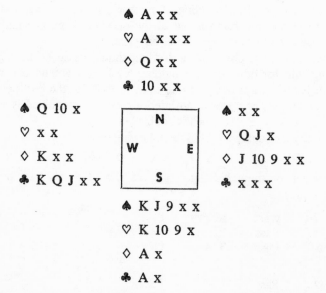

                    ♠ A x x
                    ♡ A x x x
                    ◊ Q x x
                    ♣ 10 x x

♠ Q 10 x   ┌─────────┐   ♠ x x
♡ x x   │   N   │   ♡ Q J x
◊ K x x   │ W   E │   ◊ J 10 9 x x
♣ K Q J x x   │   S   │   ♣ x x x
                  └─────────┘
                    ♠ K J 9 x x
                    ♡ K 10 9 x
                    ◊ A x
                    ♣ A x

YOUR ANSWER: South could make a four heart contract because there would be no heart loser.

No, a heart loser is unavoidable in either case. Try it for yourself. Then return to **507** and select the correct answer.

320

Answer
Letter

(A) Two spades. See Rule No. 3.
(F) One no trump. See Rule No. 4.
(K) One club. See Rule No. 8.
(D) One spade. See Rule No. 5.
(H) Pass. See Rule No. 7.
(B) One no trump. See Chapter II.
(J) Two spades. See Rule No. 6.
(E) Three diamonds (or three spades). See Rules No. 1 and 7.
(I) Two no trump. See Chapter III.
(C) One spade. See Rule No. 5.
(G) Two spades. See Rules No. 1 and 4.

Go on to **498**.

♠ K Q 10 x   ♡ A Q x x x   ◊ void   ♣ A J x x

SOUTH	WEST	NORTH	EAST
1 ♡	Pass	2 ◊	Pass
2 ♠	Pass	3 ♣	Pass
?			

YOUR ANSWER: As South, I would pass after this bidding sequence.

You must have reached this page by mistake. Responder has just bid a brand-new suit, clubs. This is a one-round force. North may not be able to support your hearts or spades, but he must have strength in the minor suits or he wouldn't be mentioning a new one at the three level.

To be sure, three no trump may be makable, but if you bid it you might miss slam in a suit. Bid four clubs; this will give partner a complete picture of your hand.

So return to **493** and find the right answer.

Protection Bidding

When the opponents' bidding clearly shows that they lack the balance of power, great liberties may sometimes be exercised in entering the auction. The requirements for the takeout double and the simple overcall are considerably reduced in these so-called "protective" situations.

What action would you take with the following hands?

You are South. West opens with one heart and the next two hands pass.

♠ Q x x x ♡ x x	◇ A J x x	♣ K x x	(A)
♠ K J x x ♡ x x	◇ A x x x x	♣ x x	(D)
♠ x x ♡ K x	◇ A Q J 9 x x x	♣ K x	(F)
♠ Q x x x ♡ K Q x x	◇ Q J 9 x	♣ x	(H)

The bidding has been:

EAST	SOUTH	WEST	NORTH
1 ♡	Pass	1 NT	Pass
Pass	?		

♠ x	♡ A J x x	◇ K Q 10 x	♣ Q J x x	(B)
♠ K x x	♡ K x	◇ J x x x	♣ A x x x	(E)

The bidding has been:

EAST	SOUTH	WEST	NORTH
1 ♡	Pass	2 ♡	Pass
Pass	?		

♠ A J 10 x x	♡ x x x	◇ K 10 x	♣ J x	(G)
♠ A 9 x x	♡ A x x x	◇ A x x	♣ Q 10	(C)

Please turn to **501** to check your answers.

♠ K Q 10 x   ♡ A Q x x x   ◊ void   ♣ A J x x

	SOUTH	WEST	NORTH	EAST
(A)	1 ♡	Pass	2 ◊	Pass
	2 ♠	Pass	3 ♣	Pass
	?			
(B)	1 ♡	Pass	2 ◊	Pass
	2 ♠	Pass	3 ◊	Pass
	?			
(C)	1 ♡	Pass	2 ◊	Pass
	2 ♠	Pass	3 ♡	Pass

YOUR ANSWER: As South, with this hand I would pass after bidding sequence B.

Right. You can't pass North's forcing bid of three clubs in sequence A and you surely won't pass his supporting heart bid in C. But in B you are obviously dealing with a misfit.

In B you have shown partner that you have five hearts, four spades, and at least 19 points. Yet he has continued to bid his diamonds. Why? Because he has diamonds and nothing else. With three hearts or four spades he would surely have shown preference for one of your majors. With club strength he would have assayed no trump. His hand was:

♠ x x x   ♡ x x   ◊ A Q 10 x x x   ♣ Q x

Go on to **500**.

The Forcing Pass

At times, a pass is a sign of strength rather than weakness. For example, you and your partner have announced great power by your bidding and your right-hand opponent interjects an overcall. If you are unsure whether to bid further over the overcall or to double it, you may pass and leave the decision to partner.

It is not always easy to recognize a forcing pass. The most clear-cut examples occur when the overcall follows a game-forcing bid. If, for example, your partner makes an opening bid of two in a suit or a jump response to your opening bid, you are both committed to reaching a game contract. If he passes following an overcall before you have reached game, you are obliged to go on to game or double.

Let us say that you are South and the bidding has proceeded thus:

SOUTH	WEST	NORTH	EAST
1 ♡	Pass	3 ♡	3 ♠

With which of these hands would you now pass?

♠ x   ♡ K Q x x x x   ◇ Q x x x   ♣ A x   **494**

♠ x x   ♡ A K Q x   ◇ 10 x x x   ♣ A Q 10   **502**

♠ J x x x   ♡ A Q x x   ◇ Q x x   ♣ K x   **506**

Answer
Letter

(A) Double. The requirements for a takeout double may be reduced to 11 points for purposes of reopening the bidding.

(B) Pass. You have the necessary points for a double, but partner is too apt to bid spades.

(C) Double. Partner can have no more than one heart. Game is a distinct possibility if he has any length in spades.

(D) Bid one spade. Competition should be offered, and the safest course of action is to bid one spade rather than two diamonds. It is cheaper and affords competition in a higher-ranking suit.

(E) Double. You had nearly enough for a double on the first round, and the slight distributional feature is in your favor.

(F) Bid three diamonds. A two diamond call would merely sound competitive. This is an excellent hand for offensive purposes and a display of strength is indicated. *Note that when used in a protective position, the jump overcall is not considered preemptive.* (How could it be?)

(G) Bid two spades. Partner must have a few high cards and is probably short in hearts. Competition is therefore reasonably safe.

(H) Pass. Partner cannot have much strength, since he clearly has nothing in hearts and was unable to make an overcall. To reopen the bidding might permit the opponents to find a better contract.

Now go on to **507**.

502

[*from 500*]

(A)	♠ x	♡ K Q x x x x	◇ Q x x x	♣ A x
(B)	♠ x x	♡ A K Q x	◇ 10 x x x	♣ A Q 10
(C)	♠ J x x x	♡ A Q x x	◇ Q x x	♣ K x

SOUTH	WEST	NORTH	EAST
1 ♡	Pass	3 ♡	3 ♠

YOUR ANSWER: As South, I would now pass with hand B.

Good for you. This would be a good forcing pass. Partner can now bid four hearts, three no trump, or double. He is in a better position to judge what to do. With hand A, you should say four hearts; with hand B, you should double.

Part-Score Bidding

Some of the principles of bidding must be modified when either side has a part score:

1. The new-suit (by responder) forcing principle does not apply when responder's bid is sufficient to produce game.

2. Responder's jump shift is forcing for one round only.

3. An opening demand bid is forcing for one round only and hence may be based on slightly less playing strength.

4. With a part score of 60, responder should stretch a point to keep the bidding alive.

5. With an advanced part score, the opening bidder need not have a convenient rebid, since he can pass partner's response; likewise, short club suits should not be bid.

6. With an advanced part score, responder should not pass with a good hand simply because the bid completes game. At least one response is in order, lest slam be missed.

7. Any raise beyond game suggests interest in slam.

8. Doubtful hands should be opened when the opponents have a part score, for fear they will steal the game before you can enter the auction.

Go on to **503**.

With these rules in mind, how would you handle these bidding problems?

You are the dealer, with a part score of 60.

(A) ♠ A K Q x x x   ♡ A x   ◇ K x   ♣ K x x

(B) ♠ K x x   ♡ A J x x   ◇ K J x   ♣ A x x

(C) ♠ A Q x x   ♡ A Q x   ◇ x x x x   ♣ x x

(D) ♠ A K x x   ♡ x x   ◇ x x x x   ♣ K Q x

You have a part score of 60, partner has opened with one spade, and your right-hand opponent has passed.

(E) ♠ A x x x   ♡ Q x x   ◇ A K Q x x   ♣ x

(F) ♠ x x   ♡ Q x x   ◇ Q x x x   ♣ J x x x

(G) ♠ 10 x x   ♡ x x   ◇ Q J x x   ♣ K x x x

You have a part score of 70, partner has opened with one spade, and your right-hand opponent has passed.

(H) ♠ A Q x   ♡ x x   ◇ Q x x x   ♣ x x x x

(I) ♠ x x x   ♡ A J x   ◇ A Q x   ♣ K J x x

(J) ♠ Q x x x   ♡ x x   ◇ A x x x   ♣ K x x

The opponents have a part-score of 60; you are the dealer.

(K) ♠ A Q x x   ♡ x x   ◇ x x x   ♣ K Q 10 x

Check your answers on **496**.

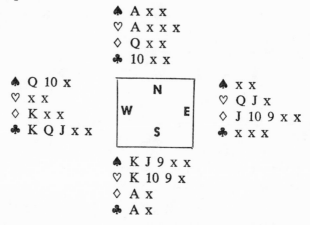

♠ A x x
♡ A x x x
◇ Q x x
♣ 10 x x

♠ Q 10 x
♡ x x
◇ K x x
♣ K Q J x x

♠ x x
♡ Q J x
◇ J 10 9 x x
♣ x x x

♠ K J 9 x x
♡ K 10 9 x
◇ A x
♣ A x

YOUR ANSWER: South can make a four heart contract because the spade suit will permit the discard of two of dummy's losers.

Correct. With spades as trump, South must lose one trick in each suit. With hearts as trump, however, he will lose one heart, one spade, one club, but no diamonds. Dummy's two losing diamonds will be thrown off on the established spade suit.

If there is a choice for trump between one suit split 4–4 and another split 5–3, the former is preferable, since the five-card side suit will provide discards for two losers in the other hand.

This principle does not apply when there is a choice between eight trumps divided 6–2 and 5–3. The 6–2 division is preferable; declarer, with six trumps, is better able to withstand repeated forces by the opponents.

The Weak No Trump

Some players open with one no trump on hands containing only 12–14 high-card points. This deprives the opposition of a certain amount of bidding room, achieving its best results when the outstanding strength is evenly divided and the opponents can be goaded into entering the auction. It is subject to great risk, when the no trumper's partner is broke, and should be used rarely when vulnerable.

The values required for an overcall of a weak no trump bid are the same as those for any other two-level overcall. For a takeout double, 14 points are needed.

Go on to **508**.

♠ K Q 10 x   ♡ A Q x x x   ◇ void   ♣ A J x x

SOUTH	WEST	NORTH	EAST
1 ♡	Pass	2 ◇	Pass
2 ♠	Pass	3 ♡	Pass

YOUR ANSWER: As South, I would pass after this bidding sequence.

No, your answer is wrong, and with 20 points in your hand and a promise of at least ten more points plus heart support from partner, slam is on the horizon, and you should inform partner of this fact by bidding four clubs.

So return to **493** and find the right answer.

♠ J x x x   ♡ A Q x x   ◇ Q x x   ♣ K x

SOUTH	WEST	NORTH	EAST
1 ♡	Pass	3 ♡	3 ♠

YOUR ANSWER: As South, I would now pass with this hand.

With such a minimum opening bid and length in the adverse suit, we would recommend an immediate double. It is a sure bet. If you pass, how is partner to know you have four spades and only 13 points?

You will find a better forcing-pass situation on **500**.

Four Opposite Four

Partnership possession of eight trumps is usually considered the minimum for suit play. Many players like the feeling of security that comes from holding a five-card trump suit, but it is often better to have them distributed four in each hand. Look at this deal:

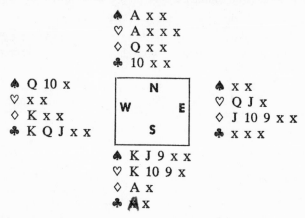

♠ A x x
♡ A x x x
◇ Q x x
♣ 10 x x

♠ Q 10 x
♡ x x
◇ K x x
♣ K Q J x x

♠ x x
♡ Q J x
◇ J 10 9 x x
♣ x x x

♠ K J 9 x x
♡ K 10 9 x
◇ A x
♣ A x

The bidding proceeded:

SOUTH	NORTH
1 ♠	2 ♠
3 ♠	4 ♠

Declarer had to lose a trick in each suit and was down one. The partners consoled each other with the observation that it all depended on the spade finesse; but with a little resourcefulness, South could have scored a game despite this.

South should have rebid three hearts instead of three spades, just in case North made his raise with only three spades while he had four hearts as well. With hearts as trump, the contract cannot be defeated.

Why does four hearts make and four spades go down one?

Because there is no trump loser in the heart contract. **495**

Because with hearts as trump the spade will provide discards in dummy. **504**

Because there is no spade loser when hearts are trump. **509**

The Weak Two Bid

Some players employ an opening bid of two diamonds, hearts, or spades as a pre-emptive measure, describing a hand with a good six-card suit and only 6–11 high-card points. An opening bid of two clubs is an artificial call which is used to cover all hands that would normally qualify for a demand bid. The negative response is two diamonds, instead of two no trump, and the opener names his suit when he rebids.

Whatever success the weak two bid has enjoyed, stems largely upon the rashness of opponents who feel compelled to overcall at dangerously high levels rather than be shut out of the bidding. Restraint should be exercised in this regard.

Overcalls should be calculated upon the usual basis of suit strength and anticipated losers. Takeout doubles should be based upon at least 16 points.

Let's say that you are South with each of the following hands, and East has opened with one no trump (weak). What action do you take?

♠ x	♡ A J 10 x x x	◊ K Q J x	♣ x x	(A)
♠ K Q x x x	♡ A Q x x x	◊ x x	♣ 10	(D)
♠ K x x	♡ A x x	◊ A J x x	♣ J 10 9	(F)
♠ A J 9 x x	♡ A 10 x x	◊ J	♣ A x x	(B)

Now the player on your right has opened with a weak bid of two hearts.

♠ A Q x	♡ K 10 x	◊ A x x	♣ J 10 x x	(E)
♠ A J 10 x	♡ 10 x	◊ K Q 9 x x	♣ A J	(G)
♠ K Q 10 9 x	♡ x x	◊ x x	♣ A Q J x	(C)

Check your answers on **510**.

509
[*from 507*]

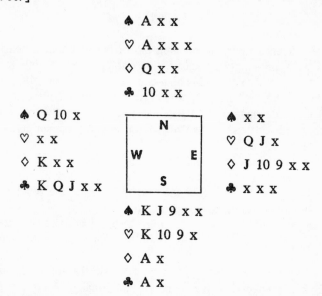

♠ A x x
♡ A x x x
◇ Q x x
♣ 10 x x

♠ Q 10 x
♡ x x
◇ K x x
♣ K Q J x x

N
W   E
S

♠ x x
♡ Q J x
◇ J 10 9 x x
♣ x x x

♠ K J 9 x x
♡ K 10 9 x
◇ A x
♣ A x

YOUR ANSWER: South could make a four heart contract, because there would be no spade loser.

No, this is not true. A spade loser is unavoidable in either case.
But after South loses a spade trick, the suit is established. He will be able to win tricks with the two little spades in his own hand. Can you guess what this means?

Turn back to **507** and choose the correct answer.

Answer
Letter

(A) Bid two hearts. You have the requirements for a normal over-call at the two level.

(B) Double. If partner responds in diamonds, you can bid your spades. It's quite possible that you will be able to score a game or a substantial set.

(C) Bid two spades. You should take at least six tricks.

(D) Pass. Your suits are not good enough for offensive action. Any contract on the two level would be risky.

(E) Pass. Your hand is too well balanced to justify any offensive action.

(F) Pass. You should have at least 14 high-card points for an immediate takeout double. Remember that the hand of the doubler should be at least as strong as the hand of the player who opened. When you have even distribution, you require an extra point for safety's sake.

(G) Double. Your hand calls for offensive action of some sort, and the takeout double gives the most flexible approach.

Go on to **511**.

We hope that in the preceding pages we have been able to give you a better understanding of how, what, and when to bid in bridge. But every game is different from the last and each new hand requires individual attention, so we could not hope to cover all the problems and possibilities you might encounter in bidding. If we have succeeded in making the intricacies of bidding understandable, then your game will not only noticeably improve but your appreciation and enjoyment of bridge will increase as well.

If you have answered all the questions correctly and properly as you worked through this TutorText, you should now have an excellent knowledge of the art of bidding in bridge. However, should you want to clarify a point, the index will quickly refer you to the proper page. Or you might want to review what you have learned by going over the quizzes that are scattered throughout the book. In any case, you are on your own now, so good luck and good bidding!

APPENDIX

SCORING TABLE

POINTS SCORED BELOW THE LINE

Trick Score—Tricks bid for and made count toward game:

	Not Doubled	*Doubled*	*Redoubled*
Each trick over 6 (Book)			
Spades or Hearts	30	60	120
Diamonds or Clubs	20	40	80
No Trump—first trick over 6 (Book)	40	80	160
Each additional No Trump trick	30	60	120

POINTS SCORED ABOVE THE LINE

Tricks made over the number bid (overtricks) do not count for game, but are scored above the line as follows:

	Not Vulnerable	*Vulnerable*
Overtricks not doubled	Trick Value	Trick Value
" doubled	100	200
" redoubled	200	400

First side to score 100 points in trick score (below line) wins game. Having made game, a side is vulnerable.
First side to win two games wins the rubber.

For winning rubber, if opponents have no game	700
For winning rubber, if opponents have a game	500
If rubber is unfinished, for winning a game	300
If game is unfinished, for having a part score	50

Premiums (scored above the line)

	Not Vulnerable	Vulnerable
Bidding and making small slam (12 tricks)	500	750
Bidding and making grand slam (13 tricks)	1000	1500
Holding 4 trump honors in one hand	100	100
Holding 5 trump honors in one hand	150	150
Holding 4 Aces in one hand at No Trump	150	150
Making any doubled or redoubled contract	50	50

Penalties (scored by opponents above the line)
If declarer fails to make his contract, opponents score:

	Not Vulnerable			**Vulnerable**		
	Not Doubled	Doubled	Redoubled	Not Doubled	Doubled	Redoubled
1 Down	50	100	200	100	200	400
2 Down	100	300	600	200	500	1000
3 Down	150	500	1000	300	800	1600
Add for each additional trick down:						
	50	200	400	100	300	600

TUTORTEXTS

ADVANCED BIDDING
by Charles H. Goren

ADVENTURES IN ALGEBRA
by Norman A. Crowder and Grace C. Martin

THE ARITHMETIC OF COMPUTERS
by Norman A. Crowder

BASIC COMPUTER PROGRAMMING
by Theodore G. Scott

COMPUTER PROGRAMMING TECHNIQUES
by Theodore G. Scott

EFFECTIVE EXECUTIVE PRACTICES
by Neely D. Gardner

EFFECTIVE WRITING
by Kellogg Smith and Jane Stapleford

THE ELEMENTS OF BRIDGE
by Charles H. Goren

FRACTIONS: A Basic Course in Arithmetic
by Betty K. Friel

FUNDAMENTALS OF ELECTRICITY
by Paul Sanborn and James B. Owens

INTRODUCTION TO ELECTRONICS
by Robert J. Hughes and Peter Pipe

THE MEANING OF MODERN POETRY
by John Clark Pratt

PARLIAMENTARY PROCEDURE
by Warren Lehman

PRACTICAL LAW: A Course in Everyday Contracts
by Warren Lehman

PRACTICAL MATHEMATICS
by Grace C. Martin and Ann Smalley

PROPER PUNCTUATION
by Kellogg Smith and Leighton G. Steele

THE SLIDE RULE
by Robert Saffold and Ann Smalley

TRIGONOMETRY: A Practical Course
by Norman A. Crowder and Grace C. Martin

YOUR LIFE INSURANCE
by Barbara H. Hathaway

INDEX